I0014609

Jaume Rigau Vilalta

Information-Theoretic Refinement Criteria for Image
Synthesis

Jaume Rigau Vilalta

Information-Theoretic Refinement Criteria for Image Synthesis

An Intersection between Computer Graphics,
Information Theory, and Complexity

VDM Verlag Dr. Müller

Imprint

Bibliographic information by the German National Library: The German National Library lists this publication at the German National Bibliography; detailed bibliographic information is available on the Internet at http://dnb.d-nb.de.

Cover image: www.purestockx.com

Publisher:
VDM Verlag Dr. Müller Aktiengesellschaft & Co. KG , Dudweiler Landstr. 125 a, 66123 Saarbrücken, Germany,
Phone +49 681 9100-698, Fax +49 681 9100-988,
Email: info@vdm-verlag.de

Zugl.: Barcelona, Technical University of Catalonia, Diss., 2006

Produced in USA and UK by:
Lightning Source Inc., La Vergne, Tennessee, USA
Lightning Source UK Ltd., Milton Keynes, UK
BookSurge LLC, 5341 Dorchester Road, Suite 16, North Charleston, SC 29418, USA

ISBN: 978-3-8364-7731-4

Preface

It is already six years since I started graphics research thanks to Miquel Feixas and Mateu Sbert, who were studying the application of the information theory to computer graphics within the Girona Graphics Group. I have the personal impression that only a few months have passed since then. This is not a paradox of the Theory of Relativity[1] but rather a consequence of the effort and dedication that we have all invested. This thesis, and other lines of research that have been opened up, is the fruit of this collaboration.

Abstract

This work is framed within the context of computer graphics starting out from the intersection of three fields: *rendering*, *information theory*, and *complexity*.

Initially, the concept of scene complexity is analysed considering three perspectives from a geometric visibility point of view: *complexity at an interior point*, *complexity of an animation*, and *complexity of a region*.

The main focus of this dissertation is the exploration and development of new refinement criteria for the global illumination problem. Information-theoretic measures based on Shannon entropy and Harvda-Charvát-Tsallis generalised entropy, together with *f*-divergences, are analysed as kernels of refinement. We show how they give us a rich variety of efficient and highly discriminative measures which are applicable to rendering in its pixel-driven (ray-tracing) and object-space (hierarchical radiosity) approaches.

Firstly, based on Shannon entropy, a set of *pixel quality* and *pixel contrast* measures are defined. They are applied to supersampling in ray-tracing as refinement criteria, obtaining a new *entropy-based adaptive sampling* algorithm with a high rate quality versus cost. Secondly, based on Harvda-Charvát-Tsallis generalised entropy, and generalised mutual information, three new refinement criteria are defined for hierarchical radiosity. In correspondence with three classic approaches, oracles based on *transported information*, *information smoothness*, and *mutual information* are presented, with very significant results for the latter. And finally, three members of the family of Csiszár's *f*-divergences (*Kullback-Leibler*, *chi-square*, and *Hellinger* divergences) are analysed as refinement criteria showing good results for both ray-tracing and hierarchical radiosity.

Acknowledgements

This thesis would not have been possible without the support of Miquel Feixas and Mateu Sbert, who have always believed in the project and have given me all the necessary encouragement. Miquel Feixas' energy in the search for answers to the continual questions we posed has been essential. Equally, Mateu Sbert's multi-disciplinary knowledge has often put the pieces together. All in all, I have to be grateful for the many hours of discussion we have had, and for what they have provided me with from a scientific and a personal point of view. I would especially like to thank their constant availability, more often than not outside the working day.

---

[1] Time dilates in a factor of $\sqrt{1 - \left(\frac{v}{c}\right)^2}$, where v and c are our velocity and that of light, respectively (Hendrik A. Lorentz, 1904). Albert Einstein, complementing the work of Hendrik A. Lorentz and Henri Poincaré, developed the Special Theory of Relativity published in 1905 [55].

I also wish to thank all my coauthors for the opportunity that I have had to work with them. I have learnt from all of them and they have helped me when ever necessary: Anton Bardera, Philippe Bekaert, Imma Boada, Miquel Feixas, László Neumann, and Mateu Sbert.

With regard to my University, I would like to thank Girona Graphics Group for its support and facilities, especially their director, Xavier Pueyo; all the colleagues of my Department of *Infomàtica i Matemàtica Aplicada* and in particular Miquel Bofill, Francesc Castro, Roel Martínez, Jordi Palau, and Mateu Villaret for their encouragement; the administrative staff, Mercè Bautista, Maria Brugue, Jordi Fontrodona, and Montse Vila, for helping me in bureaucratic tasks; and the system managers team, Marc Franquesa, Joan J. Pujol, and Robert Valentí, for solving me all software problems.

I also thank my tutor at the *Universitat Politècnica de Catalunya*, Horacio Rodriguez, for the time he has given me; Joaquim Gelabertó, for his comments and revision of my thesis; and Carlos Andújar, Philippe Bekaert, Dimitri Plemenos, Xavier Pueyo, and László Szirmay-Kalos for agreeing to be members of my tribunal.

This thesis was printed in English in order to widen its diffusion in the context of computer graphics. However, I would like it to be known that all the ground work of this thesis, carried out over these years, have been done in Catalan[2]. I would like to thank Vivien Greatorex-Davies for her effort in the difficult task converting the bilingual and technical text into English; also Elisa Serra, who suffered a part of it; and Miquel Feixas and Mateu Sbert, for the linguistic apprenticeship that I have experienced with them.

I also wish to thank all those people and institutions who appear in the credits of this work for the permission they have either given me or which they have offered for the use of their material. With regard to the images resulting from the work of the thesis itself, I thank the team of the Computer Graphics Research Group of the Katholieke Universiteit Leuven, Belgium —for the creation of and permission to use Renderpark software [33] as a test-bed system for physically based photo-realistic image synthesis—, and the authors of Materials and Geometry Format [246] —for making the scene design easy for me—.

Finally, I would like to thank my family, Mariàngels, Marc, and Judit, for the understanding and help that they have always given me.

Grants

The work that has led to this thesis has been funded in part with grant numbers: 2001-SGR-00296 of the Department of Universities, Research and Society of Information (Catalan Government), TIC-98-586-C03, TIC-98-973-C03, and TIC-2001-2416-C03-01 of the Ministry of Science and Technology (Spanish Government), and joint action numbers HU-1998-0015 and HU-2000-0011 of the Ministry of Foreign Affairs (Spanish and Austrian Governments).

---

[2] Catalan is one of the Romance or Neolatin languages formed immediately after the dissolution of Latin between the 8th and the 10th centuries in the territories of the Carolingian Empire. Geographically, it is spoken in the north-west of the Iberian Peninsula in areas such as Catalonia, Valencia, and the Balearic Islands. In order to promote Catalan culture and help to conserve it for the future, the Internet domain *cat* has been created. General information about Catalan can be found at http://www.gencat.cat/catalunya/eng/ (Catalan Government).

Contents

Acronyms

Acronym	Refinement criterion
CC	Classic contrast
CS	Chi-square f-divergence
CS$^{\frac{1}{2}}$	Square root of CS
CT	Confidence test
EC	Entropy contrast
HL	Hellinger f-divergence
HL$^{\frac{1}{2}}$	Square root of HL
IC	Importance contrast
IS	Information smoothness
KL	Kullback-Leibler f-divergence
KL$^{\frac{1}{2}}$	Square root of KL
KS	Kernel smoothness
MI	Mutual information
RS	Received radiosity smoothness
TI	Transported information
TP	Transported power
VT	Variance test

Acronym	Description
AURA	Association of Universities for Research in Astronomy
BRDF	Bidirectional reflectance distribution function
BTDF	Bidirectional transmittance distribution function
CIE	Commission Internationale de L'Éclairage
ESA	European Space Agency
HCT	Harvda-Charvát-Tsallis
HST	Hubble Space Telescope
IEC	International Electrotechnical Commission
MSE	Mean square error
NASA	National Aeronautics and Space Administration
pdf	Probability density function
PSNR	Peak signal-to-noise ratio
$PSNR_a$	Peak signal-to-noise ratio (channel average)
$PSNR_p$	Peak signal-to-noise ratio (channel perceptual average)
RMSE	Root mean square error
$RMSE_a$	Root mean square error (channel average)
$RMSE_p$	Root mean square error (channel perceptual average)
SDM	Sampling density map
SPD	Spectral power distribution
STScI	Space Telescope Science Institute

Definitions

Id.	Description	Def.	Page
$H_{\mathrm{c}}(S,x)$	Discrete cross entropy field at point $x \in \mathcal{I}_S$	31	57
$H_{\mathrm{c}}(S,x)$	Discrete cross entropy field at point $x \in \mathcal{I}_S^{\mathrm{2D}}$	37	59
$H^{\mathrm{c}}(X)$	Entropy of continuous random variable X	8	43
$H^{\mathrm{c}}(X|Y)$	Conditional entropy of continuous random variables (X,Y)	9	43
$H^{\mathrm{g}}(\mathsf{P})$	Image plane geometry entropy	55	80
$H^{\mathrm{g}}(\mathsf{p})$	Pixel geometry entropy	56	80
$H_{\mathrm{J}}(S)$	Discrete scene joint entropy of S	14	45
$H_{\mathrm{J}}(S)$	Discrete 2D-scene joint entropy of S	23	49
$H_{\mathrm{P}}(S)$	Discrete scene positional entropy of S	11	44
$H_{\mathrm{P}}(S)$	Discrete 2D-scene positional entropy of S	20	48
$H_{\mathrm{p}}(S,x)$	Discrete entropy field at point $x \in \mathcal{I}_S$	28	55
$H_{\mathrm{p}}(S,x)$	Discrete entropy field at point $x \in \mathcal{I}_S^{\mathrm{2D}}$	34	58
$H_{\mathrm{s}}(S)$	Discrete scene entropy of S	13	45
$H_{\mathrm{s}}(S)$	Discrete 2D-scene entropy of S	22	48
$H_{\mathrm{s}}(S,i)$	Discrete scene entropy of patch $i \in S$	12	45
$H_{\mathrm{s}}(S,i)$	Discrete 2D-scene entropy of patch $i \in S$	21	48
$H_{\alpha}(S)$	Discrete scene HCT entropy	70	104
$H_{\alpha}(X)$	HCT entropy of discrete random variable X	66	100
$H_{\alpha}(X,Y)$	HCT entropy of systems X and Y	67	101
HL	Hellinger oracle	79	132
$\mathsf{HL}^{\frac{1}{2}}$	Hellinger refinement criterion in adaptive ray-tracing	80	136
$I(X,Y)$	Mutual information of discrete random variables (X,Y)	7	42
$I^{c}(X,Y)$	Mutual information of continuous random variables (X,Y)	10	43
$I_{\mathrm{p}}^{c}(\mathcal{S},x)$	Continuous mutual information field at point $x \in \mathcal{I}_S$	30	56
$I_{\mathrm{p}}^{c}(\mathcal{S},x)$	Continuous mutual information field at point $x \in \mathcal{I}_S^{\mathrm{2D}}$	36	59
$I_{\mathrm{s}}^{c}(\mathcal{S})$	Continuous scene mutual information of $\mathcal{S}$	16	46
$I_{\mathrm{s}}^{c}(\mathcal{S})$	Continuous 2D-scene mutual information of $\mathcal{S}$	25	49
$I_{\mathrm{s}}^{c}(\mathcal{S},s)$	Surface-to-surface complexity of region $s \subseteq S$	43	70
$I_{\mathrm{s}}^{c}(\mathcal{S},s)$	Length-to-length complexity of 2D-region $s \subseteq \mathcal{S}$	45	71
$I_{\mathrm{s}}^{c}(\mathcal{S},s,s')$	Surface-to-surface complexity between regions $s,s' \subseteq \mathcal{S}$	44	71
$I_{\mathrm{s}}^{c}(\mathcal{S},s,s')$	Length-to-length complexity between 2D-regions $s,s' \subseteq \mathcal{S}$	46	71
$I_{\mathrm{p}}(S,x)$	Discrete mutual information field at point $x \in \mathcal{I}_S$	29	55
$I_{\mathrm{p}}(S,x)$	Discrete mutual information field at point $x \in \mathcal{I}_S^{\mathrm{2D}}$	35	58
$I_{\mathrm{s}}(S)$	Discrete scene mutual information of S	15	45
$I_{\mathrm{s}}(S)$	Discrete 2D-scene mutual information of S	24	49
$I_{\mathrm{s}}(S,s)$	Surface-to-surface complexity of region $s \subseteq S$	47	72
$I_{\mathrm{s}}(S,s,s')$	Surface-to-surface complexity between regions $s,s' \subseteq S$	48	72
$I_{\alpha}(S)$	Discrete scene generalised mutual information of S	73	116
$I_{\alpha}^{c}(\mathcal{S})$	Continuous scene generalised mutual information of $\mathcal{S}$	74	116
$I_{\alpha}(X,Y)$	Generalised mutual information of discrete random variables (X,Y)	69	102
IS	Information smoothness oracle	72	110
KL	Kullback-Leibler oracle	79	132
$\mathsf{KL}^{\frac{1}{2}}$	Kullback-Leibler refinement criterion in adaptive ray-tracing	80	136
MI	Mutual information oracle	76	118
$Q^{c}(\mathsf{p})$	Pixel channel quality	53	79
$\mathbf{Q}^{\mathbf{c}}(\mathsf{p})$	Pixel colour quality of colour system $\mathbf{c}$	54	79
$Q^{\mathrm{g}}(\mathsf{p})$	Pixel geometry quality	57	80
S^{n}	Animation of S with n-frames	38	65
TI	Transported information oracle	71	104

Figures

Tables

Chapter 1

Introduction

This work has been carried out in the context of computer graphics and in particular within the field of image synthesis. Its aim is to apply information theory to rendering problems. Three sets of new refinement criteria for global illumination are introduced using different information-theoretic tools and divergence measures. Previous to introducing these criteria and from a geometric visibility perspective, we present a group of information-theoretic complexity measures of a scene based on the interaction between its different parts.

Three fundamental areas are involved in this dissertation: *rendering*, *information theory*, and *complexity*. The relationship between them is discussed in this chapter (§1.1) where the objectives (§1.2) and an overview (§1.3) are also presented.

1.1 Framework

Let us situate the content of this work by presenting the three foundations on which it is based: rendering (§1.1.1), information theory (§1.1.2), and complexity (§1.1.3). As we shall see later on, each one of these fields is multidisciplinary. This work is in itself an example of this (Fig. 1.1).

1.1.1 Rendering

According to László Szirmay-Kalos, *"the ultimate objective of image synthesis or rendering is to provide the user with the illusion of watching real objects on a computer screen"* [223][1]. Given that obtaining an exact representation of the illumination is an insurmountable objective, the algorithms of rendering do not have any option other than to search for an approximation to the solution. To produce realistic images, the precise treatment required for lighting effects can be achieved by "simulating" the underlying physical phenomena of light emission, propagation, and reflection [215]. It is along these lines that rendering algorithms are developed becoming a blend of concepts from three fields: physics, signal processing, and vision [74]. This produces multiple working alternatives and, as a consequence, different techniques are used to solve the rendering problem [30, 215, 74].

Figure 1.1: The framework with some multidisciplinary interactions. Our work is placed in the common intersection.

---

[1] We choose this definition for the aptness of the word "illusion" which reminds us explicitly that we have an uncomputable problem: how "to recreate" the behaviour of nature. Objective reasons are: the exact simulation of the light perceived by the eye requires infinite computations, the discretisation of a continuous function produces errors, and the colours produced by an output device are limited with respect to the infinite variety of the real world.

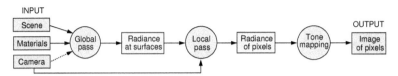

Figure 1.2: Phases of rendering process.
Credit: Adapted from László Szirmay-Kalos [223].

Within rendering, the context of this work is *physically-based global illumination*. Next, we comment on its meaning followed by an analysis from the perspective of the *signal theory*.

Physically-Based Global Illumination

The first part of the term makes a reference to the physical description of the world to be rendered. Thus, the input of the problem remains determined [12]:

Scene Geometric description of a set of 3D objects from a primitive surface set (e.g., triangles, spheres, and cylinders).

Materials Assignation of materials to the surfaces of the scene and description of the physical properties of each one:

- *Colour*. Modelled by a colour space (§2.2.4).
- *Emissivity*. Spontaneous emission of light modelled by an emittance distribution function (§2.2.3).
- *Light scattering*. Reflectance and transmittance. Modelled by a bidirectional reflectance and transmittance distribution functions (§2.2.3).

Camera A description of a virtual camera that includes:

- The virtual observer position in 3D space with a viewing direction: *eye*.
- A geometric description of an *image plane*[2] with resolution and pixel data.

A surface of the scene that has non-zero emission is called a *lightsource*. There is a set of abstract lightsources with an important role in rendering: point-lightsource, directional lightsource, and sky-light illumination [223].

The second part of the term, *global illumination*, refers to how the light within the scene is treated. The global illumination takes the interactions of the light with all the surfaces of the scene into account (e.g., shadows and reflections), as against a *local illumination*, where only the interactions between a lightsource, a surface and a viewing position are considered [12].

Once our input is determined, we consider the output: *"physically-based illumination computations are used in order to generate a photo-realistic image of the scene corresponding to the virtual camera data"* [12]. In order to attain this objective, it is necessary to measure the intensity of the light of the scene which the camera is gathering accurately. We describe the generic process of rendering in three well differentiated phases [223] (Fig. 1.2):

Global pass Determines the light reflected off the surface points at different directions. It is represented by a wavelength-dependent function [251]. The intensity of the light on a given wavelength is the *radiance* (§2.2.3). For the scenes without participating media, the radiance is only on the surface point and therefore we must consider the material properties exclusively. Under this consideration, the behaviour of light becomes formalised by the *rendering equation* (2.46). The process by which its solution is calculated is the global pass.

---

[2] Without loss of generality, we consider a plane being aware that every mechanism of output has a specific, often uneven, geometry. We also assume that the light distribution of the scene is not influenced by the observer (i.e., *virtual image plane*).

Local pass This is the measurement of the global radiance function by a camera understood as a set of light measuring devices (usually pixels). They are characterised by a function describing the points and directions involved in the measuring.

Tone-mapping It is necessary to visualise the values of the image plane in a display. To do this, the radiance must be converted into a colour space appropriate for the device, taking into account the technical characteristics and the human visual system [236] (§2.2.4).

The critical task of the rendering for obtaining a photo-realistic image of quality is well identified: *"the average radiance perceived through each pixel of the image needs to be computed"* [12]. Next, following Bekaert [12], we recall the approaches used to attain this goal[3]:

Pixel-driven Search for the radiance of the scene, sampling only in the specific areas that are necessary for creating the image. The usual situation consists in sampling each pixel of the image plane in directions determined by the observer. Applying the sampling theory, the final radiance value per pixel is obtained. The *ray-tracing* algorithms belong to this approach (§2.3).

The advantage consists in the storage necessary being little more than that related to the description of the scene and the main disadvantage is that at any movement of the viewing plane or the observer, we need a new set of samples and so, they are *view-dependent* solutions.

Object-space Sample a representation of the radiance function on all surfaces of the scene. After this, we need only sample the function on each pixel of the image plane using the sampling theory. In order to achieve this, algorithms to obtain the visible surfaces (e.g., projection, ray-casting, and Z-buffer) through each pixel are used. The *radiosity* algorithms belong to this approach (§2.4).

One advantage is that we can move the viewing plane or the observer through the scene with minimum computation and so, they are *view-independent* solutions[4]. Another advantage is the possibility of reusing the previous computations with a change of physical description. The disadvantage is the amount of storage required for complex scenes.

Multi-pass Compute the radiance in object-space while the resources allow it and then use a pixel-driven approach. It is a hybrid option presented by Wallace et al. [245] and continued by other authors [102, 222].

The Signal of Light

The synthetic images can be considered to be 2D signals where, in the image plane, the "image" corresponds to the signal and the "pixel" to a region of domain [74]. This point of view is very important because it has allowed the application of aspects of *signal processing theory* to rendering (§2.1). From this perspective, we can consider the process of collecting the signal transmitted through a 3D scene in a 2D image plane in two phases: the *sampling* and the *reconstruction* process. The two phases are of equal importance, so when one of the processes is not carried out correctly, the signal obtained contains unwanted energy that shows visually notable errors. The term *aliasing* (§2.1.1) is employed, sometimes erroneously, to refer to all of these: jaggies, motion strobing, moiré patterns, blurring, and many other objectionable artifacts in images and animations. It is important for any rendering method to reduce the effects of aliasing.

Descriptively, if f is the 2D signal seen from the image plane, $p = (x, y)$ is any point in this plane, P any finite set of points p, and $S(P) = \{(p, f(p)) \mid p \in P\}$ the samples set over P, we can consider an initial $S(P_0)$ that is evaluated to reconstruct an estimation $\hat{f}$ of the signal that may later be *resampled* over a new set of points P_1 in order to obtain the final set of samples $\hat{S}(P_1)$ (Fig. 1.3).

By the theory of the signal, in order to be able to evaluate it optimally, it is essential for it to be *band-limited*[5] (§2.1.1). In rendering, we have an important handicap, we cannot assume that the signal

---

[3] The global pass and local pass can be mixed but the tone-mapping is independent of the rendering equation solution.

[4] In classic radiosity, the projection step is efficiently made by hardware and therefore, the visualisation of a change of view is very fast.

[5] The spectrum $F(\omega)$ of a signal $f(t)$ has finite support: $\forall |\omega| > \omega_F . F(\omega) = 0$. The ω_F frequency is the *cut-off* frequency and the *bandwidth*.

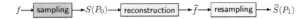

Figure 1.3: Discretisation of a continuous signal.

coming from a scene actually is band-limited, basically due to the make up of finite objects and the need to obtain sharpness images. This implies that the direct techniques of sampling and reconstruction cannot be strictly employed. The signal can be prefiltered before beginning the process of sampling but the actual scenes contain more and more complex geometry, surface textures, and shading models, and other components besides (e.g., light, fire, smoke, and fog), which are not at all easy to handle and which make the process unapproachable. For the same reason any analytic technique is also discarded. Thus, the current methods of rendering have to be based on *point sampling* so as to obtain information and take decisions on the value of visualising.

However, a new handicap appears: the complexity of the scene carries with it a very high cost for the sampling due to the value of the function being determined by the modelling of all the physical phenomena of light which occur inside the scene, complex enough in themselves. As Glassner says so well: *"Every sample is precious"* [74]. This is more certain every day, as in computer graphics more and more sophisticated scenes are manipulated, we distance ourselves from more analytical solutions and get closer to more costly samplings. Using a closer semantic to our objectives (§1.2), we can rewrite the previous claim as:

$$\textit{Minimise the number of samples and maximise its information.} \qquad (1.1)$$

That is, reduce the costs and improve the quality.

To attain a correct discretisation of the signal, techniques have been designed which tackle each process independently (Fig. 1.3), or otherwise, all at the same time. The majority of methods contain a common scheme called *adaptive refinement* (details in §2.1.3 and §4.4.1). There are two subjacent ideas:

- The signal of the image can present wide regions where there may be values that are constant or with few variations. This would mean that the signal is band-limited and so, within this neighbourhood, with a density of sampling which is not very high, we can collect the signal accurately. On the other hand, in other regions the signal can be very complex and will need a more detailed analysis. That will lead to increasing the sampling density in order to extract from it high frequencies and to reduce aliasing.

- In the majority of signals used in computer graphics, the intensity decreases on increasing the frequency, then as we increase the sampling rate we decrease the aliasing.

A standard process includes a test necessary, the *refinement criterion*, for determining when we consider the density of sampling, for capturing the signal, to be right. On finalising the *sampling*, the signal is sent to the *reconstruction* process by afterwards applying, if the occasion should arise, a *filtering* process before finally undergoing *resampling* to obtain the final datum (Fig. 1.3).

In rendering, the essential objective is to put a unique value on a pixel, so that the final resampling will coincide with the pixel grid (e.g., the centre of a pixel). With the pixel-driven approach, in order to estimate the signal, each sample takes the role of a ray of light which simulates physical laws. The whole image must be sampled from a viewpoint and the final resampling is included in the local process by every pixel. With the object-space approach, the signal has been reconstructed over the whole scene and the last part of the process consists in a global resampling from the viewpoint.

1.1.2 Information Theory

Developed in 1940s by Shannon [200], the *information theory* deals with the transmission and compression of data in any communication system [37] (§2.5). Currently, information theory is applied to many fields of science and technology such as communication theory, probability theory, physics, computer science, mathematics, economics, and statistics. It has brought fundamental contributions to other fields like biology, linguistics, neurology, learning, etc. [18, 37, 239]. In particular, it is also applied successfully to

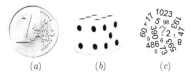

Figure 1.4: In an intuitive way, the entropy corresponds to the average number of binary questions to find out the result (§2.5.1). (*a*) The entropy of an Euro is 1: heads or tails (i.e., we only need one binary question for two options: $\log_2 2$). (*b*) For a dice, the entropy is 2.585 ($\log_2 6$). (*c*) To guess a number between 1 and 1,024 we need 10 questions (entropy of 10).
Credit: (*a*) © 2000 European Commission.

fields closely related to computer graphics such as medical image processing [247, 221, 165] or computer vision and robot motion [244, 5].

The basic concept in a communication system is *information*. It is simply the outcome of a selection from among a finite number of possibilities [243]. *Entropy* (§2.5.1) is the classical measure of information and expresses the *information content* or *uncertainty* (Fig. 1.4) of a random variable (§B). In other words, it is also a measure of the variation, dispersion, or diversity of a probability distribution of observed events. *Mutual information* (§2.5.2), a derived measure of entropy, expresses the *information transfer* in a communication channel. It is also a measure of the *dependence* or *correlation* between two random variables.

Recently, it has been demonstrated that we can apply information-theoretic measures in order to capture characteristics of the complexity of a scene [61, 63]. Thus, within a scene, the entropy measures its degree of randomness or uncertainty and the mutual information quantifies its degree of structure or correlation. In this work, we use information-theoretic measures to capture new types of scene complexity and to obtain new refinement criteria to improve the quality of the rendering.

1.1.3 Complexity

The study of *complexity* (§2.7) has become a very active research area in many different fields: automata, information theory, computer science, physics, biology, neuro-science, etc. The problem of characterising complexity in a quantitative way is a vast and rapidly developing subject and various interpretations of the term have been given in different disciplines.

In a generic way, in a first instance we dispose of the dictionary definition of "complex" object or system [134]: *"a whole made up of complicated or interrelated parts"*, and for "complicated" we obtain: *"consisting of parts intricately combined"* or *"difficult to analyse, understand, or explain"*. All the possible definitions of complexity employed seem to converge towards the measure of "difficulty" of performing any action or task on the object or system in question (i.e., construction, description, compression, updates, queries, etc. [121]). This difficulty will depend directly on how many parts there are and how the system is made up. From this perspective, and in agreement with Badii [9], the simultaneous presence of elements of *order* and *disorder*, some degree of *unpredictability*, and interactions between subsystems which change in *dependence* on how the system is subdivided, can be good parameters in the evaluation of its complexity.

Within the context of physically-based rendering (§1.1.1), a scene is a perfectly defined system. From the perspective of global illumination, given that in the behaviour of the simulation of the light propagation in the scene it is necessary to take all the interreflections between all the surfaces in the environment into account, the scene complies with all the characteristics of a complex system and there is no doubt that we can consider that we are faced with a problem of elevated "complexity". Thus, from both geometric visibility and illumination points of view, measures can be obtained which allow us to evaluate its complexity [61]. In this thesis, the study of new complexity measures in a scene helps us to better understand the structure and dependence of its elements (Fig. 1.5).

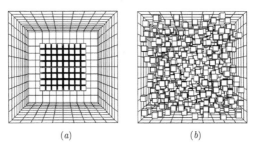

(a) (b)

Figure 1.5:   Visibility complexity of a discrete scene (§2.7.3). Which scene do you feel to be more "complex" from a visibility point of view?
Credit: Miquel Feixas [60].

(a) Measured scene   (b) Simulated scene   (c) Difference scene

Figure 1.6:   The rendering transforms a 3D world into a 2D image. We show the *Cornell Box*, the first scene in rendering. (a) The image was captured from a physical model under controlled lighting conditions using a photometric CCD camera. (b) The image was rendered using a geometric model with material properties and lighting set to identical values to the physical conditions of (a). (c) The difference image is simply a pixel-by-pixel subtraction of one image from the other.
Credit: © 1998 Cornell University Program of Computer Graphics, Cornell University, Ithaca (NY), USA.

1.2   Objectives

Over the last few decades, the field of action of computer graphics has become increasingly more important. This area covers a wide range of activities in society today: engineering, architecture, design, medicine, chemistry, biology, animation, photography, etc. The common factor is the description of real or virtual scenes through their analysis and transformation into digital image (Fig. 1.6). It is in this direction that this work is focused and is trying to make its contribution.

In 1998, within our research group, the possibilities of the application of information theory to computer graphics started to be studied. Acebo et al. [48] presented the first work in which its viability became clear and in Feixas [60] specific applications are shown. Following this line of research, this thesis was motivated by the analysis of the complexity of a closed scene. Thus, our first objective is:

> To present the study of complexity from a point of a scene (interior and on the surface) and also the interaction between different parts, from a geometric visibility point of view.

The second, and main objective, arises out of the difficulty in obtaining an accurate computation of the global illumination of a scene (§1.1). From this goal, we analyse the application of the information-theory to the kernel of the algorithms of rendering. Given the diversity of the existent methods, we evaluate the most representative of the pixel-driven and object-space approaches (§1.1.1): ray-tracing and radiosity, with the path-tracing and hierarchical modalities, respectively.

On the one hand, the ray-tracing method (§2.3.1) attempts to solve the equation of rendering (2.46) by an implicit function, evaluating for each pixel a set of point samples of the unknown radiance function. Like all point sampling algorithms, ray-tracing leads to the potential problem of aliasing (§2.1.1). To reduce this problem, the number of samples, the method of sampling, where they are cast, and also the mixed system used to assign the final colour of a pixel, are important. Many combinations of different techniques have been studied, but one critical factor amongst all of them is the search for a balance between the cost, proportional to the number of samples, and the image obtained (1.1). In order to attain this, one question is fundamental: what is the criterion in deciding when more samples are needed or not? And if more are needed, where? These questions are answered by the *refinement criteria* (§2.1.4).

On the other hand, the radiosity method (§2.4.2) attempts to solve the rendering equation by the construction of an explicit function that approximates the unknown radiance function. Classical radiosity eases the problem making some relaxations. The rendering equation is transformed into a radiosity equation (2.62) which is solved by an algorithm from the discretisation of the surfaces of the scene into a mesh of polygons, called *patches*, and the *form factors* (§2.2.2) between them. The main problems of the radiosity method are meshing and form factor computation. Scene meshing not only has to represent illumination variations accurately, but it also has to avoid unnecessary subdivisions of the surfaces that would increase the number of form factors to be computed, and consequently the computational time. Even though many variants of these techniques exist, yet again, one of the most common problems they have is in determining when a good balance has been reached between the cost and a good level of accuracy (1.1). The response to this critical factor is closely related to the *refinement criteria*, responsible for deciding when the computation is sufficient (§2.4.4). In this context, it is usual to refer to them as *oracles*.

Summarising, let us assume that a generic problem of rendering methods is taking decisions with respect to when we dispose of sufficient quality on the signal coming from the scene. More specifically, how many samples are necessary and where (ray-tracing), or how much discretisation is lacking (radiosity)? The study of the refinement criteria attempts to give an answer to these questions. In this work, the solutions are designed from information-theoretic concepts. Thus, our main objective is:

To introduce new refinement criteria in global illumination for rendering techniques (ray-tracing and radiosity) from information-theory-based tools.

Basically, only two groups of measures will be used to reach our objectives:

- *Information-theoretic measures* (§1.1.2 and §2.5).

    – Entropy.
        * Shannon entropy: classic version defined initially for communication analysis (§2.5.1).
        * Harvda-Charvát-Tsallis entropy: generalised version used in many fields of physics (§5.1).
    – Mutual information. Classic (§2.5.2) and generalised (§5.1.2) versions.

- *f-Divergences.* Family of convex functions that measure the divergence between probability distributions (§6.2).

    – Kullback-Leibler: Shannon relative entropy (2.77 and 6.7).
    – Chi-square: Classic divergence used in statistical areas (6.8).
    – Hellinger: Important divergence whose square root is a true metric (6.9).

In conclusion, in this dissertation we show the feasibility of the set of measures mentioned to deal with scene rendering problems. Our work is the natural step to be taken following Feixas [60] in the application of information theory to computer graphics, and we believe that other applications can be derived from the concepts introduced here (§7.4). Just as Glassner foresaw: *"when a photon is emitted from a lightsource and then strikes an object, that photon has effected the transfer of some* information *... it also tells us something about the relative visibility of the two points, and the amount of impact that lightsource will have on the final image"* [74].

1.3   Overview

Our previous objectives are developed in four chapters preceded by a summary of the concepts related in the framework. The work ends with a chapter of conclusions. Therefore, it is organised into the following chapters:

The foundations of the framework The foundations of the framework are reviewed to obtain a starting point for the continuing chapters and, at the same time, this gives us the opportunity to recognise existent problems. Also, the common necessary background is introduced leaving the most specific previous work for each corresponding chapter so these become more self-contained. First, an introduction to sampling theory is reviewed. Next, rendering tools are presented followed by an brief and specific overview of techniques of global illumination of ray-tracing and radiosity. An information-theoretic section is also presented following its applications to the scene as an information channel. The last section is dedicated to the complexity concept as well as its application in a scene.

Scene complexity measures From a geometric visibility point of view, three typologies of complexity on a scene are presented. Previously, the definition of measures to compute the "fields" of both information content and information transfer existing in the interior space of a scene, entropy field and mutual information field respectively, are introduced. From this latter, the *point complexity* is presented. Also, the concept of *animation complexity* is analysed. Finally, the *region complexity* is shown from two perspectives: from the surface points and from the interior points of the space which the region encloses.

Entropy-based sampling for ray-tracing By sampling, we capture radiance information, as well as geometric information, from the scene through the pixel in order to evaluate the homogeneity of the information and measure the necessity of taking samples from a double perspective: geometry and illumination. To do this, an appropriate information-theoretic tool is the Shannon entropy because of its properties. From it, we define the measures of *pixel quality* and *pixel contrast* both in relation to geometry and colour. We obtain, using the pixel contrast, new refinement criteria which are directly applicable to any supersampling ray-tracing technique. In addition, the recursive property of entropy enables us to present a new stochastic adaptive scheme: *entropy-based ray-tracing*.

Oracles based on generalised entropy for hierarchical radiosity We investigate the use of generalised information-theoretic measures to obtain better and cheaper oracles for hierarchical radiosity. Thus, new oracles in hierarchical radiosity based on Harvda-Charvát-Tsallis generalised entropy and generalised mutual information are introduced. Alongside three classic approaches (based on transported power, kernel smoothness and smoothness of received radiosity), we obtain the oracles based on *transported information*, *information smoothness*, and *mutual information*. The performance of these oracles is compared with the classic ones and with each other, the mutual information based oracle being the one which stands out.

Refinement criteria based on *f*-divergences The *f*-divergences are successfully used as measures of discrimination or distance in different scientific and engineering areas (e.g., multi-modal image registration [165]). Thus, we study their application to ray-tracing and hierarchical radiosity techniques for three members of the family of Csiszár's *f*-divergences: Kullback-Leibler, chi-square, and Hellinger divergences. Their behaviour is analysed with satisfactory results in both techniques.

Conclusions The conclusions and the main contributions of these previous chapters are presented, as well as some indications of connected works and future research. Also, the publications related with this thesis are referred to.

The appendixes give support at specific concepts of the framework. They review the preliminary mathematics employed throughout the work and establish notational aspects.

By default, all the considerations are made from a geometric visibility point of view of the modelled scene. When colour is considered, this is indicated explicitly[6]. All the results contained in this dissertation have been obtained with the same software. For the input, the Materials and Geometry Format[7] developed by Ward et al. [246], and for the output, the *RenderPark*[8] developed at the Computer Graphics Research Group of the Katholieke Universiteit Leuven, Belgium [33].

Summary

This dissertation belongs to the computer graphics field and deals with the application of the information theory to rendering problems. The framework of this work is three-rooted: *rendering* (image synthesis in computer graphics), *information theory*, and *complexity*.

The objectives of this thesis are: to present a study of the *complexity* in a scene from the interactions between its different parts and to introduce new *refinement criteria* for ray-tracing and radiosity techniques, from information-theoretic and *f*-divergence measures. This last goal constitutes the kernel of our work.

This work has been structured into the following chapters: the foundations of the framework, scene complexity measures, entropy-based sampling for ray-tracing, oracles based on generalised entropy for hierarchical radiosity, refinement criteria based on *f*-divergences (ray-tracing and radiosity), and conclusions.

---

[6] The term geometric visibility must be considered implicit in all the definitions of information-theoretic tools which do not consider colour.

[7] *"A least common denominator language for describing scenes and objects suitable for physically-based rendering applications"* [246].

[8] *"A photorealistic rendering tool"* [33].

Chapter 2

The Foundations of the Framework

In this chapter, we present the concepts that we consider to be essential for the development of the following chapters. The foundations of the three fields which make up the framework of this work (i.e., rendering, information theory, and complexity) are reviewed and, at the same time, the more important problems are formulated (§1.1). Initially we revise the sampling theory which includes the basis for understanding the handicaps that have to be faced in the digitisation of an image (§2.1). Following this, there are three specific rendering sections: rendering tools are presented (§2.2) together with two specific techniques, ray-tracing (§2.3) and radiosity (§2.4). Next, general concepts about information theory are reviewed (§2.5) followed by an interpretation of the scene as an information channel (§2.6). Finally, a special section about complexity and its application in a scene is presented (§2.7). More specific concepts will be introduced later according to the needs of each chapter.

2.1 Sampling Theory

In the previous chapter we remembered how important the signal processing is within the rendering theory (§1.1). Because a computer image is a digital signal, one of the most important areas in signal processing is the sampling theory, whose goal is to study the conversion of a continuous signal[1] to a discrete one. Therefore, we will focus our review on those specific aspects directly related to rendering. We follow the discussion of Glassner [74] closely.

2.1.1 Aliasing

The acquisition process of an continuous signal and converting it into digital can often lead to errors. These are the outcome of both the errors coming out of the sampling phase and the reconstructed signal. The latter, also called *reconstruction errors*, are particularly complex and often misinterpreted as sampling errors. Studying them falls beyond our scope so we will focus specifically on the sampling phase.

A basic question is: how many samples are necessary to ensure we are preserving the information contained in the signal? If the signal contains high frequency components, we will need to sample at a higher rate to avoid losing information that is in the signal. If we sample a band-limited continuous signal with a sampling frequency that is higher than twice the bandwidth of the input signal, then the *sampling theorem*[2] provides that we are able to reconstruct the original signal perfectly from the sampled data. Consequently, the maximum measurable frequency, called the *Nyquist limit*, is half of the sampling frequency. When a signal is sampled at a lower frequency than required by the sampling theorem, we say

---

[1] In general, computer graphics deals with continuous-time (or analytic) signals. They have a representation that enable us to evaluate them for any parameter value. We use only the term "continuous" due to the fact that the parameter may represent anything, not necessarily time.

[2] The theorem was formulated initially by Nyquist [143] (1928). It was later published by Kotelnikov (1933), Whittaker (1935), and Gabor (1946). Finally, it was proved by Shannon [201] (1949). It is also known as the Nyquist-Shannon sampling theorem.

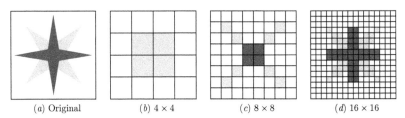

(a) Original   (b) 4 × 4   (c) 8 × 8   (d) 16 × 16

Figure 2.1: Image undersampling with three uniform grids. The sample set corresponds to the central point of each cell set. The jaggies appear at any level of the grid.

that the signal is *undersampled* (Fig. 2.1), and if it is sampled more than necessary, it is *oversampled*. If the signal frequency is higher than the Nyquist limit, then a phenomenon called *aliasing* takes place. This problem was presented in rendering by Crow [38, 39] and it can show up either in static images (spatial aliasing) or animated ones (temporal aliasing).

Aliasing is the presence of unwanted components in the reconstructed signal. These components were not present when the original signal was sampled and, moreover, some of the frequencies in the original signal may be lost in the reconstructed signal. That happens because different copies of the signal, called *alias*, can overlap if the sampling frequency is too low. If an image is sampled with a regular pattern that is too low, a variety of aliasing structures are visible in the result because the pattern inherent in the signal combines with the pattern created by the sampling geometry to produce a new pattern (e.g., a moiré pattern[3]). When we sample edges, we get a typical kind of aliasing, called *jaggies*, which cause stair steps. Notice that increasing the sampling frequency does not help to avoid this phenomenon (Fig. 2.1).

To solve the aliasing issue in rendering we cannot consider analytical answers, since they would only be efficient for those situations that present very simple conditions of geometry and colour (e.g., flat polygons and text). The signal usually has a finite width (e.g., square side length or height and radius of cylinders) and therefore, the continuous representation of the objects cannot be captured without error because the signal has an infinite support in frequency domain[4]. Thus, in general, it is unknown and not band-limited [74]. Nevertheless, a *low-pass filter* allows all frequencies over a specified frequency to be cut[5], and we could apply it before sampling to ensure that no components with frequencies greater than half the sample frequency remain. The ideal 2D low-pass filter is the *box function*:

$$\Pi_a^b(x,y) = \begin{cases} 1, & \text{if } |x| \leq \frac{a}{2} \wedge |y| \leq \frac{b}{2}, \\ 0, & \text{otherwise,} \end{cases} \tag{2.1}$$

where (a, b) is the bandwith. The Fourier transform is (Fig. 2.2):

$$F_a^b(u,v) = ab\,\text{sinc}(ua)\,\text{sinc}(vb) \qquad \text{sinc}(x) = \begin{cases} \frac{\sin(\pi x)}{\pi x}, & \text{if } x \neq 0, \\ 1, & \text{if } x = 0. \end{cases} \tag{2.2}$$

---

[3] Interference pattern created by two grids (different angles or sizes). The term originates from the French word "moiré", a type of textile with a rippled or watered appearance.
[4] Fourier analysis allows to prove that a signal cannot, simultaneously, have finite width (i.e., compact support in signal space) and be band-limited (i.e, compact support in frequency space).
[5] A *high-pass filter* is the opposite and a *band-pass filter* is a combination of both.

Since the sinc function has infinite support[6], applying an ideal low-pass filter to the frequency domain, besides a loss in quality, it requires infinite spatial support and so is not computable[7]. If we take the approach of truncating this spatial support with another box filter[8] then we get a new filter in the frequency domain that involves loss of information and the appearance of new artifacts (e.g., ringing or Gibbs phenomenon). And, to make things more difficult, assuming that we could meet the theoretical conditions for applying the sampling theorem, the reconstruction process is by convolution of the sinc function[9] so, there is no easy way to remove the issues referred to here. Summing up, the optimal reconstruction is theoretically possible, but in practise, the conditions cannot be met or, it is not computable.

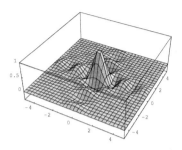

Figure 2.2: The Fourier transform of Π_1^1.

2.1.2 Point Sampling

As an alternative to the conclusion of the previous section, we can think of a simple and cheap approach that consists of taking a *point sample* within each pixel to capture the signal (usually the centre of the pixel). Given the possibility that this sampling frequency is not enough, we can sample at a higher frequency: *supersampling*. This means that each pixel will take more than one sample that will be later converted into a single value. The number of samples that we may need depends on the spatial distribution of the samples, the quality of the reconstruction method, and the complexity of the scene. The simplest way to implement supersampling consists of taking a $n \times n$ grid of samples for each pixel, and an easy way to get a single value is by weighting each sample proportionally to the area it represents (i.e., by using a reconstruction box filter for each region). Thus,

$$\overline{S} \approx \sum_{i=1}^{n^2} a_i s_i, \tag{2.3}$$

where s_i is the function value sampled, a_i is the proportional area representative of sample s_i ($\sum_{i=1}^{n^2} a_i = 1$), and $\overline{S}$ is the estimated value. Now, if we consider the image in Fig. 2.1.a as an individual pixel, we can observe the evident gain of quality with the use of supersampling. Obviously, supersampling offers many possibilities (grid size, sample location, low-pass filter, reconstruction filter, etc.) and, at the same time, the combination of them offers many variants [49, 74]. It is important to bear in mind that we should strive for a balance between the computational cost and the outcome (1.1), for we will never be able to represent a continuous signal on a discrete plane with precision.

2.1.3 Sampling Methods

There are two main groups of sampling methods[10]:

Uniform Also called regular or periodic. The sampling pattern can be described with respect to a *lattice* (i.e., a set of points generated by combining a basis of vectors in all possible ways): rectangular [248, 189], hexagonal [49], triangular [211], diamond [22], etc.

---

[6] It can also be expressed as $\Pi_{k=1}^{\infty} \left(1 - \frac{x^2}{k^2}\right)$, $\Pi_{k=1}^{\infty} \cos \frac{x}{2^k}$, or $(\Gamma(1+x)\Gamma(1-x))^{-1}$ (C.1). Fourier analysis allows it to be proved that any near-ideal low-pass filter has infinite support in the spatial domain.

[7] Real options employed for sinc consist in a tabulated sampling at a predetermined rate.

[8] The set of functions used to truncate the sinc functions are called *windows* (e.g., rectangular or box, Bartlett, Welch, and Parzen).

[9] This is no surprise since the sampling theorem filters with the inverse Fourier transform of ideal filter: a box function.

[10] We follow the classification of Glassner [74].

Nonuniform Also called stochastic or aperiodic. Any sampling technique that produces a pattern that is not periodic: Poisson-disk sampling [49, 135, 133], jittered sampling [35, 49], hierarchical sampling [106], importance sampling [205], N-rooks sampling [207, 206], complete stratification at each refinement level [198], quasi-Monte Carlo sampling [110, 144], etc.

The advantage of uniform sampling is that if we assume that the signal is band-limited, then the reconstruction process can be theoretically driven (sampling theorem) and the original signal can be reconstructed with its corresponding losses and artifacts (§2.1.1). We also have aliasing[11] because this assumption is not valid within our context. The search for patterns that help to avoid this is the source of a great variety of nonuniform sampling methods. The origins go back to Yen [254] and Leneman [119] and were applied to rendering by Cook [34], Dippé and Wold [49], Bouville et al. [22], etc. The nonuniform methods are used in computer graphics for two basic reasons: they offer the chance to use variable sampling density, and they allow structured aliasing for noise to be traded. As a result of this, the reconstructed signal is still wrong but now it is important to take into account that the human visual system is able to ignore a large amount of noise, with the exception of the structural errors. This major tolerance to noise makes nonuniform sampling the most widely used method. We mention here the basic strategies of nonuniform sampling (combinations of them are also used).

Poisson Sampling The basic nonuniform sampling method. The goal is just to place the samples out of the regular uniform pattern (Fig. 2.3.a). To achieve this, the samples are placed, randomly, anywhere and so, are aperiodic (i.e., there is no single structure that is repeated across the domain). The advantage, as we said above, is that the highly structured aliasing artifacts that intrude in uniformly sampled signals turn into noise. A disadvantage is that, in those cases where the number of samples is minimised, a worst case sample distribution can generate a wrong reading of the signal.

Stratified Sampling The method of stratification is a particular case of Poisson sampling. The objective is to avoid the problem mentioned above, where a group of samples occur in the same region. To solve this, the domain is broken into *strata* or regions that do not necessarily have the same size or shape. Each of these regions will receive one sample (Fig. 2.3.b). However, a poor design of the strata can still clump the samples together locally. The advantage of stratified sampling is the guarantee that the samples are not all clumped together in one region, and the disadvantage is that we must decide on the number and shape of strata.

Importance Sampling The importance sampling consists in distributing the samples in such a way that each one represents the same amount of energy (Fig. 2.3.c). Thus, they are located more densely in regions where the signal has a large value, but this requires knowing the function in advance. To lessen the problem, a filter function is used in rendering which controls the density over the domain, in the hope that the filtered signal will have about the same shape as the filter. In practise, the filter is divided into regions which are evaluated by determining its importance. The process can be recursively repeated for each region.

Adaptive Sampling The adaptive sampling methods attempt to put samples where they will do the most good by concentrating them in "complex" regions and leaving them sparse in simple regions (Fig. 2.3.d). It is often implemented by first sampling with a base pattern of some predetermined density. This set of samples is our first estimate of the signal. Afterwards, the samples are evaluated with respect to any refinement criterion. If required, a refinement strategy creates and evaluates additional samples in the selected region. This process is applied recursively until the criterion is met or some upper limit on the recursion level is achieved. The two important issues in adaptive refinement are where to place the new samples and what criteria to use to stop the refinement. Kirk and Arvo [111] show that the simple form of refinement process introduces a bias into the final result. The problem is a connection between the values of the base samples, the test, and the final set of samples. It is not quite clear whether this

---

[11] We understand aliasing as the result of all artifacts that occur.

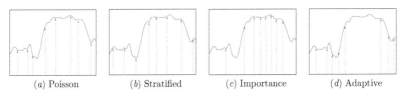

| (a) Poisson | (b) Stratified | (c) Importance | (d) Adaptive |

Figure 2.3: Four types of nonuniform sampling.

theoretical issue has much effect on the problems of computer graphics. Regardless of this, the same authors presented a solution for correcting the bias.

2.1.4 Refinement Criteria

In any adaptive strategy, the critical factor is the selection of a good refinement criteria that will be used in the process of subdivision[12]. The objective of the process is to work out the best characterisation of the signal of a region. So, when the captured values are homogeneous enough, we may consider that the signal is a good representation of the region. Otherwise, if it is too heterogeneous, we understand that the signal is not very clear and we proceed to apply a refinement. We present a basic selection of the refinement criteria according to the type of information: *intensity* (image-space based) or *geometry* (object-space based). Over-refined variants and hybrid methods have been designed, while at the same time we always looked for the right balance between cost and efficiency (1.1).

Image-Space

The intensity is the signal in the image-space sampling. We consider two subgroups: those that are based on intensity comparisons and those based on statistical measures. Let $S = \{s_1, \ldots, s_n\}$ be the set of values obtained by sampling which are put in the test.

Intensity Comparison   A representation can be:

- *Intensity difference.* The difference between the minimum and maximum values are compared with a constant parameter:
$$S_{\min} - S_{\max} < \epsilon. \tag{2.4}$$
  If the test fails, the refinement continues[13]. Whitted presented this test in his first paper on adaptive point-sampling [248].

- *Intensity groups.* A variant of the intensity difference is used by Jansen and van Wijk [99]. The minimum and maximum values are compared separately with a new constant parameter t:
$$|S_{\max} - t| < \epsilon \wedge |S_{\min} - t| < \epsilon. \tag{2.5}$$
  If one of these differences is not lower than a predefined ϵ, then the test fails and a new subdivision will be generated. In order to reduce the computational time, the ϵ value can be increased as the recursion level increases[14]. This means that first levels of recursion are more important than the rest.

- *Intensity contrast.* Mitchell [135] presents one of the most widely used intensity measures, the *contrast* [25]:
$$C(S) = \frac{S_{\max} - S_{\min}}{S_{\max} + S_{\min}}. \tag{2.6}$$

---

[12] By default, if the criterion fails, more refinement is necessary.

[13] A common rule at the image plane is to use $\epsilon = \frac{1}{2^d}$, where d is the depth of the colour value. Beyond this limit, the human eye cannot perceive the difference.

[14] The authors obtained good results with a sequence of 0, 0.05, and 0.15 for ϵ values.

Mitchell observes that, in an RGB colour system (§2.2.4), the different contrast values can be used for each channel, thus allowing each component to be weighted according to the human system of vision, where the eye is more sensitive to green, red, and blue, in this order. Mitchell computes a separate contrast for each channel and the test fails when any contrast is higher than a given threshold[15]. Other definitions of contrast can be used (e.g., $(S_{\max} - S_{\min})/S_{\max}$).

This method presents problems when the values are all zero or very small. In the latter case, the test is too sensitive (e.g., for $S = \{1, 3\}$ and $S = \{0.01, 0.03\}$, we obtain the same result: $C(S) = 0.5$). It is possible that we may not be interested in continuing the sampling when the values are very small and the test should control this. A solution consists of weighting the contrast by the mean of the samples: $\overline{C}(S) = C(S)\overline{S}$ [74] (e.g., for the previous case, $\overline{C}(S)$ will be 1 and 0.01 coinciding with what we would like to happen).

Simmons and Séquin [216], within an interactive rendering context, present a *priority-value* based on the above concepts (contrast and perception) for their refinement test in a RGB space. With regard to the colour, they use

$$p_c = 0.4\overline{C}(R) + 0.3\overline{C}(G) + 0.6\overline{C}(B), \tag{2.7}$$

where R, G, and B represent the subset of intensity values for the red, green, and blue components of set S, respectively. The p_c value is combined with a geometric datum (2.14) in order to get a more accurate priority-value (2.15).

Intensity Statistics   Representative examples are shown here:

- *Variance test.* The variance σ_n^2 (B.1) of a set S of n samples is the base of this method proposed by Lee et al. [117]. The test evaluates the quality of S by checking if the variance is below a predetermined threshold t:

$$\sigma_n^2 < t. \tag{2.8}$$

The sampling process finishes when the test is true. They also suggest a less precise variant which tests if the probability that the variance is less than t is within some probability tolerance β:

$$\frac{\sigma_n^2}{\chi_\beta^2} < t, \tag{2.9}$$

where χ^2 is the chi-square function (C.6). If the test fails, another sample is made and the test is repeated.

From a visual perception perspective, Mitchell [135] considers that variance is a poor measure of local variation. Bolin and Meyer [20] control the variance with an error metric to determine the optimal number of samples in Monte Carlo ray-tracing and also present an interesting adaptive sampling algorithm based on a visual perception model that estimates the error as a function of variance [21].

- *Confidence test.* This method was presented by Purgathofer [169]. The idea is to continue sampling until the confidence level or probability that the true value $\overline{S}_T$ is within a given tolerance t of the estimated value $\overline{S}$ is $1 - \alpha$ (§C):

$$Pr\{\overline{S}_T \in [\overline{S} - t, \overline{S} + t]\} \geq 1 - \alpha. \tag{2.10}$$

When only the sample standard deviation s (B.2) is known, the true mean lies within the interval of width $2t$ around $\overline{S}_T$ with minimum probability α if

$$t_{1-\alpha,n-1}\frac{s}{\sqrt{n}} \leq t, \tag{2.11}$$

---

[15] The author suggests $\epsilon = (0.4, 0.3, 0.6)$ for an RGB colour system.

where $t_{1-\alpha,n-1}$ is the parameter of the t-distribution with $n-1$ degrees of freedom with an error probability of $1-\alpha$ (C.4).

The predefined parameters are studied by Purgathofer and

$$n \geq \frac{\log(1-\alpha)}{\log(1-t)} \qquad (2.12)$$

is a suggested number of samples to start the test. Observe how n grows fast as the confidence increases and the interval decreases.

Painter and Sloan [151] also use a confidence level together with the variance to compare the t-test with a threshold. Tamstorf and Jensen [224] use the confidence interval in the same way as Purgathofer but with the inclusion of a tone-operator included in the formula with the objective that the samples be concentrated in those regions where they contribute most to the final appearance of the image.

- *Sequential analysis test.* Maillot et al. [126] presented this method to guide their sampling process. The idea is to assume that the range of intensity values of S with respect to the mean $\overline{S}$ is a good measure of homogeneity. The test calculates the probability p that the value of a sample s_i is within a margin ϵ of $\overline{S}$:

$$p = Pr\{|s_i - \overline{S}| < \epsilon\}. \qquad (2.13)$$

The way this method works consists in initially taking a sample set as base and determining $\overline{S}$. For each of the samples s_i we check if they are within the range $[\overline{S} - \epsilon, \overline{S} + \epsilon]$ and we calculate the percentage of those that fall inside, p_{in}, and outside, p_{out}. If p_{in} is greater than a threshold t_{in}, it suggests that the domain of samples is sufficiently homogeneous and the process can be stopped. If p_{out} is greater than a threshold t_{out}, the process can also be stopped because we assume that the region is heterogeneous and the actual set of samples is representative enough of this variety. Finally, if the percentages are not big enough to take a decision, then we need more sampling, and the process continues[16].

Many other possible valid tests using similar or different statistical measures and combinations of them can be used (e.g., Dippé and Wold [49] present an error estimator based on the root-mean-square signal-to-noise ratio of the sample set).

Object-Space

If we consider the sample as a ray that crosses the scene we will obtain data on the objects that are found along the way: an object-intersection history. This history can be gathered either by considering the path of the sample as a simple beam or a bounced-off beam of light. In both cases, the sample set can provide much additional information about the contents of the scene besides the intensity. The refinement methods that are designed using this information are known as *object-based refinement tests* and are typically ray-tracing techniques (§2.3). Some examples: object-difference test [189], four-level test [6], object-count test [87], mean-distance test [240], Cooks's test [34], and ray-tree comparison [2].

Here we only comment on a useful and simple geometric measure for refinement: the *depth difference*, used recently in the image based rendering field to weight pixel colour for reconstruction purposes [168], adaptive sampling strategies [45, 46], and interactive rendering [216]:

$$p_d = 1 - \frac{D_{\min}}{D_{\max}}, \qquad (2.14)$$

where D is the set of distances of the first object hits. Note that $p_d \in [0,1]$ plays the role of depth of field of the camera.

Simmons and Séquin [216] combine this measure with colour using p_c (2.7) in order to obtain a better priority-value:

$$p_v = \delta p_c + (1-\delta)p_d, \qquad (2.15)$$

where $\delta \in [0,1]$. They obtained good results with $\delta = 0.9$.

---

[16] Based on the human visual system, Maillot [73] proposes $t_{\text{in}} = 0.7$ i $t_{\text{out}} = 0.9$ as good threshold values.

2.1.5   Refinement Geometry

While the refinement test tells us when we need to sample at a higher rate, the *refinement geometry* tells us where we should address the new set of samples. The range of methods is very wide since there is a strong dependency on the sampling process that has been chosen. Below we present a selection of three groups with the understanding that there is an intersection of certain criteria. More or less to a degree, all methods follow an adaptive strategy searching for the geometric location of the most complex signal:

Cell Partition   Initially we consider a group of cells that is made up of a grid on the image plane, which does not necessarily have to match the grid of pixels. These cells are the basis for starting the sampling, and the methods that divide them up, one way or another, belong to this group. One straightforward way to reconstruct the signal, which is done quite often by these methods, consists of weighting the values representative of each subcell proportionally by its area (2.3).

Roth [189] presents a bipartition system that looks for edges with the help of an object-difference test for refinement. Searching for edges too, Hashimoto et al. [87], in the case where there are more than two objects, split the cell into four subcells and this is repeated until the object-count refinement test is achieved.

On a separate approach, the following references mostly use a refinement test based on intensity comparison. Whitted [248] assigns the cell to the pixel and samples at each corner. If we need to sample more, the cell is partitioned off into four equal subcells and the process is repeated at each new quadrant. Triangular partitions have been analysed by Shu and Liu [211]. A diamond pattern based on adaptive refinement is used by Bouville et al. [22] in a similar way to that of Whitted. Similarly, Akimoto et al. [2] show a method that starts with supercells, where at each level of refinement they switch between square and diamond patterns. Jansen and Van Wijk [99] propose a grid of cells at a high level and a grid of pixels at a low level. From now on the positions of the sampling set and the refinement test are totally predetermined. If a subdivision is required, they are also partitioned off into four subcells and the process goes to a lower level.

Multiple-Level   The main feature of this group consists of having several sampling patterns with different densities available. It is started with the lowest level and while the refinement test requires it and not all the levels have run out, the following pattern in density will be employed. Therefore, the geometry is explicit in the definition of the pattern. Examples of these models are Cook [34], Mitchell [135], and Dippé and Wold [49].

Tree-Based   These are methods which base the geometric distribution of the samples on a tree structure. Here the refinements and the structure base are closely related. A binary tree which is scanned breadth-first was presented by Kajiya [106]. Every node (region) is sampled once and if refinement is necessary, the node is split in two, now sampling the empty subnode and re-evaluating the two subnodes. This type of structure allows us to estimate the signal for adaptive hierarchical integration, weighting the sample values by the areas of their nodes (e.g., piecewise-continuous (2.16)). Similarly, the approach of Painter and Sloan [151] also uses a tree. Starting from the pixel level, the adequate density is approached by refining the structure. Other factors apart from homogeneity are taken advantage of in considering refinement tests: areas, means of samples, variances, etc. Some of these measures can be employed by designing levels of priority between the nodes or sub-trees (e.g., the variance weighted by the area).

2.1.6   Reconstruction

As we have already mentioned in the previous chapter (§1.1), all the effort of the process of sampling could be devalued if there is not enough care taken in the process of reconstruction. New artifacts can appear along with the aliasing: ripple, anisotropic effects, ringing, blurring, etc. These are the *reconstruction errors*.

We have seen (§2.1.1) that, in theory, certain functions can be perfectly reconstructed from a set of samples (i.e., uniform sampled, band-limited ones) but that, in practise, this approach cannot be used due to the complexity of the function sinc (2.2). So it is necessary to get close to a balance between the difficulty of implementing the process and the perfection of the filter within the spatial domain. We are entering the field of *filter design*. There are simple and complex possibilities in all the fields of application but we must not lose sight of two aims: reducing the aliasing introduced in the sampling process and capturing the original undistorted signal.

In uniform sampling, simple and usual reconstruction filters are[17]: rectangular or box (2.1), linear interpolation or tent function, quadratic functions, cubic functions, Gaussian functions, etc. Discussions on the problem can be found in Oppenheim and Schafer [145], Gabel and Roberts [70], Dudgeon and Mersereau [51], Wolberg [250], etc. In our context, we focus on the nonuniform sampling which allows us to deal with a sample rate variable and, as a consequence, to obtain a reduction in aliasing at the cost of the introduction of noise (§2.1.3). A type of noise at high-frequency is the *shot noise*, which is due to the fact that several samples, called *rogues* or *outliers*[18], have an excessive value with respect to the rest.

We should remember that the reconstruction process is followed by a resampling process at lower density (§1.1.1). This creates the need for a low-pass filter after the reconstruction filter so that there are no frequencies over the Nyquist limit (e.g., shot noise). Whenever it is possible, for practical reasons[19], the two processes are combined. Therefore, the methodology of the *reconstruction point* is characterised by evaluating the set of samples and obtaining one value from the signal which has already been reconstructed and filtered. In this way, we save carrying out the final resampling process. This reconstruction point refers to the neighbourhood corresponding to the set of samples which have been evaluated.

In rendering, we are interested in local approximation to the specific signal: the pixel. The resampling process always coincides with the pixel grid and usually at the centre of the pixel. When the neighbourhood coincides with the pixel, the reconstruction phase and resampling can be joined together by considering the reconstruction point to be the centre of the pixel. Regarding the filter, it is usual to assume that the values of the estimated signal near the centre of pixels are more important than the values in the zones that are further away from this centre. What is happening is that we are applying importance sampling to the resampling, implicitly guided by the great weight that we give to the centre of the pixel in comparison with its borders.

The possibilities of combining reconstruction and filtering for nonuniform sampling are numerous, and they vary from algorithm to algorithm, and for each of the adopted solutions many variations appear. A list of surveys and applications on nonuniform reconstruction are: Shirley and Wang [210], Feichtinger and Gröchening [59], Heckbert [90], Pratt [135], etc. We now make note of some of the techniques that are employed[20]:

Local Filters Set of techniques which apply a reconstruction filter (or a combination with a low-pass filter) directly to the sampled data, centred on the reconstruction point, just as it would be done for the phase of resampling of a uniform sampling. As a result, the filters used in uniform sampling are also valid options but, how a filter is applied to nonuniform reconstruction depends of each algorithm.

In the survey of Mitchell and Netravali [136] the characteristics of the local filters are evaluated and, with textures, in Greene and Heckbert [81]. A collection of radially symmetric filters would be: Pavicic [159] (B-splines), Cook [34] (difference of Gaussians), Dippé and Would [49] (cosinus), Max [132] (special curve), and Mitchell and Netravali [136] (splines curves). This last is one of the most frequently used in rendering because of its good behaviour and it includes a set of usual spline filters as particular cases.

Warping Techniques which convert the nonuniform sampling into uniform sampling by using an invertible mapping. If this mapping is band-limited, then the signal can be reconstructed by a nonuniform version of sampling theorem. These methods are restrictive and complex [28, 90, 250].

---

[17] The majority of them are also employed to truncate the function sinc as windows (§2.1.1).
[18] Lee and Redner [116] introduced an *alpha filter* to eliminate them.
[19] Cost in time which includes Fourier transforms.
[20] We follow the classification of Glassner [74].

Iteration An estimate of the signal and a variable of error are calculated. Afterwards, these data are worked on iteratively to obtain new estimates until convergence is attained. The results are generally good but they are high in cost. [152, 193, 131, 58].

Piecewise-Continuous The neighbourhood is tiled in regions without gaps. This method was presented by Whitted [248] using rectangular regions and a box filter to form a single flat reconstructed surface over the neighbourhood. The signal estimation is weighted by the area of each region. Wyvill and Sharp [252] opt for dividing up in accordance with one edge[21] that passes through a region. A special system weights the sample values with the areas. Painter and Sloan [151] use a tree to make the reconstruction. The tree-structure contains rectangles with a sample[22] representative of it. The structure contains complete information on a perfect partition of any region where the application of a filter is easy. We can express its calculation as

$$p(x,y) = \int_A f(x-u, y-v)s(x,y)\,du\,dv$$
$$= \sum_{i=1}^{n} \mathbf{s}_i \int_{A_i} f(x-u, y-v)\,du\,dv, \qquad (2.16)$$

where $p(x,y)$ is the value of the *reconstruction point* in a neighbourhood A, and $f(x,y)$ a filter function over a signal $s(x,y)$ represented in the last expression as a sum of n subregions with area A_i and value $\mathbf{s}_i$.

Multi-Step In situations of great changes in density and those which are far from uniform, reconstruction generates *grain noise*. Mitchell [135] contributes with a multistage filter which consists in the successive application of a box filter. The process begins by filtering at a first stage with a small step which will be doubled at every stage until it covers the whole region. Every new stage has the effect of smoothing the signal at the next level. Thus, by the last stage, the value returned by the filter should contain less grain noise.

Finally, we should consider that all the proceedings employed to produce a good signal are trying to find a trade off between the aliasing and the noise. Given that these two factors cannot be totally eliminated[23], with respect to the quality of rendering, we will never be capable of reproducing the perfect image but we will be able at least to create an illusion close enough to reality (§1.1.1).

2.2   Rendering

As we have already advanced in §1.1.1, the process of synthesising a real scene aims to transform an image of the continuous 3D world to the discrete 2D one with the greatest precision possible (Fig. 2.4). To attain this goal it is necessary to design multidisciplinary algorithms (signal processing, physics, and vision) which achieve a good approximation to the solution. Within our framework of physically-based global illumination, complementing the concepts of signal processing (§2.1), in this section we present some mathematical concepts[24] useful for rendering which are related to physics and vision: Monte Carlo integration (§2.2.1), form factors (§2.2.2), the light behaviour from the rendering equation (§2.2.3), and colour spaces (§2.2.4).

---

[21] Restriction for each region.

[22] Assumption that the whole rectangle is uniform in the sample colour.

[23] In real particle physics, the *uncertainty principle* (Werner K. Heisenberg, 1927) is fulfilled [93]. A consequence is that any pair of related physical data fulfil a strong relationship with respect to the precision of their measurement: the better the knowledge of one value, the less certain we can be about the other. Because of the product of two incertitudes has to be maintained over a universal constant, below a certain limit, reductions in aliasing will correspond to increases in noise and vice versa. As a result, the error in the signal must continue and it will be either in a regular way (aliasing), or otherwise, in an irregular way (noise) [74].

[24] See §A and §B for geometric and probabilistic notation, respectively.

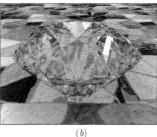

(a)   (b)

Figure 2.4: Two rendering applications: (a) engineering design and (b) diamond cutting.
Credit: (a) Mercedes-Benz SLK, © 2004 Daimler-Chrysler AG. Rendered with mental ray®, © 2005
mental images GmbH., Berlin, Germany. (b) Diamond, rendered with NuGraf®, copyright © 1995-2008
Okino Computer Graphics, Inc., Toronto (Ontario), Canada. All Rights Reserved.

2.2.1 Monte Carlo Integration

In order to obtain an image of quality we must calculate the colour of each pixel accurately. Given that we are only interested in one sole value per pixel, an efficient way of doing this is to apply the reconstruction point, simplifying the process of reconstruction of the signal (§2.1.6). A useful technique to deal with this kind of problems is *Monte Carlo integration* [84].

The aim of the Monte Carlo method is to formulate the solution of a given mathematical problem as the expected value of a given random variable. By sampling this random variable, the solution of the problem is estimated. Thus, to solve an integral by Monte Carlo we convert it to an expected value. Following, we give a brief overview. For a general and more detailed description of Monte Carlo method, see Rubinstein [190], Kalos [109], Sillion and Puech [215], Glassner [74], Bekaert [12], and Szirmay-Kalos [223].

Let us suppose we want to solve the integral of a function $f(x)$. This can be written as

$$I = \int_D f(x)\mathrm{d}x = \int_D \frac{f(x)}{g(x)}g(x)\mathrm{d}x, \tag{2.17}$$

where $g(x)$ is a pdf of a random variable X. The integral can be read as the expected value of the random variable $\frac{f(X)}{g(X)}$ with respect to the pdf $g(x)$:

$$I = E_f\left[\frac{f(X)}{g(X)}\right]. \tag{2.18}$$

The term $\frac{f(x_1)}{g(x_1)}$, where x_1 is obtained by sampling from the $g(x)$, is a *primary estimator* for the integral I:

$$I \approx \widehat{I}^1 = \frac{f(x_1)}{g(x_1)}. \tag{2.19}$$

This estimator is unbiased (i.e., $E[\widehat{I}^1] = I$). The variance of this estimator is given by

$$\sigma^2\left[\widehat{I}^1\right] = E\left[\left(\frac{f(X)}{g(X)}\right)^2\right] - \left(E\left[\frac{f(X)}{g(X)}\right]\right)^2 = \int_D \frac{f(x)^2}{g(x)}\mathrm{d}x - I^2. \tag{2.20}$$

Averaging n independent primary estimators (obtained by sampling n independent values $x_1, \ldots, x_n$ from $g(x)$), we obtain the unbiased *secondary estimator* $\widehat{I}_n^2$:

$$I \approx \widehat{I}_n^2 = \frac{1}{n}\sum_{i=1}^n \frac{f(x_i)}{g(x_i)}, \tag{2.21}$$

with variance

$$\sigma^2\left[\hat{I}_n^2\right] = \frac{1}{n}\sigma^2\left[\hat{I}^1\right] = \frac{1}{n}\left(\int_D \frac{f(x)^2}{g(x)}\mathrm{d}x - I^2\right). \tag{2.22}$$

So, we obtain better estimators as the number of samples increases. This result is according to the weak law of large numbers, which states that, for identically independent distributed random variables, $\frac{1}{n}\sum_{i=1}^n X_i$ is close to its expected value $E[X]$ for large numbers of n. Obviously the variance depends on the pdf chosen. When we use a pdf that resembles the integrand we are doing *importance sampling*, which can dramatically reduce the variance of our estimator [109].

It can be observed from (2.22) that the standard deviation $\sigma[X]$, which represents the error, decreases at a rate of $\frac{1}{\sqrt{n}}$ as the number of samples increases.

2.2.2 Form Factors

In physics, the term *form factor* describes the fraction of radiant energy which leaves one surface and reaches a second surface [212]. In other fields it is also called geometric factor, configuration factor, or shape factor. It takes into account the distance between the surfaces (the centre), their orientation in space relative to each other, and their differential of areas. It is important to note that the form factor is exclusively a geometric relationship, independent of any viewpoint or surface attributes, and that it is a dimensionless quantity.

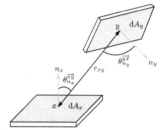

Figure 2.5: Differential to differential form factor.

Definition 1 *The form factor between two elements is given by*

- *Differential-to-differential (Fig. 2.5)*

$$F_{\mathrm{d}A_x \leftrightarrow \mathrm{d}A_y} = \frac{\cos\theta_{n_x}^{\overline{xy}}\cos\theta_{n_y}^{\overline{yx}}}{\pi r_{xy}^2}V(x,y) \tag{2.23}$$

- *Differential-to-finite*

$$F_{\mathrm{d}A_x \to A_j} = \int_{A_j} F_{\mathrm{d}A_x \leftrightarrow \mathrm{d}A_y}\mathrm{d}A_y \tag{2.24}$$

- *Finite-to-finite*

$$F_{A_i \to A_j} = \frac{1}{A_i}\int_{A_i}\int_{A_j} F_{\mathrm{d}A_x \leftrightarrow \mathrm{d}A_y}\mathrm{d}A_y\mathrm{d}A_x \tag{2.25}$$

Within the context of a discretised scene (closed environment), the previous form factors are called *point-to-point*[25], *point-to-patch*, and *patch-to-patch*, respectively, under the understanding that all the points involved belong to surfaces of the scene[26]. The intermediate point-to-patch form factor can be seen as the limit of the patch-to-patch form factor when the area of the first patch decreases to zero. The set of all form factors can be seen as a matrix $F^{N_\mathrm{p}\times N_\mathrm{p}}$ where[27] $F_{ij} = F_{i\to j}$ and all rows and columns add up to 1. The form factors play an essential role in many of the techniques used and, particularly, in radiosity (§2.4).

---

[25] Noted $F_{x\leftrightarrow y}$.
[26] This will not be the case in §3.
[27] A matrix element $F_{i,j}^{N_\mathrm{p}\times N_\mathrm{p}}$ is usually noted F_{ij} if it does not generate any ambiguity.

Form Factor Properties

We note the following properties between patches:

- *Reciprocity*

$$A_i F_{i \to j} = A_j F_{j \to i} \quad \forall i, j \qquad (2.26)$$

- *Energy conservation* (closed environment)

$$\sum_{j \in S} F_{i \to j} = 1 \quad \forall i \qquad (2.27)$$

- *Additivity*

$$F_{i \to j \cup k} = F_{i \to j} + F_{i \to k}, \qquad (2.28)$$

where i, k, and j are three disjoint patches. In general the reverse is not true: $F_{i \cup j \to k} \neq F_{i \to k} + F_{j \to k}$. In fact, if the patch i is divided into n subpatches, we obtain

$$\sum_{k=1}^{n} A_{i_k} F_{i_k \to j} = A_i F_{i \to j}. \qquad (2.29)$$

Form Factor Computation

The computation of the form factors is difficult even for simple surfaces, and the presence of occlusions makes it even more difficult (visibility function §A). The first idea, the *Nusselt analog* (1928), is based on the hemispherical projection body that allows the simple and accurate calculation of the form factor between a surface and a point on a second surface:

$$F_{dA_x \to A_j} = \frac{A_p}{\pi r^2}, \qquad (2.30)$$

where A_p is the area projected by $\Omega_{x \to A_j}$ on the base of the hemisphere of radius r centred at x. It was from the 80's that this problem was tackled in more depth. Thus, based on the Nusselt analog, Cohen and Greenberg [29] presented the hemicube, Malley [127] published a Monte Carlo approach, and Sillion and Puech [214] the method of the single-plane (a variation of hemicube).

No analytical closed-form solution exists except for very simple shapes without occlusions. Schroeder and Hanrahan [199] solved the polygon-to-polygon case, and in Siegel and Howell [212] or Glassner [74], we can find an extensive list of formulæ for simple shapes. When occlusions between patches exist, we can use deterministic numerical approximations to compute the form factors. Different methods can be found in the literature [215, 74]. We review here three different ways of computing the patch-to-patch form factor (2.25) based on Monte Carlo technique [195, 12].

- *Uniform area sampling.*

To calculate the patch-to-patch form factor (2.25) we take random points x and y on patches i and j respectively (Fig. 2.6.a). This means taking as pdf $f(x, y) = \frac{1}{A_i A_j}$, which is a uniform distribution.

A primary estimator is given by

$$\widehat{F}_{i \to j}^{1} = \frac{1}{A_i} \frac{F_{x \leftrightarrow y}}{f(x, y)} = A_j F_{x \leftrightarrow y}. \qquad (2.31)$$

It is easy to see that this estimator is unbiased ($E\left[\widehat{F}_{i \to j}^{1}\right] = F_{i \to j}$). For a set of samples represented by the pairs ($x \in A_i, y \in A_j$), that defines the nonempty set of random segments $\mathcal{S}_{i \times j}$, the form factor integral is approximated by the secondary estimator

$$\widehat{F}_{i \to j}^{2} = A_j \frac{1}{|\mathcal{S}_{i \times j}|} \sum_{(x, y) \in \mathcal{S}_{i \times j}} F_{x \leftrightarrow y}. \qquad (2.32)$$

- *Uniformly distributed lines.*

    - *Local lines.* Each one of the *local lines* is a ray with its origin uniformly distributed on the surface of i and its direction distributed according to the cosine with respect to the normal at the origin. So, we rewrite (2.25) as

$$F_{i\to j} = \frac{1}{A_i} \int_{A_i} \int_{\Omega_{x\to j}} \frac{\cos\theta_{n_x}^{\Theta}}{\pi} V(x, \Lambda(x, \Theta)) d\omega_\Theta dA_x, \qquad (2.33)$$

    and we take the pdf $f(x, \Theta) = \frac{1}{A_i} \frac{\cos\theta_{n_x}^{\Theta}}{\pi}$.

    An unbiased primary estimator $\widehat{F}_{i\to j}^1$ takes the value 1 if the local line hits the patch j directly and 0 if not. Let us recall that if a random variable X takes the values 1 and 0 with probabilities p and $1-p$, its variance is given by $\sigma^2[X] = p(1-p)$ [153]. Thus,

$$\sigma^2\left[\widehat{F}_{i\to j}^1\right] = F_{i\to j}(1 - F_{i\to j}). \qquad (2.34)$$

    A secondary estimator for F_{ij} is given by

$$\widehat{F}_{i\to j}^2 = \frac{|\mathcal{L}_{i\times j}|}{|\mathcal{L}_{i\times \mathcal{S}}|}, \qquad (2.35)$$

    where $\mathcal{L}_{i\times\mathcal{S}}$ is the set of local lines with origin on i and $\mathcal{L}_{i\times j}$ is the set of local lines with origin on i that hit j[28]. It shows clearly that the $F_{i\to j}$ can be interpreted as the fraction of local lines with origin on i that have j as the nearest patch intersected (Fig. 2.6.b). The variance is $\sigma^2[\widehat{F}_{i\to j}^1]/|\mathcal{L}_{i\times\mathcal{S}}|$.

    - *Global lines.* The *global lines* [194, 195] can be generated by putting the scene within a sphere and selecting a pair of random points on the surface of this sphere [218]. Interestingly, this uniform density generation does not have a counterpart in 2D. That is, taking pairs of points uniformly distributed on a circumference does not provide a uniform density within the circumference. In 2D, a way to get a random chord consists in choosing uniformly at random a direction on the circle and then uniformly at random a point on the corresponding radius: the chord is the line segment whose endpoints are located on the circle and perpendicular to the radius [218, 26].

    The lines connecting each pair of points are uniformly distributed throughout the scene. So, $F_{i\to j}$ can also be considered to be the probability of a global line that, crossing i, hits j (Fig. 2.6.c). It can be shown that each line can contribute to the computation of several form factors. Also, it is important to note that, from integral geometry [192, 195], the probability that, for a planar patch, a global line will intersect patch i is proportional to A_i.

    A secondary estimator for $F_{i\to j}$ is given by

$$\widehat{F}_{i\to j}^2 = \frac{|\mathcal{G}_{i\times j}|}{|\mathcal{G}_{i\times \mathcal{S}}|}, \qquad (2.36)$$

    where now, $\mathcal{G}_{i\times\mathcal{S}}$ is the set of global lines which cross i and $\mathcal{G}_{i\times j}$ is the set of global lines that crossing i, also cross j[29]. Its variance is

$$\sigma^2\left[\widehat{F}_{i\to j}^2\right] = \frac{1}{|\mathcal{G}_{i\times\mathcal{S}}|} F_{i\to j}(1 - F_{i\to j}). \qquad (2.37)$$

    To sample with global lines is equivalent to casting, for each patch, a number of local lines proportional to its area. Observe that the variance will be higher for smaller patches as $|\mathcal{G}_{i\times\mathcal{S}}|$ is proportional to A_i [195].

---

[28] $\mathcal{L}_{i\times j} \subseteq \mathcal{L}_{i\times\mathcal{S}} \neq \emptyset$.
[29] $\mathcal{G}_{i\times j} = \mathcal{G}_{i\times\mathcal{S}} \cap \mathcal{G}_{j\times\mathcal{S}}$ and $\mathcal{G}_{i\times j} \subseteq \mathcal{G}_{i\times\mathcal{S}} \neq \emptyset$.

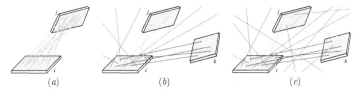

$$(a) \qquad\qquad (b) \qquad\qquad (c)$$

Figure 2.6: Form factor computations. (a) Twelve segments are used to calculate F_{ij} by uniform area sampling. (b) Twelve local lines calculate $F_{ij} = \frac{1}{6}$ and $F_{ik} = \frac{1}{3}$. (c) Twenty global lines calculate all the form factors (i.e., they add $F_{ji} = \frac{1}{4}$, $F_{jk} = \frac{1}{2}$, and $F_{ki} = F_{kj} = \frac{4}{9}$).

2.2.3 Light

Light is electromagnetic radiation with a wavelength that is visible to the eye (i.e, wavelength in [380,780] nm). Three dimensions of any electromagnetic radiation are:

- *Intensity* (or amplitude), perceived by humans as the brightness.
- *Frequency* (or wavelength), perceived by humans as the colour.
- *Polarisation* (or angle of vibration), perceived by humans in special cases.

Due to wave-particle duality, light simultaneously exhibits properties of both waves and particles. The light is quantified as particles called *photons*[30]. Electromagnetic radiation in the vacuum always travels at the speed of light, relative to the observer, independently of the observer's velocity[31]. Next, we present some necessary concepts in rendering.

Radiometry

Radiometry is a field of physics which undertakes the measurement of the intensity of electromagnetic radiation in absolute units. Next, we enumerate the basic definitions related with the flux of energy:

Radiant flux Radiant energy, defined as the energy carried by electromagnetic radiation (joule), flowing in radial direction per unit time: $\Phi = \frac{dQ}{dt}$ (watt).

Irradiance Incident flux per unit area: $E = \frac{d\Phi}{dA}$ (watt·m^{-2}).

Radiance exitance Radiated flux, called *radiosity*, from a surface per unit area: $B = \frac{d\Phi}{dA}$ (watt·m^{-2}).

Radiant intensity Radiated flux from a point source per unit solid angle in a radiant direction: $I = \frac{d\Phi}{d\omega}$ (watt·sr).

Radiance Radiant flux per unit projected area in a radial direction that arrives at or leaves from a surface [107, 85]: $L = \frac{d^2\Phi}{dA d\omega_\Phi}$ (watt·m^{-2}·sr^{-1}).

We add the following notation:

- $L(x \rightarrow \Theta)$ is the outgoing radiance from x in direction Θ.
- $L(x \leftarrow \Upsilon)$ is the incoming radiance to x from direction Υ.
- $L(x \rightarrow y)$ is the outgoing radiance from x to y (direction $\overrightarrow{xy}$).
- $L(x \leftarrow y)$ is the incoming radiance to x from y (direction $\overrightarrow{yx}$).

Two usual properties are assumed in radiometric equations:

---

[30] Its energy is related to the frequency of the wave given by Planck's relation $E = \hbar v$, where $\hbar$ is Planck's constant, and v the frequency of the wave. Electromagnetic waves were predicted by Maxwell's equations (1864) and subsequently discovered by Heinrich R. Hertz (1888).

[31] The Special Theory of Relativity, published by Albert Einstein in 1905 [55], is based on this fact.

- *Radiance invariance in vacuum*[32]

$$L(x \to y) = L(y \leftarrow x) \qquad (2.38)$$

- *Wavelength dependency*

$$L(x \to \Theta) = \int_{380\ \mathrm{nm}}^{780\ \mathrm{nm}} L(x \to \Theta, \lambda) \mathrm{d}\lambda \qquad (2.39)$$

Optics

Optics is a branch of physics that describes the behaviour and properties of light and the interaction of light with matter. On light-surface interaction, the surface illuminated by an incident ray may reflect and transmit a portion of the incoming energy and it absorbs the rest. In a physically correct model, the energy equilibrium is maintained (i.e., the reflected, transmitted, and absorbed energy must be equal to the incident energy). Here, we consider an *isotropic* model (i.e., all the surfaces reflect equally from any direction viewed from, otherwise it is *anisotropic*).

The probability theory tools (§B) are used to model the complex behaviour of the light-surface interactions. In general, the *transfer probability density* of a surface point x is [223]

$$w(\Upsilon, x, \Theta) \mathrm{d}\omega_\Theta = Pr\{\text{photon is reemitted to } \mathrm{d}\omega_\Theta \mid \text{coming from } \Upsilon\}. \qquad (2.40)$$

To obtain the total energy reemitted (i.e., reflected or refracted), we have to take all possible directions Υ into account. If the surface itself emits energy (i.e., it is a lightsource), the emission also contributes to the output flux in direction Θ [223].

The *bidirectional reflectance distribution function* (BRDF) at a point x (Fig. 2.7) is the ratio between the incident flux reflected from $\mathrm{d}\Upsilon$ into $\mathrm{d}\Theta$ over all $\mathrm{d}A_x$ ($\mathbf{sr}^{-1}$):

$$f_\mathrm{r}(\Upsilon, x, \Theta) = \frac{\mathrm{d}L(x \to \Theta)}{\mathrm{d}E(x \leftarrow \Upsilon)}. \qquad (2.41)$$

In terms of probabilities:

$$f_\mathrm{r}(\Upsilon, x, \Theta) = \frac{w(\Upsilon, x, \Theta) \mathrm{d}\omega_\Theta}{\cos \theta_{n_x}^\Theta \mathrm{d}\omega_\Theta}. \qquad (2.42)$$

We can also define for transmission the corresponding *bidirectional transmittance distribution function* (BTDF). Both BRDF and BTDF exist for each side of the surface. We note two important properties:

- *Helmholtz-symmetry.* Reversing the roles of the incident and reflected energy does not change the value of the BRDF:

$$f_\mathrm{r}(\Upsilon, x, \Theta) = f_\mathrm{r}(\Theta, x, \Upsilon). \qquad (2.43)$$

- *Energy conservation.* The energy reflected must be a fraction of the energy received (the other fraction is absorbed). The *albedo* is the ratio of the total reflected power and incoming power. Thus,

$$a(x, \Upsilon) = Pr\{\text{photon is reemitted} \mid \text{coming from } \Upsilon\}$$

$$= \int_{\Omega_x} w(\Upsilon, x, \Theta) \mathrm{d}\omega_\Theta$$

$$= \int_{\Omega_x} f_\mathrm{r}(\Upsilon, x, \Theta) \cos \theta_{n_x}^\Theta \mathrm{d}\omega_\Theta \leq 1. \qquad (2.44)$$

A lot of different models are discussed for BRDFs according to different types of reflectance and transmittance (see details in [74, 223]). They attempt to model all the types of reflection:

Specular The light is propagated without scattering. The incoming direction and outgoing direction are on the same plane with equal angles with respect to the surface normal (Fig. 2.7.a). This is also called regular or mirror reflection.

---

[32] In this work, we consider non participating media.

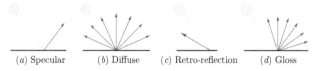

(a) Specular   (b) Diffuse   (c) Retro-reflection   (d) Gloss

Figure 2.7: Four kinds of reflectance.
Credit: Adapted from Andrew S. Glassner [74].

Diffuse The light is reflected in all directions with uniform distribution (Fig. 2.7.b).

Mixed A combination of specular and diffuse reflectance.

Retro-reflection The incident energy is mostly reflected in directions close to the incident direction (Fig. 2.7.c).

Gloss A set of mixed reflections (Fig. 2.7.d). It is what originates the production of the mirror-like effects. It is composed of different grades: from a perfect mirror (1 gloss) to perfect diffuser (0 gloss). This incoherent reflection is usually broken down into diffuse and specular components [47]. For this last, a lot of models have been presented (e.g., Phong [161], Blinn [19], and Cook-Torrance [36]).

In a similar way to reflection, transmittance can be divided into: *specular*, *diffuse*, and *mixed*. In this thesis, we are interested in perfect diffuse reflection. If the BRDF is independent of the viewing direction (i.e., isotropic), it must be independent of the direction of light (2.43) and the BRDF is constant:

$$f_r(\Upsilon, x, \Theta) = \rho_r^d(x) \quad \forall \Upsilon, \Theta. \tag{2.45}$$

Note that ρ_r^d is the ratio of outgoing radiance to incoming flux density. A more convenient quantity is the ratio of reflected radiance to incoming total flux (i.e., the albedo). This ratio is called the diffuse reflectance, or simply *reflectance*, and is given by $a_d(x) = \rho_r^d(x)\pi = \rho(x)$. Thus, taking into account (2.44): $\rho_r^d(x) \leq \frac{1}{\pi}$.

A distinction is usually made between types of origins of light in order to simplify the algorithmic designs. Thus, we have the *direct light* (L_d), which comes directly to us from the lightsources, and the *indirect light* (L_i), any type of light that is not direct.

Equation

The light transported in a virtual closed environment is described by the *rendering equation* [106], which is a second-order Fredholm integral equation. This equation, which describes all energy exchanges between surfaces, gives us the distribution of light at every point of a scene.

It expresses the radiance from point x in direction Θ with the integration over the hemisphere[33]:

$$L(x \to \Theta) = L_e(x \to \Theta) + \int_{\Omega_x} L(x \leftarrow \Upsilon) f_r(\Upsilon, x, \Theta) \cos \theta_{n_x}^{-\Upsilon} d\omega_\Upsilon, \tag{2.46}$$

where L_e is the *emitted radiance*[34] of a surface point at a given direction. Rewriting this expression over all surfaces we obtain:

$$L(x \to \Theta) = L_e(x \to \Theta) + \int_A L(x \to y) f_r(\overrightarrow{yx}, x, \Theta) G(x, y) dA_y, \tag{2.47}$$

where $G(x, y)$ is the *geometric kernel*:

$$G(x, y) = \frac{\cos \theta_{n_x}^{\overrightarrow{xy}} \cos \theta_{n_y}^{\overrightarrow{yx}}}{r_{xy}^2} V(x, y) = \pi F_{x \leftrightarrow y}. \tag{2.48}$$

---

[33] We consider radiance to be invariant in vacuum (2.38), wavelength dependency (2.39), and do not consider transmittance (a problem equivalent to that of reflectance).

[34] It depends on the physical property of emissivity of each material.

The rendering equation can be presented in slightly different forms depending on the assumptions that are made about the physical conditions [215, 74]. Observe that the radiance distribution L is described implicitly and we only know what conditions it must satisfy, but we do not know its value. The unknown radiance appears inside and outside the integral and, in order to obtain a solution, this coupling should be solved. If we consider the T to be a contraction operator[35] as the light-surface interaction, we can group together the techniques to solve it in [223]:

- *Inversion.* Group the terms that contain the unknown function on the same side of the equation and formally apply an inversion operation $(1 - T)L = L_e \Rightarrow L = (1 - T)^{-1}L_e$. This technique is not practised due to its time complexity and numerical instability.

- *Expansion.* Eliminate the coupling rewriting the equation into a Neumann series:

$$L = \sum_{i=0}^{n} T^i L_e + T^{n+1}L \overset{n\to\infty}{\equiv} \sum_{i=0}^{\infty} T^i L_e. \qquad (2.49)$$

- *Iteration.* The solution is the fixed point of an iteration scheme as

$$L_n = L_e + T L_{n-1}. \qquad (2.50)$$

Due to T operator, the scheme converges towards the solution from any initial function L_0.

Specific applications of expansion and iteration are ray-tracing (§2.3) and radiosity (§2.4), respectively, which can be complemented by forming hybrid designs belonging to the class of *multi-pass algorithms* [214, 91, 205, 204, 213] (§1.1.1), the aim of which is to differentiate phases in the rendering process as to where the best of them could be applied. It seems reasonable to consider that an algorithm which uses the best of each one must obtain superior results to each one of them separately.

The *radiance* describes the interaction between an emitter and a receiver from the point of view of the emitter (Fig. 2.8). The reverse situation is explained from the *potential* $W(y, \Upsilon)$. *"It expresses the effect of that portion of the unit power ray emitted by y in direction Υ, which actually lands at a given measuring device either directly or indirectly after some reflections or refractions"* [223]. The *potential equation* is defined by [158]

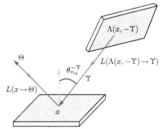

Figure 2.8: Geometry of rendering equation. Credit: Adapted from László Szirmay-Kalos [223].

$$W(y \to \Upsilon) = W_e(y \to \Upsilon) + \int_{\Omega_x} W(x \to \Theta) f_r(\Upsilon, x, \Theta) \cos \theta_{n_x}^{\Theta} d\omega_\Theta, \qquad (2.51)$$

where $x = \Lambda(y, \Upsilon)$.

2.2.4   Colour Spaces

In a strict way, we can consider the rendering process exclusively as the search for a solution to its equation and then, the tone-mapping independent of it (Fig. 1.2). We have seen how the rendering equation (2.46) reflects a simplification of the model of global illumination in order to attempt to decide the colour for each of the pixels of the image plane (§2.1.6). In any case, for the process of rendering itself as much as for tone-mapping, we must consider the spaces of colour in the framework.

Colour is the human perception of light in the visible domain of the spectrum incident on the retina (§2.2.3). The intensity of energy, radiance, received through every wavelength is expressed by the *spectral*

---

[35] For $\lambda < 1$, $\| TL \| < \lambda \| L \|$ and then $\lim_{n\to\infty} T^{n+1}L = 0$.

	R	G	B	white
x	0.64	0.30	0.15	0.3127
y	0.33	0.60	0.06	0.3290
z	0.03	0.10	0.79	0.3583

Table 2.1: The xyz values for sRGB (D65).

power distribution (SPD). In rendering equations we assume a unique luminance for all the SPD (2.39), but in practise, systems of colour must be established for the output devices. We will comment on the two systems of colour which we use in this work (XYZ and sRGB).

Based on the system of perception of the eye, through *photometry* different models on colour have been created and studied [27, 251, 83, 166]. Because of the nature of the human eye, energy is sampled and integrated in three overlapping frequency ranges by three types of photoreceptors. As a consequence of this, any colour perception can be represented by three scalars, called *tristimulus* values, instead of complete SPD. One important result is that different SPDs can become the same tristimulus values and so the same colour. In fact, any colour has an infinite number of SPDs, called *metamers*.

The Commission Internationale de L'Éclairage (CIE) defines *luminance* as the radiant power (cd·m^{-2} in photometry) weighted by a spectral sensitivity function that is characteristic of vision. The SPD integrates with the luminance weighting function resulting in the CIE luminance Y that is normalised with respect to a specified white reference (e.g., the standard daylight defined by CIE as illuminant D65). In 1931, the CIE created the tristimulus system XYZ to represent the SPD [251]. It is based on luminance Y and two components X and Z so that a value XYZ describes any colour.

On considering pure colours with an absence of brightness, the CIE defines a normalisation process, (x, y, z), to compute the *chromaticity coordinates* (x, y) (i.e, a projection of 3D space on the 2D plane X+Y+Z=1)[36]. Thus, a colour is well determined by its chromaticity and luminance: CIE xyY[37]. Other more specific spaces are: L*u*v*, L*a*b*, YCbCr, HSL, etc. The mapping between the different spaces is always easy if, and only if, they have correspondence. The process of this correspondence is called *gamut mapping*. In rendering, it is usual for the characteristic of the colour of a material to be specified in the chromaticity coordinates (device-independent).

The current technology for monitors is based on screens where a pixel is drawn with three phosphor layers which are stimulated to produce red, green and blue light: (r,g,b). It is necessary to find the stimulus values to produce a metamer of the energy desired. Also, before sending the signal to the monitor, a correction of the intensities is necessary in order to adapt them to the specific characteristics of the human perception system [167, 166]. This process is called *gamma correction*.

An RGB space is a system based on physical devices where a range of colours is produced by an additive mixture of the three primary spectra of phosphors (i.e., adding the corresponding fractions of the XYZ components). The systems based on subtraction are, in general, more complex (e.g., CMY is the complementary one for RGB). One RGB system is specified by the chromaticities of its primaries and its white point. So as to unify the definition of spaces RGB, the International Electrotechnical Commission (IEC) has defined the standard sRGB (IEC 61966-2-1) [220, 32]. The expected primary colours on phosphorous and the white setting of an sRGB on D65 are shown in Table 2.1 for an xyz system[38].

The conversion between sRGB and XYZ tristimulus D65 values is

$$\begin{bmatrix} R \\ G \\ B \end{bmatrix} = \begin{bmatrix} 3.2406 & -1.5372 & -0.4986 \\ -0.9689 & 1.8758 & 0.0415 \\ 0.0557 & -0.2040 & 1.0570 \end{bmatrix} \times \begin{bmatrix} X \\ Y \\ Z \end{bmatrix}. \qquad (2.52)$$

The negative coefficients are due to the fact the some XYZ colours are out of the gamut of sRGB space[39].

---

[36] $x = \frac{X}{X+Y+Z}$, $y = \frac{Y}{X+Y+Z}$, and $z = 1 - x - y$.
[37] $X = \frac{x}{y}Y$ and $Z = \frac{1-x-y}{y}Y$.
[38] Following the previous recommendation of the ITU-R BT.709 [237].
[39] All values are clipped between 0 and 1.

(a)   (b)

Figure 2.9: Ray-tracing of two scenes with different material types. (a) Still life picture rendered by the Radiance ray-tracing research software. (b) Five transparent chess figures rendered by the NuGraf® commercial software.
Credit: (a) © 1994 Dr. Martin Moeck[41], Pennsylvania State University, University Park (PA), USA. Radiance © 2005 University of California Regents. (b) © 1995-2008 Okino Computer Graphics, Inc., Toronto (Ontario), Canada. Original 3D Studio model was obtained from the 3D Cafe Internet website and was created by Renzo Del Fabbro of Italy.

The inverse transformation is:

$$\begin{bmatrix} X \\ Y \\ Z \end{bmatrix} = \begin{bmatrix} 0.4124 & 0.3576 & 0.1805 \\ 0.2126 & 0.7152 & 0.0722 \\ 0.0193 & 0.1192 & 0.9505 \end{bmatrix} \times \begin{bmatrix} R \\ G \\ B \end{bmatrix}, \tag{2.53}$$

where the middle row adds up to 1 due to the white normalisation[40]. For details about nonlinear sR'G'B' transformation (gamma of the monitor of 2.2) and more specification of the viewing environment, see IEC 61966-2-1 [32].

In practise, the process of obtaining the final colour of the pixel of a device consists in computing the pixel value by initiating a rendering process (usually with a CIE XYZ space colour) and finishing with a gamut mapping for a specific nonlinear RGB device system (usually sR'G'B'). This colour process is the basis of tone-mapping.

2.3   Ray-Tracing

The aim of the pixel-driven approach is to obtain the final colour of each pixel of the image plane (§1.1.1). To achieve this, we can use Monte Carlo integration techniques (§2.2.1) with point sampling (§2.1.2). It is necessary to estimate the scene radiance signal integrating within the solid angle formed by the position of the camera and the pixel (Fig. 2.9). In this section, we follow the work of Szirmay-Kalos [223].

2.3.1   Method

The expansion technique to solve the rendering equation is based on Neumann series (2.49). The measured power is

$$\mathcal{M}L = \sum_{i=0}^{\infty} \mathcal{M}T^i L_e, \tag{2.54}$$

---

[40] To recover the primary chromaticities, transform the values RGB (1,0,0), (0,1,0), and (0,0,1) to XYZ and normalise. The same for RGB (1,1,1) to obtain the white reference.
[41] Contact address: Pennsylvania State University, Department of Architectural Engineering, 104 Engineering A, University Park (PA) 16802, USA, e-mail: mm12@psu.edu.

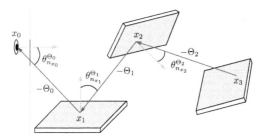

Figure 2.10: The gathering ray-tracing expansion.
Credit: Adapted from László Szirmay-Kalos [223].

where $\mathcal{M}$ is a measuring operator. The term $\mathcal{M}\mathcal{T}^i L_e$ is used to determine the radiance going through a pixel and can be seen as a single multi-dimensional integral:

$$\mathcal{M}\mathcal{T}^i L_e = \int_A \int_{\Omega_{x_1}} \cdots \int_{\Omega_{x_i}} \frac{c(x_0)}{A} w_0 \cdots w_i L_e(x_{i+1} \to -\Theta_i) \mathrm{d}\omega_{\Theta_i} \cdots \mathrm{d}\omega_{\Theta_1} \mathrm{d}A_{x_0}, \qquad (2.55)$$

where A is the pixel area, x_0 is the sample point of the pixel, $c(x_0)$ is the camera parameter function, Θ_0 is the sample direction (from observer to x_0), $\Theta_{k \in \{1,\dots,i\}}$ are directions of the reflections, $x_{k \in \{1,\dots,i+1\}}$ is $\Lambda(x_{k-1}, \Theta_{k-1})$, and the weight $w_{k \in \{1,\dots,i\}}$ is $f_r(x_k, -\Theta_k \to -\Theta_{k-1}) \cos \theta_{n_{x_k}}^{\Theta_k}$ (Fig. 2.10).

For $i = 0$, the term of the series represents the emission intensity, but at level $i > 0$, i reflections have been taken into account. This infinite theoretical process can be implemented algorithmically for a finite number of reflections: a ray is cast recursively from a visible point at a direction Θ_1 and onto the next surface, at direction Θ_2, and this continues until Θ_i. The emission intensity of the last point is achieved and attenuated according to the cosine weighted BRDFs of the stages of the walk. If the emission is transferred from all points of the walk, we have an estimation of i-bounce transfer thanks to this random walk (§B).

This process constitutes the basis for a calculation of Monte Carlo integration with one multi-dimension sample. Another interpretation of the term (2.54) is a recursive evaluation of many directional integrals:

$$\mathcal{M}\mathcal{T}^i L_e = \frac{c(x_0)}{A} \int_A w_0 \left(\int_{\Omega_{x_1}} w_1 \left(\cdots \int_{\Omega_{x_i}} w_i L_e(x_{i+1} \to -\Theta_i) \mathrm{d}\omega_{\Theta_i} \cdots \right) \mathrm{d}\omega_{\Theta_1} \right) \mathrm{d}A_{x_0}. \qquad (2.56)$$

Note that if n sample points are considered for computing each Monte Carlo integral, the cost is exponential along the path: n^i. With the independence of a possible stratification for the integration, in order to speed up the calculations, one of the simplest options is to consider one strata and one single sample for each one (i.e., only one random walk is used to estimate a specific irradiance). For this simplification an important price must be paid: the estimate of the result is worse. On the other hand, the relationship between quality and cost is very good (1.1), and this is why this method and its variations are often used at the present time.

The walks are generated in a *ray-tracing* process and can be interpreted as the inverse walk of a photon (ray of light) that bounced around the scene. The camera gathers the illumination of the path and consequently, the methods using this approach are called *gathering walks* or *backward ray-tracing* (§2.3.2).

The same technique of expansion can be applied in a similar way to the potential equation (2.51) obtaining the *shooting walks* or *forward ray-tracing* (§2.3.3), where the random walks are generated from lightsources.

No matter what type of approach (gathering or shooting), the difficulty of the calculation of intersections in the current complex scenes, plus the difficulty of the calculations of illumination themselves for each of the rays, makes the total computational cost for the image high and as a result many techniques have been developed in order to accelerate the processes.

Among others, in Arvo and Kirk [8], Shirley [209, 208], Glassner [73, 74], and Szirmay-Kalos [223] there is a good collection of ideas and methods for producing ray-tracers (e.g., Sbert et al. [196] presents a technique of reusing paths for the speeding up of the calculation in problems of global illumination which could be adapted to methods for backward as well as for forward ray-tracing).

Both approaches have advantages and disadvantages of calculation, and as a consequence, taking into account that the two modalities vary in their design but not in their results (the physics laws of light transport do not change if paths are reversed), the *bidirectional random walks* methods have come up. They are based on the combination of shooting and gathering walks and take advantage of the strong points only. Some examples are: bidirectional path-tracing [114, 241], Metropolis light transport [242], and photon map [103, 102, 104].

2.3.2   Gathering Random Walks

In theory, the expansion is applied to the radiance equation (2.46). In practise, it results in generating random walks from the camera through the pixel approaching a Monte Carlo solution (backward ray-tracing §2.3.1). The evaluation of the set of rays employed by each one of the random walks will determine the final colour of the pixel. The general scheme of a gathering random-walk algorithm would be [223]:

```
for each pixel p do
    colour = 0
    for each sample s_{i∈{1,...,n}} do
        r_c^Θ = sample ray from camera through p
        colour_s = (c/A)×Trace(r_c^Θ)
        colour = colour + colour_s/n
    endfor
    display(p, colour)
endfor
```

The Trace function calculates the radiance carried by the ray to the camera, the value c is a scaling camera parameter according to the display settings, and A is the size of the integration domain. This function ends by determining the quantity of random walks in play depending on the precision which is desired and on the kinds of illumination involved. Thus, each possibility of implementation of Trace gives way to a different method of gathering. Next, following Szirmay-Kalos [223], we revise the most important.

Ray-Casting

The *ray-casting* algorithm replaces the unknown radiance inside the integral of the rendering equation by an approximation of the emission function. Thus, the Trace function computes the irradiance in the first intersection point only due to the lightsources (L_d) and the function accumulates it to the point's own emissivity (L_e) in order to obtain the final radiance. It is a particular case: local-illumination and no recursive ray-tracing.

The Trace process is:

```
function Trace(r_x^Θ)
    y = Λ(x, Θ)
    if ∄y then return L_e(background)
    colour = L_e(y → −Θ)+DirectLightsource(y, −Θ)
    return colour
end
```

The DirectLightsource returns

$$\sum_{i=1}^{N_\ell} L_{d_i}(y \leftarrow -\Upsilon_{d_i}) f_r(-\Upsilon_{d_i}, y, -\Theta), \qquad (2.57)$$

obtained by casting a shadow ray $r_y^{\Upsilon_d}$ on each one of the N_ℓ lightsources.

The indirect illumination L_i must be calculated so that the process will become recursive. This is the case of the three following techniques. Recursivity will finalise the attainment of certain predetermined conditions of stop such as: a fully absorbing surface, escape from the environment, recursion level, Russian roulette, values less than a predefined threshold, and other options which are strongly dependent on the algorithms used.

Visibility Ray-Tracing

The *visibility ray-tracing* or *classic ray-tracing* is a recursive ray-tracing algorithm where we can follow multiple light paths for ideal reflection and refraction. The rays cast from the camera through a pixel are weighted from an appropriate filter and we obtain an estimate of the radiance of the pixel. The concept was introduced by Whitted [248].

If ρ_r and ρ_t are the ideal reflection and refraction coefficients, respectively, the Trace process is:

```
function Trace(r_x^Θ)
    y = Λ(x,Θ)
    if ∄y then return L_e(background)
    colour = L_e(y→ -Θ)+DirectLightsource(y, -Θ)
    if ρ_r > 0 then colour = colour+Trace(r_y^{Υ_r})
    if ρ_t > 0 then colour = colour+Trace(r_y^{Υ_t})
    return colour
end
```

The computation of the direct illumination at each point of the random walk using a ray towards the lightsources is called *next event estimation*. Any of the stopping criteria mentioned previously are valid for stopping the recursivity (e.g., recursion level). From Whitted's contribution, many combinations and variants of calculation opened up. Two of the most important are *distributed ray-tracing* and *path-tracing* which we show below.

Distributed Ray-Tracing

It was introduced by Cook [34] and it is generically called *stochastic ray-tracing*. It is a recursive ray-tracing of global illumination algorithm which can model all the possible paths. When a ray hits a diffuse surface, child rays are generated randomly according to the BRDF characterising the surface. The values returned for this set of rays are averaged to obtain the final result.

Let BRDFSampling be a function that selects, with a low-variance estimator, an elementary BRDF with the probability of its albedo in order to generate an out direction Υ_{r_i} (from an in direction and a surface normal) and to return the selection probability[42] (details in Szirmay-Kalos [223, p. 64]). Then, the process Trace for reflectance[43] is:

```
function Trace(r_x^Θ)
    y = Λ(x,Θ)
    if ∄y then return L_e(background)
    colour = L_e(y→ -Θ)+DirectLightsource(y, -Θ)
    for each sample s_{i∈{1,...,n}} do
        p = BRDFSampling(Θ, n_y, Υ_{r_i})
        if p > 0 then colour = colour+Trace(r_y^{Υ_{r_i}}) × w(-Υ_{r_i}, y, -Θ)/(p × n)
    endfor
    return colour
end
```

---

[42] 0 indicates that the walk has to be stopped.
[43] Process analogous for the transmittance.

Path-Tracing

Apart from distributed ray-tracing, *path-tracing* is the other very important Monte Carlo approach. It was proposed by Kajiya [106] and consists of creating a path history for a single particle interacting with the surfaces of the object of the scene until its absorption (e.g., using BRDF sampling and Russian roulette). Differing from the distributed ray-tracing, now instead of spawning new rays at each surface intersection, a random direction is chosen according to a density which is approximately proportional to the weight w (2.40) (e.g., the BRDF).

An implementation[43] of the `Trace` sampling with a BRDF would be:

```
function Trace(r_x^Θ)
    y = Λ(x, Θ)
    if ∄y then return L_e(background)
    colour = L_e(y → −Θ)+DirectLightsource(y, −Θ)
    p = BRDFSampling(Θ, n_y, ϒ_r)
    if p > 0 then colour = colour+Trace(r_y^{ϒ_r}) × w(−ϒ_r, y, −Θ)/p
    return colour
end
```

2.3.3 Shooting Random Walks

As with the gathering algorithms, now the expansion (2.49) is applied to the potential equation (2.51). The random walks are generated at the lightsource and they try to find the camera (forward ray-tracing §2.3.1). The general scheme of a shooting random-walk algorithm would be:

```
image = black
for each sample s_{i∈{1,...,n}} do
    r_x^Θ = sample ray from a lightsource with probability p
    power = L_e(x → Θ) × cos θ_{n_x}^Θ/(p × n)
    Shoot(r_x^Θ, power)
endfor
```

The function `Shoot` is that which is responsible for obtaining the power to send to the camera and also for identifying the pixel when the random walk finishes. We mention two variants of `Shoot` function:

Photon tracing A random walk is followed if ideal reflection or refraction exist (Pattanaik [156]). It is the opposite method to visibility ray-tracing (§2.3.2).

Light tracing When a photon hits a surface, a ray is traced to the camera to add its contribution to the corresponding pixel, if this is deemed necessary (Dutre [54]). Veach and Guibas [242] present Metropolis light transport, an important variant inspired by the Metropolis sampling method in physics which consists in randomly mutating a single path.

2.4 Radiosity

The *radiosity* is an important object-space approach for solving a simplified equation of the global illumination in a scene based on iteration (2.50). The method was introduced in Goral et al. [75] with later developments [29, 142]. It obtains an approximate solution to the problem of illumination for the environment of diffuse surfaces (Fig. 2.11). In this section, we look at the radiosity equation (§2.4.1), the general method (§2.4.2), the hierarchical radiosity technique (§2.4.3), and some refinement criteria for the latter (§2.4.4).

2.4.1 Equation

For diffuse surfaces, the BRDF does not depend on the outgoing and incoming directions (2.45). Thus, the outgoing radiance $L(x → Θ)$ and the self-emitted radiance $L_e(x → Θ)$ are also independent of the outgoing direction (Fig. 2.7.b). This simplification is applied to the rendering equation (2.47).

 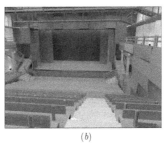

(a) (b)

Figure 2.11: Two scenes rendered with hierarchical radiosity.
Credit: (a) Pat Hanrahan, David Salzman, and Larry Aupperle [86]. © 1991 Association for Computing Machinery, *A Rapid Hierarchical Radiosity Algorithm*, July 1991. (b) Philippe Bekaert [12]. Community Theatre (unbuilt) of the Candlestick Point State Recreation Area. © 1989 University of California Regents. Designed by Mark Mack Architects and modelled by Charles Ehrlich and Greg Ward. This work was conducted as a research project during the Architecture 239X course taught by Kevin Matthews formerly at UC Berkeley, College of Environmental Design.

Continuous Equation

The rendering equation (2.47) for diffuse surfaces can be expressed as

$$L(x) = L_e(x) + \int_A \rho_r^d(x) L(y) G(x,y) \mathrm{d}A_y. \tag{2.58}$$

If we integrate $L(x)$ on the whole hemisphere Ω_x of the outgoing directions, we obtain the radiosity at point x [215, 74]:

$$B(x) = \int_{\Omega_x} L(x) \cos\theta_{n_x}^\Theta \mathrm{d}\omega_\Theta = \pi L(x). \tag{2.59}$$

In addition, the total self-emitted flux per unit area is expressed by $E(x) = \pi L_e(x)$, and is called the *emittance* at point x. The *radiosity equation* is then obtained by multiplying the equation (2.58) by π and applying (2.59) and the definition of the reflectance (2.45):

$$B(x) = E(x) + \frac{\rho(x)}{\pi} \int_A B(y) G(x,y) \mathrm{d}A_y, \tag{2.60}$$

where, according to the previous definitions,

- $B(x)$ and $B(y)$ are, respectively, the radiosities at points x and y ($\texttt{watt·m}^{-2}$).

- $E(x)$ is the emittance or emitted flux of energy per unit area at point x ($\texttt{watt·m}^{-2}$).

- $\rho(x)$ is the diffuse reflectance at point x (dimensionless).

The corresponding directional form of the radiosity equation is

$$B(x) = E(x) + \frac{\rho(x)}{\pi} \int_{\Omega_x} B(y) \cos\theta_{n_x}^\Theta \mathrm{d}\omega_\Theta, \tag{2.61}$$

where $y = \Lambda(x, \Theta)$.

Discrete Equation

To solve the radiosity equation we can use a finite element approach, discretising the scene S into S (N_p patches) and considering the radiosities, emissivities and reflectances constant over the patches. With these assumptions, the integral equation (2.60) becomes the system of radiosity equations [75]:

$$B_i = E_i + \rho_i \sum_{j \in S} F_{ij} B_j, \tag{2.62}$$

where

- B_i, E_i, and ρ_i are respectively the radiosity, emittance (or emissivity), and reflectance of patch i.

- B_j is the radiosity of patch j.

- F_{ij} is the $F_{i \to j}$ from the patch-to-patch form factor matrix (§2.2.2), which is only dependent on the geometry of the scene.

Power Equation

The radiosity equation (2.62) can be rewritten[44] as the *power equation*:

$$P_i = \Phi_i + \rho_i \sum_{j \in S} F_{ji} P_j, \tag{2.63}$$

where

- $P_i = B_i A_i$ and $P_j = B_j A_j$ are, respectively, the total powers emitted by patches i and j (**watt**).

- $\Phi_i = E_i A_i$ is the self-emitted power of patch i (**watt**).

In the power equation, the form factor represents the fraction of power leaving patch j which goes directly to patch i (§2.2.2).

2.4.2   Method

The *classic radiosity* method consists of the following steps [30, 215, 74]:

- Discretise the environment into patches.

- Compute the form factors F_{ij} for each pair of patches i and j (form factors matrix).

- Solve the system of linear equations.

- Display the solution.

In this method, the input data is the geometric information about the scene (for the form factors), the physical properties of the materials (for the emissivities and reflectances), and viewing conditions [215].
    The radiosity equation (2.62), which refers to a single patch, can be expressed as a system of N_p linear equations:

$$\begin{pmatrix} B_1 \\ \vdots \\ B_{N_\mathrm{p}} \end{pmatrix} = \begin{pmatrix} E_1 \\ \vdots \\ E_{N_\mathrm{p}} \end{pmatrix} + \begin{pmatrix} \rho_1 F_{11} & \cdots & \rho_1 F_{1 N_\mathrm{p}} \\ \vdots & \vdots & \vdots \\ \rho_{N_\mathrm{p}} F_{N_\mathrm{p} 1} & \cdots & \rho_{N_\mathrm{p}} F_{N_\mathrm{p} N_\mathrm{p}} \end{pmatrix} \begin{pmatrix} B_1 \\ \vdots \\ B_{N_\mathrm{p}} \end{pmatrix}.$$

This linear system can be written in the form

$$\mathbf{B} = \mathbf{E} + \mathbf{R}\mathbf{B}, \tag{2.64}$$

---

[44] Multiplying both sides by A_i and applying the reciprocity relation (2.26).

where $\mathbf{B}$ and $\mathbf{E}$ are, respectively, the vectors of radiosities and emittances, and $\mathbf{R}$ is the $N_p \times N_p$ matrix of the terms $\rho_i F_{ij}$. The solution $\mathbf{B}$ of such a system can be written as a Neumann series. As ρ_i is strictly less than 1, the matrix $\mathbf{R}$ has a norm[45] strictly less than 1. In this case, the Neumann series converges and we can write the radiosity vector as a sum of an infinite series:

$$\mathbf{B} = \mathbf{E} + \mathbf{R}\mathbf{E} + \mathbf{R}^2\mathbf{E} + \cdots + \mathbf{R}^n\mathbf{E} + \cdots \tag{2.65}$$

Since $\mathbf{R}$ represents the effect of one reflection on all the surfaces of the scene, $\mathbf{R}^n\mathbf{E}$ can be interpreted as the radiosity obtained after n rebounds from the emitted light through the scene.

In the literature, different iterative solution methods [215, 74] are available for solving the radiosity and power systems: Jacobi relaxation, Gauss Seidel relaxation, Southwell relaxation, and also their respective stochastic versions [205, 139, 215, 138, 140, 12].

2.4.3 Hierarchical Radiosity

The two most important problems to solve in radiosity technique are meshing and form factor computation. A fine mesh determines a good accuracy in the solution, but a lot of computation due to the high number of form factors. On the other hand, a thick mesh reduces the calculation time of its form factors, but its solution does not capture the illumination variations enough. It is necessary to find a strategy to balance the reduction in the number of patches and the precision of the illumination. To solve this, some techniques have been introduced: progressive refinement, substructuring, adaptive refinement, and hierarchical refinement. Other techniques are an attempt to reduce the number of form factors arriving at a solution within a given error boundary. Additional information can be found in [215, 74, 12].

The *hierarchical refinement* method was introduced by Hanrahan et al. [86]. The concept is based on the existent analogy between the problem of gravitational forces between various bodies (n-body physics problem) and the radiosity between several patches. It is worth noting that both problems are based on the interaction between all pairs of objects and also that the gravitational force and the form factor have a similar mathematical expression. The idea is that if the interaction between two bodies decreases with the distance and the size of the body, then, a distance will exist from which a pair of bodies may be considered a single body, and then this new body may be joined with another body (or set of bodies). This system is called *clustering interactions* and it can be applied recursively. If each one of the n bodies exerts interactions on the other $n-1$, then there are $\mathcal{O}(n^2)$ interactions to account for, and with clustering $\mathcal{O}(n)$ can be attained. The clustering ideas of the n-body problem are reversed (i.e., splitting instead of clustering) and then can be applied to radiosity, resulting in the *hierarchical radiosity* algorithm. The bodies are substituted by patches and these are subdivided into smaller elements if necessary, in order to achieve accurate light transport between them.

The main objective is to obtain an accurate piecewise constant approximation of the radiosity on all the elements. To do this, the mesh is generated adaptively: when a constant radiosity assumption on patch i is not valid for the radiosity due to another patch, the refinement algorithm will refine i in a set of subpatches or elements (Fig. 2.12). However, we could still have a lot of unnecessary computation due to the fact that the last level of refinement which patch i has attained, due to its interaction with a patch j, is certainly unnecessary for its interaction with another patch k. In order to solve this problem, hierarchical refinement radiosity uses a *multi-resolution element mesh* representing the radiosity on each patch at multiple levels of detail. Contrary to a single-level element mesh, an element hierarchy allows the computation of the light transport at the right level of detail for each source instead of just one level of detail which suffices for all sources [74, 12].

Given that the two basic pillars of the algorithm are the creation of an adaptive mesh and the use of a multi-resolution representation of the radiosity function on a hierarchy of elements, it is clear that the accuracy of the oracle of refinement is essential. The oracle collects geometric and visibility information about the patches and also the source radiosity and receiver reflectance, and answers whether or not the interaction is valid (Fig. 2.12). Some of these patches will need further refinement, up to a certain level where no more refinement is needed or a previously imposed limit on the area of the patches is reached.

---

[45] The norm of $\mathbf{R}$ can be defined by $\| \mathbf{R} \| = \max_i \{ \sum_j |\rho_i F_{ij}| \} = \max_i \{ \rho_i \} < 1$. Then, $\mathbf{R}$ represents a contraction operator (2.50).

Figure 2.12: Three levels of a hierarchical radiosity subdivision from Fig. 2.11.a. The refinement is based on the energy transported between patches. The colour of the interaction segments indicates the visibility factor used in the estimation of the form factor: completely visible (white), partially visible (green), cut by aeroplane (pink), and relatively visible (blue).
Credit: Pat Hanrahan, David Salzman, and Larry Aupperle [86]. © 1991 Association for Computing Machinery, *A Rapid Hierarchical Radiosity Algorithm*, July 1991.

Its cost should not make the method prohibitive. Bekaert et al. [13] have incorporated hierarchical refinement in Monte Carlo radiosity (stochastic Jacobi radiosity). Given its importance, the following section deals specifically with the refinement criteria in hierarchical radiosity.

2.4.4   Refinement Criteria

We review some refinement criteria for hierarchical radiosity[46]. The cheapest and most widely-used oracle has been the power-based oracle [86]. However, it leads to unnecessary subdivisions in smoothly illuminated unoccluded regions receiving a lot of power. As an alternative, oracles based on the smoothness of the geometric kernel and on received radiosity have been proposed [217, 76, 124, 123, 157, 14, 219, 96, 63]. Nevertheless, oracles based on kernel smoothness also have the problem of unnecessary subdivisions where the kernel is unbounded, and the ones based on received radiosity rely on a costly accurate computation of form factors. All in all, the additional cost invested in both smoothness-based oracles, mainly through visibility computations, may outweigh the improvements obtained.

The application of a good refinement criterion and strategy is fundamental for the efficiency of the hierarchical refinement algorithm. Next, we review some oracles based on different approaches.

Transported Power

The initial version of hierarchical refinement radiosity was presented for constant radiosity approximations by Hanrahan et al. [86]. The F_{ij} is calculated, by estimating the subtended solid angle, in order to measure the accuracy of an interaction between an element j and an element i. If $\max\{F_{ij}, F_{ji}\}$ exceeds a given threshold ϵ, the larger of the two elements i and j is subdivided using regular quadtree subdivision. Otherwise, the candidate link is considered admissible.

On this basis of refinement, three added values are incorporated. Firstly, one more level of precision using a correction of the form factor for a factor of visibility between the two patches. Secondly, refinement of the hierarchy as the iteration proceeds (multigridding implemented reducing the ϵ by levels). Finally, the number of refinements is reduced considerably without affecting image quality by weighting the F_{ij} with the source element radiosity B_j, which is the total amount of energy transported between the patches (Fig. 2.12).

Weighting with receiver element area A_i and reflectance ρ_i also further reduces the number of links without deteriorating image quality. Thus, the power-based criterion to stop refinement can be given by

$$\rho_i A_i F_{ij} B_j < \epsilon. \tag{2.66}$$

---

[46] This section is a summary of the discussion in Bekaert [12] and Feixas [63].

The left hand expression can be rewritten (2.26) as $\rho_i A_j F_{ji} B_j$, representing the power emitted by i thanks to j (2.63).

Other strategies can also be used to reduce the number of form factors [229, 68]. We can see that power-based refinement criterion uses no information about the variation of the received radiosity across the receiver element. This results, for instance, in sub-optimal shadow boundaries and excessively fine refinement in smooth areas. The main advantage of this criterion is its very low computational cost while yielding a fair image quality.

Kernel Smoothness

In order to improve on power-based refinement, the variation of the radiosity kernel between a pair of elements is taken into account. In Smits et al. [217], the refinement criterion is given by

$$\rho_i (F_{ij}^{\max} - F_{ij}^{\min}) A_j B_j < \epsilon, \qquad (2.67)$$

where $F_{ij}^{\max} = \max\{F_{x \leftrightarrow y} \mid x \in A_i, y \in A_j\}$ and $F_{ij}^{\min} = \min\{F_{x \leftrightarrow y} \mid x \in A_i, y \in A_j\}$ are the maximum and minimum radiosity kernel values[47] estimated by taking the maximum and minimum value computed between pairs of random points on both elements.

A similar approach was used in Gortler et al. [76] in order to drive hierarchical refinement with higher-order approximations. When applied to constant approximations, the refinement criterion is given by

$$\rho_i \max\{F_{ij}^{\max} - F_{ij}^{\mathrm{avg}}, F_{ij}^{\mathrm{avg}} - F_{ij}^{\min}\} A_j B_j < \epsilon, \qquad (2.68)$$

where $F_{ij}^{\mathrm{avg}} = F_{ij}/A_j$ is the average radiosity kernel value. Kernel variation is a sufficient condition for received radiosity variation, but not a necessary condition [12].

Smoothness of Received Radiosity

Because bounding kernel variation is not a necessary condition for bounding received radiosity variation, we can expect that hierarchical refinement based on kernel smoothness will yield hierarchical meshes with more elements and links than required. Optimal refinement can be expected by directly estimating how well the radiosity B_j, received at $x \in A_i$ from A_j, is approximated by a linear combination of the basis functions on A_i (i.e., by estimating the discretisation error directly).

This approach was first proposed by Lischinski et al. [124] for constant approximations:

$$\rho_i \max\{F_{ij} - \min_{x \in A_i}\{F_{x \to j}\}, \max_{x \in A_i}\{F_{x \to j}\} - F_{ij}\} B_j < \epsilon. \qquad (2.69)$$

Pattanaik and Bouatouch [157] proposed a similar strategy for linear basis functions. Other approaches are given in [123, 14, 219, 96]. The computational cost of kernel and radiosity smoothness-based oracles has not yet been found to compensate for the gain in mesh quality [12].

Mutual Information

Feixas et al. [63] introduced an information-theoretic oracle based on the mutual information (§2.5.2) between two patches or elements. The fundamental idea is that the difference between continuous and discrete patch-to-patch (or element-to-element) mutual information gives us the loss of information transfer or, equivalently, the maximum potential gain of information transfer between two elements (§2.6.1). This difference is the *discretisation error* δ_{ij} (2.97) and can be interpreted as the benefit to be gained by refining and can be used as a criterion for a decision.

The oracle takes a similar approach to the classic smoothness-based oracles (2.68 and 2.69). In these, the term $\rho_i B_j$ from the radiosity equation (2.62) is weighted by an expression of the visibility gradient between the two patches involved. Now, the visibility gradient is substituted by the discretisation error, which, in a way, also represents the variation of the radiosity kernel. So, the mutual information based oracle is given by

$$\rho_i \delta_{ij} B_j < \epsilon, \qquad (2.70)$$

---

[47] The point-to-point form factor is also referred to as the radiosity kernel value.

where δ_{ij} can be computed with area-to-area sampling between i and j (2.32):

$$\delta_{ij} \approx \frac{A_i A_j}{A_{\mathrm{T}}} \left(\frac{1}{|\mathcal{S}_{i \times j}|} \left(\sum_{(x,y) \in \mathcal{S}_{i \times j}} F_{x \leftrightarrow y} \log F_{x \leftrightarrow y} \right) \right.$$
$$\left. - \left(\frac{1}{|\mathcal{S}_{i \times j}|} \sum_{(x,y) \in \mathcal{S}_{i \times j}} F_{x \leftrightarrow y} \right) \log \left(\frac{1}{|\mathcal{S}_{i \times j}|} \sum_{(x,y) \in \mathcal{S}_{i \times j}} F_{x \leftrightarrow y} \right) \right). \tag{2.71}$$

Observe that in this expression the receiver area appears to be weighting the oracle and thus avoiding an excessively small receiver subdivision.

2.5   Information Theory

The *information theory* studies the transmission and compression of data (§1.1.2). It is considered to have begun with Shannon in 1948 when he introduced the basic laws on communication [200]. Currently, thanks to computers, information theory has extended its applicability to many other fields besides electrical engineering: physics, statistics, mathematics, computer science, etc. In this section, we present a selection of measures of information theory[48]. We follow the excellent reference of Cover and Thomas [37] (other good references are Blahut [18] and Lubbe [239]).

2.5.1   Entropy

The Shannon entropy is the classical measure of *information*, where information is simply the outcome of a selection from a finite number of possibilities. Let X be a discrete random variable $(\mathcal{X}, p_X)$ where $\mathcal{X}$ is the alphabet $\{x_1, \dots, x_n\}$ and p_X the corresponding probability distribution (§B).

Definition 2 *The entropy of a discrete random variable X is given by*

$$H(X) = -\sum_{i=1}^{n} p_i \log p_i. \tag{2.72}$$

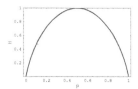

Figure 2.13: Binary Entropy. The minimum value is 0 when $P \in \{0, 1\}$ and the maximum is 1 when $P = \frac{1}{2}$.

The logarithms are taken in base 2 (entropy is expressed in bits), and we use the convention that $0 \log 0 = 0$, which is justified by continuity. We can use the notation $H(X)$ or $H(p)$ interchangeably for the entropy. In the particular case of a binary alphabet, the *binary entropy* is

$$H(X) = -P \log P - (1 - P) \log(1 - P), \tag{2.73}$$

where $p = \{(x_1, P), (x_2, 1 - P)\}$ (Fig. 2.13).

Some interpretations of entropy are:

- We can think of the value $-\log p_i$ as the information associated with the result x_i. Thus, the entropy gives us the *expected information* or *uncertainty* of a random variable. Information and uncertainty are opposites. Uncertainty is considered before the event, information after. So, information reduces uncertainty.

- The term $-\log p_i$ can also be interpreted as the *surprise* associated with the outcome x_i. The value of p_i and the surprise are inversely related to one another (i.e., if one is small it implies the other is large). Thus, the entropy is expectation of surprise [64].

---

[48] Basic and notional concepts about probability and convexity are shown in §B and §D, respectively.

- Entropy is also related to the difficulty of guessing the outcome of a random variable. Thus, it can be seen [37, 64] that $H(X) \leq \overline{N}_q < H(X) + 1$, where $\overline{N}_q$ is the average minimum number of binary questions for determining X (Fig. 1.4). This idea agrees with the interpretation of entropy as a measure of uncertainty and also with the important results in information theory for storing or transmitting efficiently [200].

- An important interpretation comes from the classical thermodynamics where the term "entropy"[49] was coined[50]. In the late 19th century, James C. Maxwell, Ludwing Bolzmann, and Josiah W. Gibbs extended the thermodynamic concept of entropy, through the molecular theory of gases, into the domain actually called *statistical mechanics*. The Boltzmann-Gibbs entropy is $S = -k \sum_i p_i \log p_i$, where p_i is the probability that particle i will be in a given microstate (all of the probabilities are evaluated for the same macrostate of the system) and k is the Boltzmann's constant which determines the units[51]. The important role of entropy is reflected in the second law of thermodynamics: the total entropy of any isolated thermodynamic system tends to increase over time, approaching a maximum value.

Some relevant properties of the entropy are:

- $H(X)$ is concave[52] in p_X.

- Range[53]: $0 \leq H(X) \leq \log n$.

  - $H(X) = 0 \Leftrightarrow \exists i.\, p_i = 1$ (i.e., we are certain of the outcome).
  - $H(X) = \log n \Leftrightarrow \forall i.\, p_i = \frac{1}{n}$ (i.e, the most uncertain situation).

- If we equalise the probabilities, entropy increases.

- Grouping:

$$H(\{p_1, \ldots, p_n\}) = H(\{p_1 + p_2, p_3, \ldots, p_n\}) + (p_1 + p_2)H\left(\frac{p_1}{p_1 + p_2}, \frac{p_2}{p_1 + p_2}\right). \tag{2.74}$$

Now, we consider another discrete random variable $Y = (\mathcal{Y}, q_Y)$ where $\mathcal{Y} = \{y_1, \ldots, y_m\}$ is the alphabet. Then, with respect to the pair (X, Y), we have the joint p_{XY}, and conditionals $p_{X|Y}$ and $p_{Y|X}$ probability distributions. From this, we can define:

Definition 3 *The joint entropy of discrete random variables (X, Y) is given by*

$$H(X, Y) = -\sum_{i=1}^{n} \sum_{j=1}^{m} p_{ij} \log p_{ij}. \tag{2.75}$$

Definition 4 *The conditional entropy of discrete random variables (X, Y) is given by*

$$H(Y|X) = -\sum_{i=1}^{n} \sum_{j=1}^{m} p_{ij} \log p_{j|i}. \tag{2.76}$$

The conditional entropy can be thought of in terms of a *discrete channel*. This is a system $X \to Y$ consisting of an input alphabet $\mathcal{X}$, output alphabet $\mathcal{Y}$, and a probability transition matrix $p_{Y|X}$ that expresses the probability of observing the output symbol y given that we send the symbol x. The $H(X|Y)$ corresponds to the uncertainty in the channel input from the receiver's point of view, and vice versa for $H(Y|X)$. Note that in general $H(X|Y) \neq H(Y|X)$. The following properties are also met:

---

[49] Greek word meaning "transformation", also chosen for its similarity to the word energy.

[50] Rudolph Clausius (1865) defined the change in entropy (S) of a thermodynamic system, during a reversible process in which an amount of heat (Q) is introduced at constant absolute temperature (T): $\Delta S = \frac{\Delta Q}{T}$.

[51] Ludwig Boltzmann interprets the entropy as an statistical form of disorder but his proposal was met with scepticism and not accepted in his lifetime. Suffering from poor health and despondent over the rejection of his work, Boltzmann committed suicide (the famous equation is engraved at the top of his tombstone).

[52] Concavity: from log-sum inequality (D.5).

[53] The discrete entropy is bounded: from Jensen's inequality (D.4) and $f(x) = \log x$ concave, with equalities in the specified cases.

- $H(X,Y) \leq H(X) + H(Y)$.
- $H(X,Y) = H(X) + H(Y|X) = H(Y) + H(X|Y)$.
- Conditioning reduces entropy[54]: $H(X) \geq H(X|Y) \geq 0$.
- Independence bound on entropy[55]: $H(X_1, \ldots, X_n) \leq \sum_{i=1}^{n} H(X_i)$.

Finally, we introduce two special entropies to measure the distance between two distributions.

Definition 5 *The relative entropy or Kullback-Leibler distance between two probability distributions p_X and q_X is given by*

$$D_{\mathrm{KL}}(p,q) = \sum_{i=1}^{n} p_i \log \frac{p_i}{q_i}. \tag{2.77}$$

We use the convention that $p_i \log \frac{p_i}{0} = \infty$ and $0 \log \frac{0}{q_i} = 0$ (based on continuity). The relative entropy is a measure of the inefficiency of assuming that the distribution is q when in reality it is p. It is convex in the pair (p,q)[56] and satisfies the information inequality[57] $D_{\mathrm{KL}}(p,q) \geq 0$. It has a drawback when the distribution q contains a 0. Note that it is not a true distance (§6.1.1) because it does not complete the triangle inequality and it is not symmetric[58].

Definition 6 *The cross entropy between two probability distributions p_X and q_X is given by*

$$H_{\mathrm{C}}(p,q) = \sum_{i=1}^{n} p_i \log q_i. \tag{2.78}$$

It measures the overall difference between the two distributions. Cross entropy is closely related to the relative entropy since it is equivalent to $H(p) + D_{\mathrm{KL}}(p,q)$. When comparing a distribution q with a fixed reference distribution p, cross entropy and relative entropy are only different in an additive constant. Both take on their minimal values when $p = q$, which is 0 for the relative entropy and $H(p)$ for cross entropy [249].

2.5.2 Mutual Information

We introduce here a measure of the amount of information that one random variable contains about another random variable. It represents a reduction in the uncertainty of one random variable due to knowledge of the other.

Definition 7 *The mutual information between two discrete random variables (X,Y) with a joint probability distribution p_{XY} and marginal probability distributions p_X and q_Y is defined as the relative entropy between p_{XY} and $p_X q_Y$:*

$$I(X,Y) = D_{\mathrm{KL}}(p_{XY}, p_X q_Y) = \sum_{i=1}^{n} \sum_{j=1}^{m} p_{ij} \log \frac{p_{ij}}{p_i q_j}. \tag{2.79}$$

Therefore, $I(X,Y)$ is a measure of the shared information between X and Y. From a channel perspective $X \to Y$, the knowledge of X decreases the uncertainty of Y, and vice versa.

---

[54] From Jensen's inequality (D.4) and $f(x) = \log x$ concave, with equality if (X,Y) are independent.
[55] From Jensen's inequality (D.4) and $f(x) = \log x$ concave, with equality if X_i independent.
[56] Convexity: from log-sum inequality (D.5).
[57] Non-negativity: from Jensen's inequality (D.4) and $f(x) = x \log x$ convex, with equality if $p = q$.
[58] Kullback and Leibler themselves defined a symmetric version as $D_{\mathrm{KL}}(p,q) + D_{\mathrm{KL}}(q,p)$. Defined from the Kullback-Leibler distance, the Jensen-Shannon divergence is symmetric and it is the square of a metric [232].

From Bayes' theorem (B.5), we can rewrite the mutual information in the following expressions:

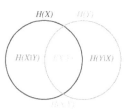

- $I(X,Y) = H(X) - H(X|Y) = H(Y) - H(Y|X)$
- $I(X,Y) = H(X) + H(Y) - H(X,Y)$

This strong relationship between entropy and mutual information can be expressed by Venn diagrams (Fig. 2.14). The following properties are satisfied by the mutual information:

- $I(X,Y) \geq 0$ (Non-negativity[59])
- $I(X,Y) \leq H(X)$ and $I(X,Y) \leq H(Y)$
- $I(X,Y) = I(Y,X)$
- $I(X,X) = H(X)$

Figure 2.14: Venn diagram of the relationship between entropy and mutual information of random variables (X,Y).

A special mention must be made of the following property:

Theorem 1 (Data processing inequality) *If $X \to Y \to Z$ is a Markov chain (i.e., $p_{XYZ} = p_X p_{Y|X} p_{Z|Y}$), then $I(X,Y) \geq I(X,Z)$. In particular, $I(X,Y) \geq I(X, f(Y))$.*

Proof in [37, p. 32–33]. This result demonstrates that no processing of Y, deterministic or random, can increase the information that Y contains about X.

2.5.3 Continuous Channel

In this section, entropy and mutual information are defined for continuous sources of information. For a continuous source X, messages are taken from a continuous set S. In a similar way to the entropy of a discrete random variable (2.72), we define

Definition 8 *The continuous entropy of a continuous random variable X with a pdf p_X is defined by*

$$H^c(X) = - \int_S p(x) \log p(x) \mathrm{d}x. \tag{2.80}$$

Similarly, for a pair of continuous random variables (X,Y) with p_X and q_Y as marginal pdfs, and p_{XY} and $p_{X|Y}$ as the joining and conditional pdfs, respectively, we have:

Definition 9 *The continuous conditional entropy of two continuous random variables (X,Y) is given by*

$$H^c(X|Y) = - \int_S \int_S p(x,y) \log p(x|y) \mathrm{d}y \mathrm{d}x. \tag{2.81}$$

Definition 10 *The continuous mutual information of two continuous random variables (X,Y) is given by*

$$I^c(X,Y) = \int_S \int_S p(x,y) \log \frac{p(x,y)}{p(x)p(y)} \mathrm{d}y \mathrm{d}x. \tag{2.82}$$

If we divide the range of the continuous random variable X into n bins of length Δ, and we consider its discretised version X^Δ, two relevant facts can be observed (proofs in [37, 64]):

Theorem 2 *The entropy of a continuous random variable does not equal the entropy of the discretised random variable within the limit of a finer discretisation:*

$$\lim_{\Delta \to 0} H(X^\Delta) \to H^c(X) - \log \Delta. \tag{2.83}$$

---

[59] From non-negativity of Kullback-Leibler distance.

Theorem 3 *The mutual information between two continuous random variables X and Y is the limit of the mutual information between their discretised versions. Thus, when the number of bins tends to infinity:*

$$\lim_{\Delta \to 0} I(X^\Delta, Y^\Delta) = I^c(X, Y). \tag{2.84}$$

In addition, the mutual information is defined as $\sup_{PQ}\{I([X]_P, [Y]_Q)\}$ by Kolmogorov [112] and Pinsker [162], where the supremum is over all finite partitions P and Q. Together with the previous theorems, two important properties have been deduced [80]:

- The continuous mutual information is the least upper bound for the discrete mutual information.
- Refinement can never decrease the discrete mutual information.

2.6   Scene Information Channel

This section is an intersection between the fields of rendering (§2.2) and information theory (§2.5). The study of a scene from an information-theoretic perspective was introduced by Acebo et al. [48] and Feixas et al. [62, 61]. It has represented the first step in the application of Shannon's concepts to computer graphics obtaining measures of complexity (§2.7.3) and introducing specific applications for the techniques of radiosity (2.70). For detailed information about the use and behaviour of these measures, see Feixas [60].

From a visibility geometric perspective, measures for a discrete and continuous scene are defined for 3D and 2D scenes. They are based on the existence of a Markov chain and the knowledge of its stationary distribution (§B). The most outstanding information-theoretic definitions were applied in [61, 175]. An analogous study for the radiosity setting appears naturally with the null variance probability transition matrix [60].

2.6.1   Information-Theoretic Measures in 3D

We present here the information-theoretic definitions corresponding to a discrete and continuous 3D-scene. After, we review the discretisation error based on the scene mutual information.

Discrete Scene

Let S be a discretisation of scene $\mathcal{S}$, with area A_T, and let A_i and a_i be, respectively, the area and the relative area $(\frac{A_i}{A_T})$ of patch $i \in S$ (§A). The scene can be modelled in two equivalent ways[60]:

A random walk A discrete random walk in a discretised scene is a discrete Markov chain where the states correspond to the N_p patches of a scene, the transition probabilities P_{ij} are the patch-to-patch form factors (i.e., F_{ij}), and the stationary distribution is given by the relative area of patches [195] $\{a_i\}$ (or length in 2D, Fig. 2.15.a) (§B).

An information channel A scene can be interpreted as a discrete information channel $X \to Y$ where the input and output variables take values over the set of patches with probability distribution $\{a_i\}$ and the conditional probabilities $p_{Y|X}$ are the patch-to-patch form factors matrix F_{ij} (§2.5).

Below we present the basic definitions.

Definition 11 *The discrete scene positional entropy of S is given by*

$$H_P(S) = -\sum_{i \in S} a_i \log a_i. \tag{2.85}$$

It is the Shannon entropy of stationary distribution and it expresses the uncertainty on the position (patch) of a particle travelling an infinite random walk. Thus, $H_P(S) = H(X) = H(Y)$, where $p_X = p_Y = \{a_i\}$.

---

[60] By default, our framework is taken from a geometric visibility point of view (§1.2).

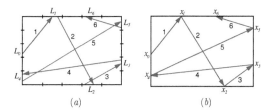

Figure 2.15: Random walk into a 2D-scene: (a) discrete ($L_{i \in \{0,...,6\}}$ is the length of each path) and (b) continuous cases.

Definition 12 *The discrete scene entropy of a patch $i \in S$ is given by*

$$H_{\mathrm{s}}(S, i) = -\sum_{j \in S} F_{ij} \log F_{ij}. \tag{2.86}$$

It measures the uncertainty about the destination patch when the source patch is i.

Definition 13 *The discrete scene entropy of S is given by*

$$H_{\mathrm{s}}(S) = \sum_{i \in S} a_i H_{\mathrm{s}}(S, i) = -\sum_{i \in S} a_i \sum_{j \in S} F_{ij} \log F_{ij}. \tag{2.87}$$

It can be interpreted as the average uncertainty about the destination patch of a random walk that remains when the source patch is known, and vice versa: $H_{\mathrm{s}}(S) = H(Y|X) = H(X|Y)$. It is also the expected minimum number of bits per symbol required to code a random walk in a scene. Note that the Bayes' theorem (B.5) applied to a scene is expressed by the reciprocity property of the form factors (2.26): $\forall i, j. \; p_{ij} = a_i F_{ij} = a_j F_{ji}$.

Definition 14 *The discrete scene joint entropy of S is given by*

$$H_{\mathrm{J}}(S) = -\sum_{i \in S} \sum_{j \in S} a_i F_{ij} \log(a_i F_{ij}). \tag{2.88}$$

It is the Shannon entropy of a random variable with probability distribution $\{a_i F_{ij}\}$ and can be interpreted as the uncertainty about the pair position-target of a particle in an infinite random walk. Thus, $H_{\mathrm{J}}(S) = H(X, Y)$.

Definition 15 *The discrete scene mutual information of S is given by*

$$I_{\mathrm{s}}(S) = \sum_{i \in S} \sum_{j \in S} a_i F_{ij} \log \frac{F_{ij}}{a_j}. \tag{2.89}$$

It is a measure of the average information transfer or dependence between the different parts of a scene and expresses the amount of information that the destination patch conveys about the source patch, and vice versa. Thus, $I_{\mathrm{s}}(S) = I(X, Y)$.

It is especially interesting to ask about the extreme cases of maximum and minimum visibility entropy, which correspond, respectively, to the maximum and minimum unpredictability in the path. Maximum unpredictability can be obtained in scenes with no privileged visibility directions (i.e., sphere[61]) and minimum unpredictability in the contrary case. The behaviour of the entropy and mutual information is illustrated with the scenes in Fig. 2.16. Also, normalised measures for H_{s} and I_{s} were defined in this context.

---

[61] The $F_{ij} = a_j$ and implies that $I_{\mathrm{s}}(S) = 0$, for all i, j.

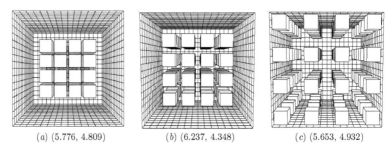

(a) $(5.776, 4.809)$ $\qquad$ (b) $(6.237, 4.348)$ $\qquad$ (c) $(5.653, 4.932)$

Figure 2.16: Three different scene visibility configurations. For each scene, the $(H_{\mathrm{s}}, I_{\mathrm{s}})$ is shown. Form factors have been computed using 10^8 global lines (§2.2.2). The scenes with the same discretisation have the same H_{p} due to the fact that the increase in entropy remains compensated by an mutual information decrease, and vice versa (10.585 in this case).
Credit: Miquel Feixas [60].

Continuous Scene

The scene is now modelled by a continuous random walk (Fig. 2.15.b) or by a continuous information channel. We can obtain the continuous information-theoretic formulæ directly from the continuous information-theoretic channel (§2.5.3) applying the following substitutions:

$$\mathrm{d}x, \mathrm{d}y \longmapsto \mathrm{d}A_x, \mathrm{d}A_y$$

$$p(x), p(y) \longmapsto \frac{1}{A_{\mathrm{T}}}$$

$$p(x|y), p(y|x) \longmapsto F_{x \leftrightarrow y}$$

$$p(x, y) \longmapsto \frac{F_{x \leftrightarrow y}}{A_{\mathrm{T}}}$$

From fundamental information-theoretic results (§2.5.3), we know that when the number of patches of $\mathcal{S}$ tends to infinity (and the size of all the patches tends to zero):

◦ The scene entropy tends to infinity: $\lim_{N_{\mathrm{p}} \to \infty} H_{\mathrm{s}}(\mathcal{S}) = \infty$ (Th. 2).
◦ The discrete mutual information of a scene converges to continuous mutual information: $\lim_{N_{\mathrm{p}} \to \infty} I_{\mathrm{s}}(\mathcal{S}) = I_{\mathrm{s}}^{\mathrm{c}}(\mathcal{S})$ (Th. 3).

For our objectives, in the continuous case we are interested exclusively in the mutual information (see [60] for continuous scene entropy). Thus,

Definition 16 *The continuous scene mutual information of* $\mathcal{S}$ *is given by*

$$I_{\mathrm{s}}^{\mathrm{c}}(\mathcal{S}) = \int_A \int_A \frac{1}{A_{\mathrm{T}}} F_{x \leftrightarrow y} \log(A_{\mathrm{T}} F_{x \leftrightarrow y}) \mathrm{d}A_y \mathrm{d}A_x. \qquad (2.90)$$

As in the discrete channel, it expresses the information transfer in the scene and the null value corresponds to the sphere[62]. One important characteristic of the introduced information-theoretic measures is that, with the exception of continuous entropy, they are invariant to a change in the scale.

This $I_{\mathrm{s}}^{\mathrm{c}}$ can be solved by Monte Carlo integration. The computation can be done efficiently by casting uniformly distributed global lines (§2.2.2). Thus, the value can be approximated by

$$I_{\mathrm{s}}^{\mathrm{c}}(\mathcal{S}) \approx \frac{1}{|\mathcal{G}_{\mathcal{S}^2}|} \sum_{(x,y) \in \mathcal{G}_{\mathcal{S}^2}} \log(A_{\mathrm{T}} F_{x \leftrightarrow y}), \qquad (2.91)$$

---

[62] Any pair (x, y) fulfils $F_{x \leftrightarrow y} = \frac{1}{A_{\mathrm{T}}}$ and then, $I_{\mathrm{s}}^{\mathrm{c}}(\mathcal{S}) = 0$: $\lim_{N_{\mathrm{p}} \to \infty} I_{\mathrm{s}}(\mathcal{S}) = I_{\mathrm{s}}^{\mathrm{c}}(\mathcal{S}) = 0$.

where $\mathcal{G}_{\mathcal{S}^2}$ is the set of global segments (x, y), joining the visible surface points x and y of $\mathcal{S}$, generated by any global line[63]. The values of I_s^c for the Fig. 2.16 are 5.678, 4.867 and 6.055, respectively.

Discretisation Error

By discretising a scene into patches, a distortion or error is introduced. Taking into account that the maximum accuracy of the discretisation is obtained when the number of patches tends to infinity (see mutual information properties in §2.5.3), we find that

- ◦ If any patch is divided into two or more patches, the discrete mutual information of the new scene increases or remains the same.
- ◦ The continuous scene mutual information is the least upper bound to the discrete scene mutual information.

Thus, a scene fulfils $I_s^c(\mathcal{S}) - I_s(S) \geq 0$. This difference expresses the *loss of information transfer* due to the discretisation. From this fact,

- • From an information-theoretic point of view, the ideal discretisation is the one that captures all the information transfer in a scene. Then, between different discretisations of the same scene, the most precise will be the one that has a higher discrete mutual information (i.e., the one that best captures the information transfer).

Definition 17 *The discretisation error of S is given by*

$$\delta(S) = I_s^c(\mathcal{S}) - I_s(S) \tag{2.92}$$

and the relative discretisation error as the quotient $\overline{\delta}(S) = (I_s^c(\mathcal{S}) - I_s(S))/I_s^c(\mathcal{S})$. *The relative discretisation accuracy is* $I_s(S)/I_s^c(\mathcal{S})$.

- • Continuous mutual information expresses the difficulty in obtaining an accurate discretisation. The higher the I_s^c (i.e., when there is more information transfer in a scene), the more difficult it is to obtain an accurate discretisation, and probably more refinements will be necessary to achieve a given precision[64].

The same arguments are valid at patch level. Thus, it is possible to calculate the difference between both continuous and discrete patch-to-patch visibility information transfers. From (2.89), we can consider the inner term as an element of an mutual information matrix and then,

$$I_{ij}(S) = a_i F_{ij} \log \frac{F_{ij}}{a_j}, \tag{2.93}$$

where each element represents the information transfer between patches i and j (note that $I_{ij}(S) = I_{ji}(S)$). Also, we can consider that

$$I_i(S) = a_i \sum_{j \in S} F_{ij} \log \frac{F_{ij}}{a_j} \tag{2.94}$$

expresses the information transfer from patch i. Using the concavity property of the logarithm function (D.5), we obtain[65] that $I_i(S) \geq 0$. Thus, we can rewrite (2.89) as

$$I_s(S) = \sum_{i \in S} I_i(S) = \sum_{i \in S} \sum_{j \in S} I_{ij}(S). \tag{2.95}$$

---

[63] Note that a global line can contribute with no, one, or more than one global segment to $\mathcal{G}_{\mathcal{S}^2}$ and that $|\mathcal{G}_{\mathcal{S}^2}|$ is half of the total number of intersections of the lines with the scene.

[64] The difficulty in discretising an empty sphere is null because the discretisation error is always zero: $I_s^c(\mathcal{S}) = I_s(S) = 0$.

[65] Substituting a_i, b_i, and n by F_{ij}, a_j, and N_p, respectively.

The information transfer between two patches can be obtained more accurately if we consider the continuous mutual information between them. Thus, from the continuous mutual information (2.90), we have

$$I_{ij}^c(S) = \int_{A_i} \int_{A_j} \frac{1}{A_\mathrm{T}} F_{x \leftrightarrow y} \log(A_\mathrm{T} F_{x \leftrightarrow y}) \mathrm{d}A_y \mathrm{d}A_x. \tag{2.96}$$

This continuous measure expresses, with maximum precision, the visibility information transfer between two elements. Then, from (2.93) and (2.96):

Definition 18 *The discretisation error between patches* $i, j \in S$ *is given by*

$$\delta_{ij}(S) = I_{ij}^c(S) - I_{ij}(S). \tag{2.97}$$

The positivity of δ_{ij} is obtained from the log-sum inequality (D.5). Observe that δ_{ij} is symmetric: $\delta_{ij}(S) = \delta_{ji}(S)$. This difference gives us the discretisation error between two elements and it is used as the kernel in an mutual information based oracle for hierarchical radiosity (2.70). Using area-to-area sampling (2.32), δ_{ij} is approximated to (2.71). Of course we can rewrite (2.92) as

$$\delta(S) = \sum_{i \in S} \sum_{j \in S} \delta_{ij}(S) = I_s^c(S) - I_s(S). \tag{2.98}$$

2.6.2   Information-Theoretic Measures in 2D

Introduced in Rigau et al. [175], the definitions of 3D-scene are adapted to flatland by only changing the area by the length. Flatland and form factors are studied in [92, 146].

Definition 19 *The differential-to-differential 2D form factor is given by*

$$F_{\mathrm{d}L_x \leftrightarrow \mathrm{d}L_y}^{2\mathrm{D}} = \frac{\cos \theta_{n_x}^{\overrightarrow{xy}} \cos \theta_{n_y}^{\overrightarrow{yx}}}{2 r_{xy}} V(x, y). \tag{2.99}$$

It has the same interpretation as its 3D expression (2.23) and all the 3D definitions and concepts related (§2.2.2) can be derived to 2D. Thus, we can consider the 2D point-to-point, point-to-patch, and patch-to-patch form factors. As a result, we also dispose of the matrix of patch-to-patch form factors $F^{2\mathrm{D}}$ of dimension $N_\mathrm{p} \times N_\mathrm{p}$.

Discrete 2D-Scene

Let S be a discretisation of 2D-scene $\mathcal{S}$, with a total length L_T, and let L_i and ℓ_i be, respectively, the length and the relative length ($\frac{L_i}{L_\mathrm{T}}$) of patch $i \in S$ (§A). By analogy with 3D (§2.6.1), with the same interpretations we have the following definitions:

Definition 20 *The discrete 2D-scene positional entropy of* S *is given by*

$$H_\mathrm{P}(S) = -\sum_{i \in S} \ell_i \log \ell_i. \tag{2.100}$$

Definition 21 *The discrete 2D-scene entropy of a patch* $i \in S$ *is given by*

$$H_\mathrm{s}(S, i) = -\sum_{j \in S} F_{ij}^{2\mathrm{D}} \log F_{ij}^{2\mathrm{D}}. \tag{2.101}$$

Definition 22 *The discrete 2D-scene entropy of* S *is given by*

$$H_\mathrm{s}(S) = \sum_{i \in S} \ell_i H_\mathrm{s}(S, i) = -\sum_{i \in S} \ell_i \sum_{j \in S} F_{ij}^{2\mathrm{D}} \log F_{ij}^{2\mathrm{D}}. \tag{2.102}$$

Definition 23 *The discrete 2D-scene joint entropy of S is given by*

$$H_{\text{J}}(S) = -\sum_{i\in S}\sum_{j\in S} \ell_i F_{ij}^{\text{2D}} \log(\ell_i F_{ij}^{\text{2D}}). \tag{2.103}$$

Definition 24 *The discrete 2D-scene mutual information of S is given by*

$$I_{\text{s}}(S) = \sum_{i\in S}\sum_{j\in S} \ell_i F_{ij}^{\text{2D}} \log \frac{F_{ij}^{\text{2D}}}{\ell_j}. \tag{2.104}$$

Continuous 2D-Scene

Following the same reasoning as in 3D (§2.6.1):

Definition 25 *The continuous 2D-scene mutual information of S is given by*

$$I_{\text{s}}^{\text{c}}(S) = \int_L \int_L \frac{1}{L_{\text{T}}} F_{x\leftrightarrow y}^{\text{2D}} \log(L_{\text{T}} F_{x\leftrightarrow y}^{\text{2D}})\mathrm{d}L_y\mathrm{d}L_x. \tag{2.105}$$

Similarly to (2.90), this integral can be solved by Monte Carlo integration with global lines:

$$I_{\text{s}}^{\text{c}}(S) \approx \frac{1}{|\mathcal{G}_{S^2}|} \sum_{(x,y)\in\mathcal{G}_{S^2}} \log(L_{\text{T}} F_{x\leftrightarrow y}^{\text{2D}}), \tag{2.106}$$

with the same considerations as in 3D.

Discretisation Error

The 2D discretisation error between continuous and discrete mutual information, and between patch-to-patch geometric visibility information transfers, can be defined and computed in the same way as in 3D expression (2.97). The mentioned changes in areas for lengths and the new definitions of 2D form factors derived from (2.99) must be taken into account.

2.7 Complexity

Given that the study of complexity is absolutely multidisciplinary, it is not our aim to analyse the extremely wide research which is going on, but rather to present, in a generic form, the concept (§2.7.1) and the measures (§2.7.2) of complexity which are used within the scene context (§2.7.3).

2.7.1 Concept

The term *complexity* is employed in many different fields, but what is "complexity"? Li [121] defines complexity as a measure of the difficulty concerning the object or the system. But, what "difficulty"? The difficulty in constructing an object, in describing a system, in reaching a goal, in performing a task, etc. We can consider this description to be accepted by the majority, but the next step is to ask: how can the difficulty be measured? The answer to this is particular to each framework and this is why we find as many definitions of complexity [79, 125, 121, 9, 66, 4] as different ways of quantifying these difficulties. It is logical then that a precise and agreed definition cannot be found [4].

Baddi and Politi [9] consider that the concept of complexity is closely related to that of understanding, in so far as the latter is based upon the accuracy of model descriptions of the system obtained using condensed information about it. They consider three fundamental points:

○ Understanding implies the presence of a *subject* having the task of describing the *object*, usually by means of model predictions.

∘ The object, or a suitable representation of it, must be conveniently divided into parts which, in turn, may be further split into subelements, thus yielding a *hierarchy*[66].

∘ Having individuated hierarchical encoding of the object, the subject is faced with the problem of studying the *interactions* among the subsystems and of incorporating them into a model[67].

In this same direction, it is important to note that among the typical characteristics of complex behaviour there is also a simultaneous presence of elements of order and disorder, some degree of unpredictability, interactions between subsystems which change in dependence on how the system is subdivided [9]. All these requirements can be considered in a scene.

2.7.2 Measures

From Lloyd [125], the complexity measures are classified in accordance with the answer to three questions about the system[68]:

How Hard Is It To Describe?

Entropy and *algorithmic complexity* are the most representative measures. Entropy is widely applicable for indicating randomness (§2.5.1). It also measures uncertainty, ignorance, surprise, information, etc. Moreover, it is closely related to statistical entropy (Boltzmann's principle, 1877) and also to algorithmic complexity[69] which can be used to measure disorder or randomness without any recourse to probabilities [120, 255]. The algorithmic complexity of an object is defined as the length of the minimal universal Turing machine program needed to reproduce it. A basic theorem states that the entropy of a random variable X taking values in S is equal, except for an additive constant, to the expected value of algorithmic complexity of elements in S.

Other measures are: Fisher information, code length (e.g., prefix-free, Huffman, Shannon-Fano, error-correcting, and Hamming), Chernoff information, dimension, fractal dimension, Lempel-Ziv complexity, etc. Typically they are measured in bits.

How Hard Is It To Create?

The *computational complexity* is the most important measure in this group. It is related to the computational resources (usually time or space) needed to solve a problem [97]. The *logical depth*, introduced by Bennett [15], measures the computational resources taken to calculate the results of a program of minimal length. And *thermodynamic depth*, introduced by Pagels and Lloyd [125], is a measure of how hard it is to put something together.

Other measures are: information-based complexity, cost, crypticity, etc. Typically these are measured in time, energy, etc.

What Is Its Degree of Organisation?

This may be divided into two quantities: difficulty of describing organisational structure and amount of shared information between the parts of a system as a result of this organisational structure.

- *Effective complexity.* Metric entropy, fractal dimension, excess entropy, stochastic complexity, sophistication, effective measure complexity, etc.

- *Mutual information.* Algorithmic mutual information, correlation, stored information, organisation, etc.

---

[66] It need not be manifest in the object but may arise in the construction of a model. Hence, the presence of an actual hierarchical structure is not an infallible indicator of complexity.

[67] Considerations of the interactions of resolution at different levels bring in the concept of *scaling*.

[68] Subtle differences distinguish measures in the same group because they are closely related.

[69] Also called *algorithmic randomness* and *Kolmogorov-Chaitin complexity* (1965-1969).

A great diversity of complexity measures have been proposed from different fields to quantify the degree of structure or correlation of a system [79, 121, 66, 65]. To avoid confusion, Feldman and Crutch-field [66] proposed calling them measures of *statistical complexity*. These researchers, from the Santa Fe Institute Research Group[70], together with Gell-Mann [71], have studied this vision of complexity in great depth. We summarise the most basic ideas below:

- Information is important in the study of complex structures.
- Randomness and unpredictability of a system (entropy) does not completely capture the correlational structure in its behaviour.
- The larger and more intricate the correlations between the system's constituents, the more structured the underlying distribution is.
- Structure and correlation, however, are not completely independent of randomness.
- Both maximally random and perfectly ordered systems possess no structure.
- Statistical complexity measures provide a measure of the regularities present in an object above and beyond pure randomness.

Diverse approaches to measuring statistical complexity have been taken. One line is based on information theory and the quantities used are related to various forms of mutual information. Another line appeals to computation theory's classification of devices that recognise different classes of formal languages. On the other hand, other researchers of the Santa Fe Institute define the statistical complexity of a system *"so as to capture the degree to which the system consists of regularities versus randomness"* [71]. This group expresses the concept of complexity that we are adopting in this work. Our complexity approach will be based on information theory and the complexity (correlation-structure-dependence) of a scene will be quantified by the mutual information.

2.7.3 Scene Complexity

Feixas et al. [62] introduced information-theoretic tools to analyse a scene from the points of view of visibility and radiosity (§2.6). It was from out of these measurements that they also presented a discussion on the statistical complexity of a scene.

Scene complexity has to answer the question of how difficult it is to compute the visibility and radiosity of a scene with sufficient accuracy. As we have seen, to solve the problem of illumination we need to simulate the interreflection of light between all the surfaces (§2.2.3). This simulation presents typical characteristics of complex behaviour. The difficulty in obtaining a precise illumination solution depends on

- The degree of dependence between all the surfaces.
- How the interaction between these surfaces changes in dependence when the system is subdivided.
- The degree of unpredictability.

The two first considerations can be represented by a statistical complexity measure (§2.7.2), which quantifies correlation, structure, or interdependence between the parts of a system, and the third one by the entropy, which measures randomness or unpredictability. The word *complexity* is reserved for a measure of statistical complexity and *entropy* is referred to as randomness.

From §2.6, the entropy, H_s (2.87), and mutual information, I_s (2.89) and I_s^c (2.90), express two basic aspects of a scene: the first measures its degree of uncertainty and the second quantifies its degree of structure or correlation. Both interpretations coincide, respectively, with the randomness and statistical complexity of a system. Since the continuous mutual information expresses the information transfer or correlation in a scene with maximum precision (§2.6.1), it has been considered to be the measure of complexity. Hence, the entropy is referred to as *scene randomness* and mutual information as *scene*

---

[70] The Santa Fe Institute, Santa Fe (NM), USA, is dedicated to basic research with emphasis on the study of problems that involve complex interactions between their constituent parts (http://www.santafe.edu).

complexity. For example, Fig. 1.5.*a* is more complex[71] than Fig. 1.5.*b*. In this case, the scene with more "order" is more complex than the one with more 'disorder".

The relationship between the discrete and continuous mutual information is shown to be closely related to the difficulty in obtaining an accurate discretisation. A scene is a continuous system, and consequently, its discretisation introduces a distortion or error (2.97). In a way, to discretise means to make it uniform, and consequently some information is lost. The aim is to model the scene with the minimum loss of mutual information. Badii and Politi [9] are in agreement with the idea that the complexity of a system is directly related to the extent to which it is intrinsically hard to model and for Li [121], an intuitively satisfactory definition of complexity should measure the amount of effort put in generating correlations. In conclusion, we assume that [61, 175]:

- The entropy and mutual information of a scene measure the degree of uncertainty and structure, respectively.

- The continuous mutual information represents the complexity of a scene (how difficult it is to discretise).

- The best discretisation is the one with the highest discrete mutual information[72] (measure of how well we have done it).

- The greater the complexity the more difficult it is to get a discretisation which expresses the visibility of a scene with precision.

This approach to complexity is different from the ones based on integral geometry results [26] and reachability graph [141].

Summary

In this chapter, we present fundamental concepts related to the framework: *sampling theory*, *rendering*, *information theory*, and *complexity*.

In the first instance, the *sampling theory* is introduced. It is essential for the conversion of continuous signals into discrete ones, such as in the case of image synthesis. It is in this theory where the bases of the problems and errors in the signal transformation of the 3D world to the 2D are formulated (e.g., sampling, aliasing, filters, and reconstruction). Different methods of sampling are presented (e.g., Poisson, stratified, importance, and adaptive samplings) and also various types of refinement criteria for sampling (based on intensity). We also comment on certain modalities of refinement geometry such as the problem of signal reconstruction (with a brushstroke of its options).

With regard to *rendering*, Monte Carlo integration and the concept of form factor are introduced. Then, the light is presented as a main character. Basic questions about radiometry, optics, and the rendering equation are reviewed. Next, we comment on the colour spaces involved in this work.

The two methodologies of rendering which solve simplifications of the rendering equation are given in their own sections. On the one hand, the *ray-tracing* technique, as a representative of the pixel-driven approach is commented on. Concept and variants are shown (e.g., visibility ray-tracing, distributed ray-tracing, and path-tracing). On the other hand, the *radiosity* technique is introduced as a representative of the object-space approach. The general method and the hierarchical radiosity modality, together with refinement criteria, are then reviewed.

Next, we introduce the *information theory* with its most important measures: entropy and mutual information. Some properties of the continuous channel are also introduced. This basis allows us to present the scene as an information channel. The analysis of the scene, in discrete and continuous version, is introduced from the perspective of geometric visibility. The measure of the discretisation error is also introduced.

Finally, we review the concept of *complexity* while enumerating its most important measures. Statistical complexity is the area where the definitions of scene complexity are presented.

---

[71] The (H_S, I_S, I_S^c) values from Fig. 1.5 are (5.271, 6.270, 7.324) and (6.761, 4.779, 5.993), respectively. The computation has been done with 10^7 global lines.

[72] Or minimum discretisation error (2.92).

Chapter 3

Scene Complexity Measures

Information-theoretic measures to study scene visibility were introduced in Feixas et al. [61]. The results of this work and others that followed constitute a well-founded theory which interprets the scene as an information channel (§2.6). While entropy gives us the average uncertainty in a scene, mutual information quantifies the average information transfer and has been proposed as a scene complexity measure (§2.7.3).

From the relationship between information theory and scene visibility, we consider that the points or patches of a scene "interact" by exchanging information, creating a dependence or correlation (§2.6). Thus, for instance, the variation of the position of the objects of a scene changes the degree of interaction between all the parts of the environment and, consequently, the information transfer between the parts also varies. Based on this *geometric information*, in this chapter we introduce new tools for studying 3D and 2D closed scenes. We analyse the application of the most basic information-theoretic measures to the set of interior points of a scene (§3.1), an animated scene (§3.2), and a region of a scene (§3.3). For each one, we define measures of statistical complexity (§2.7.2).

3.1 Point Complexity

The aim of this section is to introduce the definitions of entropy and mutual information fields at an interior point. We call an *interior point* of a scene the one which belongs to the region $\mathcal{I}_\mathcal{S}$, which is contained strictly between the enclosure and the objects included (by default, in this chapter, a point will be considered to be always interior if we do not say otherwise). We make the development for 3D (§3.1.1) and 2D (§3.1.2) scenes. Afterwards, we show some empirical results (§3.1.3) which illustrate the characteristics of the measures presented. They can be applied to areas such as rendering, computer vision, robot motion, object recognition, architecture, design, neuroimaging, crowd rendering and simulation[1], and visualisation, where it is necessary to capture information from a certain point.

3.1.1 3D-Scene

The base for defining the entropy and mutual information at a point is the introduction of a new concept of form factor: that of an interior point of a scene. From here, the information theory methodology for the study of the 3D scene is applied (§2.6.1).

Form Factor Extension

From the perspective of geometric visibility, we consider the form factor from a point $x \in \mathcal{I}_\mathcal{S}$ over a differential of area $\mathrm{d}A_y$ like the solid angle subtended by the visible part of $\mathrm{d}A_y$ from x. As the global visibility of the point is constant (i.e., solid angle of the sphere) we can normalise and define:

---

[1] Techniques for visualising, in real-time, large urban environments which are populated with as many dynamic entities (humans, cars etc) as desired. They have various relevant issues such as collision detection, rendering of the animated avatars, improved illumination, occlusion culling and simulation of pedestrian movement, etc.

Definition 26 *The point-to-differential form factor at point* $x \in \mathcal{I}_\mathcal{S}$ *is given by*

$$\mathsf{F}_{x \to \mathrm{d}A_y} = \frac{\cos \theta_{n_y}^{\overrightarrow{yx}}}{4\pi r_{xy}^2} V(x,y).\qquad(3.1)$$

In our framework, we interpret this expression as the degree of geometric visibility between an interior point x and a surface point differential $\mathrm{d}y$ of the scene (Fig. 3.1). As for each $x \in \mathcal{I}_\mathcal{S}$, $\forall y \in A_\mathrm{s}$. $\mathsf{F}_{x \to \mathrm{d}A_y} \in [0,1]$ and $\int_{A_\mathrm{s}} \mathsf{F}_{x \to y}$ $\mathrm{d}A_y = 1$, this form factor represents the visibility pdf of x. We note the similarity of this form factor with respect to the volume-to-area form factor [191, 215] used in global illumination with participating media[2]:

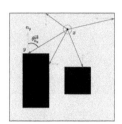

Figure 3.1:   An interior point $x \in \mathcal{I}_\mathcal{S}$. Geometry for point-to-differential form factor at point x (3.1) and complexity segments at point x (3.12).

$$F_{V_i \to A_j} = \int_{V_i} \int_{A_j} \frac{\cos \theta_{n_y}^{\overrightarrow{yx}} \kappa_t(i)}{\pi r_{xy}^2} \tau(r_{xy}) V(x,y) \mathrm{d}y \mathrm{d}x,\qquad(3.2)$$

where κ_t is the extinction coefficient (sum of absorption and scattering coefficients) of the volume, and τ is the transmittance of the medium along a path[3]. Taking into account that in our context we do not consider participating media, the extinction coefficient and the transmittance vanish and we obtain the same result, save the respective constants of normalisation, for an infinitesimal volume.

Extending (3.1) to a finite element of surface A, we have

$$\begin{aligned}
\int_A \mathsf{F}_{x \to y} \mathrm{d}A_y &= \int_A \frac{\cos \theta_{n_y}^{\overrightarrow{yx}}}{4\pi r_{xy}^2} V(x,y) \mathrm{d}A_y \\
&= \frac{1}{4\pi} \int_{\Omega_{x \to A}} V(x,y) \mathrm{d}\omega_\Theta \\
&= \frac{1}{4\pi} \int_{\Omega_{x \to A}^v} \mathrm{d}\omega \\
&= \frac{\omega_{x \to A}}{4\pi} \\
&= \overline{\omega}_{x \to A},
\end{aligned}\qquad(3.3)$$

where $\mathrm{d}\omega$ is the infinitesimal solid angle with a direction variable Θ, y is $\Lambda(x,\Theta)$, $\Omega_{x \to A}$ is the hemisphere of directions from x subtended by surface A, $\Omega_{x \to A}^v$ is the hemisphere of directions from x subtended by the visible part of A, $\omega_{x \to A}$ is the solid angle subtended by the visible part of A, and $\overline{\omega}_{x \to A}$ its normalised solid angle.

Definition 27 *The point-to-finite form factor at point* $x \in \mathcal{I}_\mathcal{S}$ *on surface A is given by*

$$\mathsf{F}_{x \to A} = \overline{\omega}_{x \to A}.\qquad(3.4)$$

If the surface is a patch of a discretised scene, we speak about a *point-to-patch form factor* at point x as $\mathsf{F}_{x \to i}$, where i is a patch of area A_i.

Field Analogy

We can consider the interior point x as a virtual spherical particle of an infinitesimal radius centred on x. Three geometric factors intervene on determining its form factor with respect to a point $y \in A_\mathrm{s}$: visibility, orientation, and distance. If there is no mutual visibility, the level of geometric relation is null otherwise its value is increasing as it improves its direction and closeness.

---

[2] Simplified case of an isotropic scattering medium where the phase function is constant (i.e., $\frac{1}{4\pi}$).
[3] For homogeneous media, it only depends on the distance r: $\tau(r) = e^{-\int_0^r \kappa_t(u)\mathrm{d}u}$.

An interesting interpretation of the extension of the form factor at a point is to consider it from the point of view of a "geometric interaction". In fact, all the information of a scene that is measured by the information-theoretic tools defined in §2.6 is based exclusively on geometric interactions. This interpretation will be of great help to us in understanding the expressions derived from the formalisms of the form factor at a point, especially from the physical concept of "field", which is perfectly adapted to our interests. The justification of this interpretation is based on the parallelism that exists with some physical interactions, such as the gravitational and electromagnetic forces. In our context, the concept of field can be interpreted in the following way: all the elements of a scene (surfaces in 3D or segments in 2D) contribute to creating a field at a point due to the geometric interaction at this point.

Using the point-to-finite form factor at a point (3.4) and the field concept, we introduce the scalar fields of entropy and mutual information of a scene.

Entropy Field

From the discrete scene visibility entropy, $\sum_{i\in S} a_i H_s(S,i)$ (2.87), we consider that the contribution of patch i to the entropy is $a_i H_s(S,i)$, where $H_s(S,i) = -\sum_{j\in S} F_{ij} \log F_{ij}$ is the entropy of patch i (2.86). By analogy, substituting in this formula patch i by point x and, consequently, the patch-to-patch form factor by the point-to-patch form factor (3.4), we can define

Definition 28 *The discrete entropy field at point $x \in \mathcal{I}_S$ is given by*

$$H_p(S,x) = -\sum_{i\in S} \mathsf{F}_{x\to i} \log \mathsf{F}_{x\to i} = \sum_{i\in S} H_p(S,x,i), \tag{3.5}$$

where

$$H_p(S,x,i) = -\overline{\omega}_{x\to i} \log \overline{\omega}_{x\to i} \tag{3.6}$$

is the contribution of patch i to the entropy field.

The measure $H_p(S,x)$ represents the information field that all the patches create at point x.

Mutual Information Field

Proceeding in a similar way to the entropy, from $I_s(S) = \sum_{i\in S}\sum_{j\in S} a_i F_{ij} \log \frac{F_{ij}}{a_j}$ (2.89), we can consider that the contribution of patch i to the discrete mutual information of S is $a_i I_i(S)$ where $I_i(S) = \sum_{j\in S} F_{ij} \log \frac{F_{ij}}{a_j}$ (2.94). By analogy, substituting in this formula patch i by point x and the patch-to-patch form factor by the point-to-patch form factor (3.4) as a new probability distribution, we obtain

Definition 29 *The discrete mutual information field at point $x \in \mathcal{I}_S$ is given by*

$$I_p(S,x) = \sum_{i\in S} \mathsf{F}_{x\to i} \log \frac{\mathsf{F}_{x\to i}}{a_i} = \sum_{i\in S} I_p(S,x,i), \tag{3.7}$$

where

$$I_p(S,x,i) = \overline{\omega}_{x\to i} \log \frac{\overline{\omega}_{x\to i}}{a_i} \tag{3.8}$$

is the contribution of patch i to the mutual information field.

Now, $I_p(S,x)$ expresses the information transfer field that all the patches of S create at point x. Following the same reasoning which is valid for the scene information channel, we can obtain finite values for the continuous mutual information. Thus, we will obtain the continuous expression using the following substitutions:

$$a_i \longmapsto \frac{1}{A_T}$$

$$\mathsf{F}_{x\to i} \longmapsto \mathsf{F}_{x\to dA_y}, \; dA_y \in A_s$$

$$\sum_{i\in S} \longmapsto \int_{x\in A_s}$$

Then, from (3.1) and (3.7), we can obtain the continuous field at point x:

Definition 30 *The continuous mutual information field at point $x \in \mathcal{I}_\mathcal{S}$ is given by*

$$I_p^c(\mathcal{S}, x) = \int_{A_S} F_{x \to dA_y} \log(A_T F_{x \to dA_y}) dA_y$$

$$= \frac{1}{4\pi} \int_{\Omega_{x \to A_S}^v} \log \frac{A_T \cos \theta_{n_y}^{\overline{yx}}}{4\pi r_{xy}^2} d\omega_\Theta, \tag{3.9}$$

where $y = \Lambda(x, \Theta)$ in the last expression.

It expresses the continuous information transfer of the whole scene at point x and we call this value the *point complexity*. We will use the notation $C_p(x)$ to refer specifically to the complexity at point x of a predetermined $\mathcal{I}_\mathcal{S}$.

This integral of (3.9) can be solved by Monte Carlo integration using a pdf equal to $\frac{1}{4\pi}$. The computation can be done efficiently by casting random lines from x in all directions (§2.2.2). These lines are converted into 3D-segments when they reach the first point of intersection and they are called *complexity segments*[4] (Fig. 3.1). Thus, the continuous visibility mutual information field can be approximated by

$$I_p^c(\mathcal{S}, x) \approx \frac{1}{|\mathcal{P}_{x \times \mathcal{S}}|} \sum_{y \in \mathcal{P}_{x \times \mathcal{S}}} \log \frac{A_T \cos \theta_{n_y}^{\overline{yx}}}{4\pi r_{xy}^2} \tag{3.10}$$

$$= \frac{1}{|\mathcal{P}_{x \times \mathcal{S}}|} \sum_{y \in \mathcal{P}_{x \times \mathcal{S}}} \left(I_p^D(\mathcal{S}, x, y) + I_p^O(\mathcal{S}, x, y) \right) \tag{3.11}$$

$$= \frac{1}{|\mathcal{P}_{x \times \mathcal{S}}|} \sum_{y \in \mathcal{P}_{x \times \mathcal{S}}} I_p^c(\mathcal{S}, x, y) \tag{3.12}$$

where

- $\mathcal{P}_{x \times \mathcal{S}}$ is the set of points $\{y \in \mathcal{S} \mid r_x^\Theta$ is a random ray $\wedge y = \Lambda(x, \Theta)\}$ where (x, y) is a complexity segment.

- $I_p^D(\mathcal{S}, x, y) = \log \frac{A_T}{4\pi r_{xy}^2}$ is the *distance component* of a complexity segment (x, y).

- $I_p^O(\mathcal{S}, x, y) = \log \cos \theta_{n_y}^{\overline{yx}}$ is the *orientation component* with respect to x of a complexity segment (x, y).

- $I_p^c(\mathcal{S}, x, y) = I_p^D(\mathcal{S}, x, y) + I_p^O(\mathcal{S}, x, y)$ is the value of complexity segment (x, y).

The contribution of any area A to $I_p^c(\mathcal{S}, x)$ is given by

$$I_p^c(\mathcal{S}, x, A) = \int_A F_{x \to dA_y} \log(A_T F_{x \to dA_y}) dA_y$$

$$\approx \frac{1}{|\mathcal{P}_{x \times \mathcal{S}}|} \sum_{y \in \mathcal{P}_{x \times A}} I_p^c(\mathcal{S}, x, y), \tag{3.13}$$

where $\mathcal{P}_{x \times A}$ is the set of complexity segments[5] that, originating at x end at a point of A which is hit by a random ray coming from x. It is important to note that the set $\mathcal{P}_{x \times A} \subseteq \mathcal{P}_{x \times \mathcal{S}}$ determines $F_{x \to A}$: $\overline{\omega}_{x \to A}$. From here, $I_p(\mathcal{S}, x)$ (3.7) can be calculated.

---

[4] The random line associated with each segment is called *complexity line*.
[5] $\mathcal{P}_{x \times A} = \{y \in \mathcal{P}_{x \times \mathcal{S}} \mid y \in A\}$ and we assume that $\mathcal{P}_{x \times A} \neq \emptyset$, otherwise $I_p^c(\mathcal{S}, x, A) = 0$.

Discrete Cross Entropy

We can also analyse the behaviour of the sum of the fields of entropy and mutual information in a discretised scene. From (3.5) and (3.7) we have

$$H_{\mathrm{p}}(S,x) + I_{\mathrm{p}}(S,x) = \left(-\sum_{i \in S} \mathsf{F}_{x \to i} \log \mathsf{F}_{x \to i} \right) + \left(\sum_{i \in S} \mathsf{F}_{x \to i} \log \frac{\mathsf{F}_{x \to i}}{a_i} \right)$$

$$= \sum_{i \in S} \mathsf{F}_{x \to i} \left(\log \frac{\mathsf{F}_{x \to i}}{a_i} - \log \mathsf{F}_{x \to i} \right)$$

$$= -\sum_{i \in S} \mathsf{F}_{x \to i} \log a_i. \tag{3.14}$$

As $\{\mathsf{F}_{x \to i}\}$ and $\{a_i\}$ are probability distributions over the same space of patches of S and according to (2.78), we obtain the cross entropy:

Definition 31 *The discrete cross entropy field at point $x \in \mathcal{I}_S$ is given by*

$$H_{\mathrm{c}}(S,x) = H_{\mathrm{p}}(S,x) + I_{\mathrm{p}}(S,x). \tag{3.15}$$

This expression can be alternatively expressed as

$$H_{\mathrm{c}}(S,x) = H(\{\mathsf{F}_{x \to i}\}) + D_{\mathrm{KL}}(\{\mathsf{F}_{x \to i}\}, \{a_i\}). \tag{3.16}$$

From this cross entropy, we obtain the following propositions:

Proposition 1 *Given a scene discretisation S and any point $x \in \mathcal{I}_S$, if the set of visible patches from x, $S^{\mathrm{v}}(x) = \{i \in S | \mathsf{F}_{x \to i} > 0\}$, have the same relative area a, then $H_c(S,x) = -\log a$.*

Proof:

$$H_{\mathrm{c}}(S,x) = H_{\mathrm{p}}(S,x) + I_{\mathrm{p}}(S,x)$$

$$= -\sum_{i \in S} \mathsf{F}_{x \to i} \log a_i$$

$$= -\log a \sum_{i \in S^{\mathrm{v}}(x)} \mathsf{F}_{x \to i}$$

$$= -\log a. \quad \square$$

From this proposition, we obtain

Proposition 2 *If all the patches of S have the same relative area $a = \frac{1}{|S|}$ (i.e., a regular discretisation), then $H_c(S,x) = \log |S|$ for all points of $\mathcal{I}_S$.*

Proof:

$$H_{\mathrm{c}}(S,x) = -\log a = \log |S| \quad \forall x \in \mathcal{I}_S. \quad \square$$

Thus, if all the patches of S have the same relative area, any increase in H_{p} is compensated by a decrease in I_{p} for any interior point, and vice versa. This property is not fulfilled for a nonregular discretisation.

3.1.2 2D-Scene

The concepts and respective definitions of information-theoretic point measures in 3D (§3.1.1) are adapted to flatland by changing the surface areas for the segment lengths (§2.6.2). The interpretation of geometric interaction continues to be valid in this new dimension. The semantics of the 3D definitions is totally maintained. As regards to the syntax, taking into account the changes mentioned, we keep the notation for the geometry (identical concepts in 2D). The only exception is the form factor extension, a critical definition which must be distinguished syntactically in order not to induce mistaken interpretations.

Form Factor Extension

Now, we can consider the interior point which belongs to the interior space $\mathcal{I}_S^{2D}$ defined by a 2D-scene. Analogously to the 3D process, from the 2D form factor (2.99) we can define

Definition 32 *The point-to-differential form factor at point $x \in \mathcal{I}_S^{2D}$ is given by*

$$\mathsf{F}^{2D}_{x \to dL_y} = \frac{\cos\theta_{n_y}^{\overline{yx}}}{2\pi r_{xy}} V(x,y), \tag{3.17}$$

where $\frac{1}{2\pi}$ is the normalisation constant (3.1). Extending the above definition to a finite element, segment L, we have

$$\int_L \mathsf{F}^{2D}_{x \to y} dL_y = \overline{\omega}_{x \to L}, \tag{3.18}$$

where $\overline{\omega}_{x \to L}$ is the normalised angle subtended by the visible part of L. Then,

Definition 33 *The point-to-finite form factor at point $x \in \mathcal{I}_S^{2D}$ on segment L is given by*

$$\mathsf{F}^{2D}_{x \to L} = \overline{\omega}_{x \to L}. \tag{3.19}$$

If the segment is explicitly a patch of a discretised scene, we will speak about a *point-to-patch form factor* at point x as $\mathsf{F}^{2D}_{x \to i}$, where i is a patch of length L_i.

Entropy Field

From the discrete scene entropy of a 2D-scene, $\sum_{i \in S} \ell_i H_s(S,i)$ (2.102), we consider that the contribution of patch i to the entropy is $\ell_i H_s(S,i)$, where $H_s(S,i) = -\sum_{j \in S} F^{2D}_{ij} \log F^{2D}_{ij}$ is the entropy of patch i (2.101). By analogy, substituting in this formula patch i by point x and, consequently, the patch-to-patch form factor by the point-to-patch form factor (3.19), we can define

Definition 34 *The discrete entropy field at point $x \in \mathcal{I}_S^{2D}$ is given by*

$$H_p(S,x) = \sum_{i \in S} H_p(S,x,i), \tag{3.20}$$

where

$$H_p(S,x,i) = -\overline{\omega}_{x \to i} \log \overline{\omega}_{x \to i} \tag{3.21}$$

is the contribution of patch i to the entropy field.

As in 3D, this measure represents the information field that all the patches create at point x.

Mutual Information Fields

From $I_s(S) = \sum_{i \in S} \sum_{j \in S} \ell_i F^{2D}_{ij} \log \frac{F^{2D}_{ij}}{\ell_j}$ (2.104), we can consider that the contribution of patch i to the mutual information of S is $\ell_i I_i(S)$ where $I_i(S) = \sum_{j \in S} F^{2D}_{ij} \log \frac{F^{2D}_{ij}}{\ell_j}$. By analogy, substituting in this formula patch i by point x and patch-to-patch form factor by the point-to-patch form factor (3.19) as a new probability distribution, we obtain

Definition 35 *The discrete mutual information field at point $x \in \mathcal{I}_S^{2D}$ is given by*

$$I_p(S,x) = \sum_{i \in S} I_p(S,x,i), \tag{3.22}$$

where

$$I_p(S,x,i) = \overline{\omega}_{x \to i} \log \frac{\overline{\omega}_{x \to i}}{\ell_i} \tag{3.23}$$

is the contribution of patch i to the mutual information field.

It expresses the transfer information field that all the patches of S create at point x. We will obtain the continuous expression using the following substitutions:

$$\ell_i \longmapsto \frac{1}{L_{\mathrm{T}}}$$

$$\mathsf{F}^{\mathrm{2D}}_{x \to i} \longmapsto \mathsf{F}^{\mathrm{2D}}_{x \to \mathrm{d}L_y}, \ \mathrm{d}L_y \in L_{\mathrm{S}}$$

$$\sum_{i \in S} \longmapsto \int_{x \in L_{\mathrm{S}}}$$

Then, from (3.22) we can obtain the continuous field at point x:

Definition 36 *The continuous mutual information field at point* $x \in \mathcal{I}^{\mathrm{2D}}_S$ *is given by*

$$I^{\mathrm{c}}_{\mathrm{p}}(S, x) = \int_{L_{\mathrm{S}}} \mathsf{F}^{\mathrm{2D}}_{x \to \mathrm{d}L_y} \log(L_{\mathrm{T}} \mathsf{F}^{\mathrm{2D}}_{x \to \mathrm{d}L_y}) \mathrm{d}L_y$$

$$= \frac{1}{2\pi} \int_{\Omega^{\mathrm{V}}_{x \to L_{\mathrm{S}}}} \log \frac{L_{\mathrm{T}} \cos \theta^{\overline{yx}}_{n_y}}{2\pi r^2_{xy}} \mathrm{d}\omega_{\Theta}, \tag{3.24}$$

where $y = \Lambda(x, \Theta)$ *in the last expression.*

This value expresses the continuous information transfer of the whole scene through point x and represents the *2D-point complexity*, $C_{\mathrm{p}}(x)$.

The integral (3.24) can be solved by Monte Carlo integration casting random lines from x in all directions (§2.2.2). Thus, if $\mathcal{P}_{x \times S}$ is now the set of 2D complexity segments we have

$$I^{\mathrm{c}}_{\mathrm{p}}(S, x) \approx \frac{1}{|\mathcal{P}_{x \times S}|} \sum_{y \in \mathcal{P}_{x \times S}} \log \frac{L_{\mathrm{T}} \cos \theta^{\overline{yx}}_{n_y}}{2\pi r_{xy}}$$

$$= \frac{1}{|\mathcal{P}_{x \times S}|} \sum_{y \in \mathcal{P}_{x \times S}} \left(I^{\mathrm{D}}_{\mathrm{p}}(S, x, y) + I^{\mathrm{O}}_{\mathrm{p}}(S, x, y) \right)$$

$$= \frac{1}{|\mathcal{P}_{x \times S}|} \sum_{y \in \mathcal{P}_{x \times S}} I^{\mathrm{c}}_{\mathrm{p}}(S, x, y) \tag{3.25}$$

where, with respect to 3D, there is only the change of the *distance component* of a complexity segment (x, y): $I^{\mathrm{D}}_{\mathrm{p}}(S, x, y) = \log \frac{L_{\mathrm{T}}}{2\pi r_{xy}}$. The contribution of any segment L to $I^{\mathrm{c}}_{\mathrm{p}}(S, x)$ is given by

$$I^{\mathrm{c}}_{\mathrm{p}}(S, x, L) = \int_L \mathsf{F}^{\mathrm{2D}}_{x \to \mathrm{d}L_y} \log(L_{\mathrm{T}} \mathsf{F}^{\mathrm{2D}}_{x \to \mathrm{d}L_y}) \mathrm{d}L_y$$

$$\approx \frac{1}{|\mathcal{P}_{x \times S}|} \sum_{y \in \mathcal{P}_{x \times L}} I^{\mathrm{c}}_{\mathrm{p}}(S, x, y), \tag{3.26}$$

where $\mathcal{P}_{x \times L}$ is the set of complexity segments[6] that hit length L coming from x. As in 3D, the set $\mathcal{P}_{x \times L} \subseteq \mathcal{P}_{x \times S}$ determines $\mathsf{F}^{\mathrm{2D}}_{x \to L}$: $\overline{\omega}_{x \to L}$. From here, $I_{\mathrm{p}}(S, x)$ (3.22) can be calculated.

Discrete Cross Entropy

We have from (3.20) and (3.22): $H_{\mathrm{p}}(S, x) + I_{\mathrm{p}}(S, x) = -\sum_{i \in S} \mathsf{F}^{\mathrm{2D}}_{x \to i} \log \ell_i$. Then,

Definition 37 *The discrete cross entropy field at point* $x \in \mathcal{I}^{\mathrm{2D}}_S$ *is*

$$H_{\mathrm{c}}(S, x) = H_{\mathrm{p}}(S, x) + I_{\mathrm{p}}(S, x). \tag{3.27}$$

---

[6] $\mathcal{P}_{x \times L} = \{y \in \mathcal{P}_{x \times S} \mid y \in L\}$ and we assume that $\mathcal{P}_{x \times L} \neq \emptyset$, otherwise $I^{\mathrm{c}}_{\mathrm{p}}(S, x, L) = 0$.

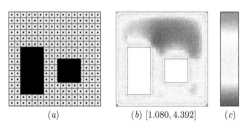

(a) (b) [1.080, 4.392] (c)

Figure 3.2: The field map for a simple scene. (a) A 16×16 square grid for computing the intensity at the central point of each square (set $\mathcal{I}_S^{d}$). (b) A continuous mutual information field map made up from a 64×64 square grid and 10^4 complexity lines for each central point. (c) Thermic colour scale. The lowest intensity corresponds to the blue and the highest to the red.

It can be alternatively expressed as

$$H_c(S,x) = H(\{\mathsf{F}_{x \to i}^{2D}\}) + D_{\mathrm{KL}}(\{\mathsf{F}_{x \to i}^{2D}\}, \{\ell_i\}). \tag{3.28}$$

From this cross entropy, Prop. 1 and Prop. 2 are also valid considering the relative distribution of areas changed for lengths. Thus, as in Prop. 2, if all the patches of S have the same relative length, any increase in H_p is compensated for a decrease in I_p for any interior point, and vice versa. We will observe this property in the next section (§3.1.3). However, it is not fulfilled for a nonregular discretisation: there are points x where $H_p(S,x) > \log|S|$ and $H_p(S,x) < \log|S|$ (Figs. 3.3.$*$.iii).

3.1.3 Results

In this section, some experiments in flatland demonstrate the behaviour of the measures introduced in the previous sections. For each scene we show its *field maps* (entropy and mutual information). The field map is a graphic representation of the intensity field at different points based on a specific thermic colour scale associated with the range of intensities (Fig. 3.2.c). The finite set of points which make up a field map is obtained by taking a square grid and computing the intensity at the central point of each square [176]. We note this finite set of points as $\mathcal{I}_S^{d}$ (Fig. 3.2.a). All the measures in this section have been computed using an $\mathcal{I}_S^{d}$ made up from a 64×64 square grid and casting 10^4 complexity lines for each central point. In all figures we specify the range of intensity obtained in each scene. Obviously, the precision of the data depends directly on how fine the grid is and the number of complexity lines used. Consequently, the intensity range also depends on these (Fig. 3.2.b).

In Fig. 3.3 and Fig. 3.4, the entropy (Figs. 3.3.$*$.i and Figs. 3.4.$*$.i) and cross entropy (Figs. 3.3.$*$.iii and Figs. 3.4.$*$.iii) field map sequences have been calibrated between the minimum and maximum intensities for each sequence. On the other hand, sequences of discrete mutual information field maps (Figs. 3.3.$*$.ii and Figs. 3.4.$*$.ii) have been calibrated together with the continuous mutual information field map (Fig. 3.2.b).

Firstly, field maps for entropy (Figs. 3.3.$*$.i), discrete mutual information (Figs. 3.3.$*$.ii), and cross entropy (Figs. 3.3.$*$.iii) are given for a scene with 208 patches and four different discretisations. We can see that:

- The entropy field maps are clearly different. The position and value of the entropy maximums depend on the discretisation. We observe a big difference between Fig. 3.3.a.i (regular discretisation), Fig. 3.3.b.i, and Fig. 3.3.d.i (very irregular discretisation). The entropy tends to infinity when the size of patches tends to zero (Th. 2).

- The discrete mutual information field maps are very similar. For example, small changes can be appreciated at the corners of the objects. The main reason for this behaviour is that, at every point, I_p is relatively near to I_p^c (Fig. 3.2.b).

- In Fig. 3.3.$a.iii$, the points with maximum entropy have minimum mutual information, as the sum of fields is constant ($\log |S|$). In the other cases (Figs. 3.3.b–$d.iii$) the sum is not constant: there are some points where the sum is greater than $\log |S|$, and other points where it is lower.

- In Figs. 3.3.c–$d.i$, where the square and the rectangle have been highly discretised, respectively, maximum entropy points are moved towards the most discretised object. Points of maximum entropy do not have to coincide with points of minimum mutual information.

- Figs. 3.3.$a.*$ and Figs. 3.3.$b.*$ are quite similar due to their discretisation similarity.

Secondly, entropy (Figs. 3.4.$*.i$), mutual information (Figs. 3.4.$*.ii$), and cross entropy (Figs. 3.4.$*.iii$) field maps are given for a scene with 26, 78, 130, and 182 patches. We can see that:

- A more precise discretisation increases entropy and mutual information fields.

- Discrete mutual information field maps converge very quickly towards the continuous mutual information field map (Fig. 3.2.b).

- The cross entropy field map is constant in Fig. 3.4.$a.iii$. In Figs. 3.4.b–$d.iii$, there are some points where the sum is greater than $\log |S|$, and other points where it is lower (see the intensity range).

And thirdly, the continuous mutual information or complexity field (Figs. 3.6.$*.iii$), and its splitting up into distance (Figs. 3.6.$*.i$) and orientation (Figs. 3.6.$*.ii$) components, are given for four different scenes (Fig. 3.6). To obtain maximum field contrast, in all figures the range has been graduated independently for each one. For the continuous mutual information field from Fig. 3.6.$d.iii$, a plot of contour lines[7] is shown in Fig. 3.5. On the one hand, we can see that the complexity and distance field maps are quite similar since the first one depends mostly on distance contribution. On the other hand, orientation component values present a small range of intensity.

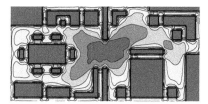

Figure 3.5: Continuous mutual information field map from Fig. 3.6.$d.iii$ with contour lines.

3.2 Animation Complexity

In the previous section we have presented a measure of point complexity based on a geometric visibility perspective. Here, we apply the same concepts to the movement of objects in a scene (i.e., dynamic environments, such as the ones presented in [17, 43]).

After considering different alternatives, we define two *animation complexity* measures (§3.2.1). Some of the applications that we envisage for animation complexity are cost prediction for visibility and radiosity recomputations and the development of meshing strategies to obtain an accurate discretisation. The study of animation complexity has also potential applications in fields such as robot motion and architectural design. We compute the complexity of different sequences of frames and analyse the main reasons for the growth in complexity (§3.2.2).

3.2.1 Measures

Within our context, we establish first what we understand by an animation:

---

[7] Quoting Feynman, *"One way of thinking about scalar fields is to imagine contours which are imaginary surfaces drawn through all points for which the field has the same value, just as contour lines on a map connect points with the same height"* [67].

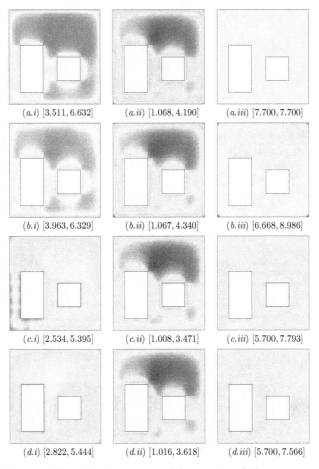

Figure 3.3: (*i*) Entropy, (*ii*) mutual information, and (*iii*) cross entropy field map sequences, corresponding to the scene in Fig. 3.2.*b*, with four different discretisations of 208 patches: (*a*) regular, (*b*) irregular, (*c*) highly discretised square, and (*d*) highly discretised rectangle. For each subfigure, the intensity range is shown.

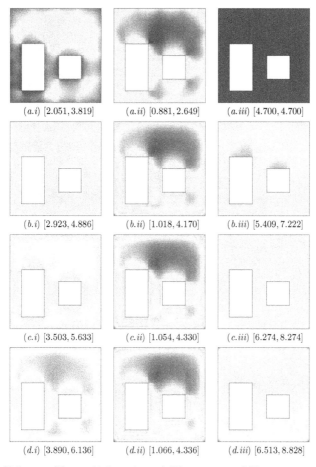

$(a.i)$ [2.051, 3.819] $(a.ii)$ [0.881, 2.649] $(a.iii)$ [4.700, 4.700]

$(b.i)$ [2.923, 4.886] $(b.ii)$ [1.018, 4.170] $(b.iii)$ [5.409, 7.222]

$(c.i)$ [3.503, 5.633] $(c.ii)$ [1.054, 4.330] $(c.iii)$ [6.274, 8.274]

$(d.i)$ [3.890, 6.136] $(d.ii)$ [1.066, 4.336] $(d.iii)$ [6.513, 8.828]

Figure 3.4: (i) Entropy, (ii) mutual information, and (iii) cross entropy field map sequences, corresponding to the scene in Fig. 3.2.b, with four different discretisations: (a) 26 (regular), (b) 78, (c) 130, and (d) 182 patches. For each subfigure, the intensity range is shown.

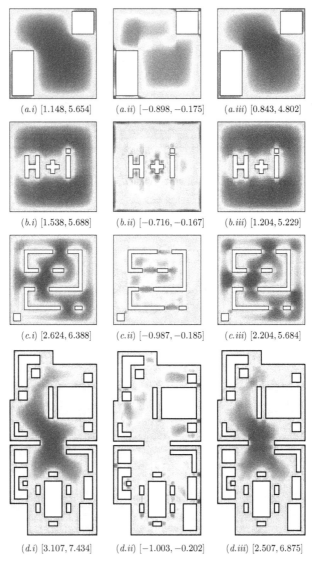

$(a.i)$ [1.148, 5.654] $(a.ii)$ [−0.898, −0.175] $(a.iii)$ [0.843, 4.802]

$(b.i)$ [1.538, 5.688] $(b.ii)$ [−0.716, −0.167] $(b.iii)$ [1.204, 5.229]

$(c.i)$ [2.624, 6.388] $(c.ii)$ [−0.987, −0.185] $(c.iii)$ [2.204, 5.684]

$(d.i)$ [3.107, 7.434] $(d.ii)$ [−1.003, −0.202] $(d.iii)$ [2.507, 6.875]

Figure 3.6: (i) Distance component, (ii) orientation component, and (iii) continuous mutual information field map sequences for four different scenes. For each subfigure, the range of intensities is shown. A contour lines plot from Fig. 3.6.$d.iii$ is shown in Fig. 3.5.

Definition 38 *We define an animation as a sequence of $n > 0$ frames on a discretised scene S: $S^n = (S_1^n, \ldots, S_n^n)$, where only the positions of objects can change (translations and rotations) and never their shapes.*

Therefore, for $S_{k \in \{2,\ldots,n\}}^n$ there is a subset of patches which are geometrically repositioned with respect to their previous frame[8]. The relationship between the points of patches changes at each frame, and consequently their complexity. Since each movement is modelled as a collection of small movements, the animation complexity will be given by the sum of the complexities of each step, and obviously the bigger the number of frames, the higher the animation complexity. This complexity (or dissimilarity between two frames) is a measure of the degree of recomputation required.

An animation complexity measure has to capture the variation of interactions between all the points or patches of a scene. With this aim we will analyse four possible dissimilarity measures. In order to compare two frames, a restriction is imposed: the discretisation should not be changed. And, obviously, the finer the discretisation the more accurate the measures.

Difference of Complexities

Since the continuous mutual information, I_s^c (2.90), represents the complexity of a frame, we could try to define the animation complexity between two successive frames as the absolute value of the difference between the respective continuous mutual information. But the difference between complexities does not express the cost of movement. For example, it is easy to imagine a scene in which the movement of an object does not change the complexity and, despite this, the transformation can have a high cost (e.g., a rotation of a symmetric object or a movement of a nonsymmetric object but which ends up in a symmetrical position with respect to the set and its initial position). This subtraction of complexities does not contain dynamic information. In fact, I_s or I_s^c express a global property of a system but there is a loss of information with respect to the diversity of the relationships between the pairs of points or patches of a scene. In conclusion, this proposal is not appropriate.

Kullback-Leibler Distance

In the context of information theory, the most used measure of discrimination between probability distributions is the Kullback-Leibler distance (§2.5.1). From (2.77), the relative entropy or Kullback-Leibler distance between two probability distributions p and q, which are defined over the same set of states $X = \{x_1, \ldots, x_n\}$, is defined by

$$D_{\mathrm{KL}}(p, q) = \sum_{i=1}^{n} p_i \log \frac{p_i}{q_i}. \tag{3.29}$$

In our case, it should be given by

$$D_{\mathrm{KL}}(p, q) = \sum_{i=1}^{N_\mathrm{P}} \sum_{j=1}^{N_\mathrm{P}} a_i' F_{ij}' \log \frac{a_i' F_{ij}'}{a_i F_{ij}}, \tag{3.30}$$

where F is the form factor patch-to-patch matrix (§2.2.2), and $p = \{a_i F_{ij}\}$ and $q = \{a_i' F_{ij}'\}$ are the joint probability distributions of two successive frames. It is easy to see that some probabilities can be zero: those corresponding to pairs of nonvisible patches which, in another frame, can become visible to each other, and then $p_i \log \frac{p_i}{0} = \infty$. In consequence, this measure fails in the majority of cases (we could adopt measures to foresee these cases but they would not reflect the geometric reality).

---

[8] If is not the case, $S_k = S_{k-1}$ and its contribution to the animation complexity should be null.

Animation Complexity

As we have seen in the interpretation of a scene as an information channel (§2.6), discrete scene visibility mutual information (2.89) is given by

$$I_s(S) = \sum_{i \in S} \sum_{j \in S} a_i F_{ij} \log \frac{F_{ij}}{a_j}. \tag{3.31}$$

Moreover, we can consider that the terms

$$I_{ij}(S) = a_i F_{ij} \log \frac{F_{ij}}{a_j} \tag{3.32}$$

form part of a symmetric mutual information matrix $(I_{ij}(S) = I_{ji}(S))$, where each term represents the exchange (or transfer) of information between the patches i and j (2.93).

We observe that negative values appear when $F_{ij} < a_j$. This situation reflects a very low interaction between the two patches involved. A case illustrating this is when the discretisation is uniform (i.e., $a_i = \frac{1}{N_p}$). Without knowledge of the scene, we would assign $F_{ij} = \frac{1}{N_p}$. This would correspond to a uniform random distribution (or visibility). Then we can interpret

- ◦ $N_p F_{ij} < 1$ Negative contribution (less interaction, occluded and far patches)
- ◦ $N_p F_{ij} = 1$ No contribution (neutral or random interaction)
- ◦ $N_p F_{ij} > 1$ Positive contribution (more interaction, high visibility and near patches)

From the mutual information matrix, we initially propose an animation complexity measure that quantifies the variation of interactions between all the patches for two frames. Thus,

Definition 39 *The animation complexity between two frames* $k, k' \in \{1, \ldots, n\}$ *of* S^n, *not necessarily consecutive, is given by*

$$C_a(S_k^n, S_{k'}^n) = \sqrt{\sum_{i \in S} \sum_{j \in S} (I_{ij}(S_k^n) - I_{ij}(S_{k'}^n))^2}, \tag{3.33}$$

where $I_{ij}(S_k^n)$ *is the exchange of information between the patches* i *and* j *in frame* k.

If $k = k'$, the measure is 0 as is desired. Then, with the sum of the complexities between two successive frames we can define

Definition 40 *The animation complexity of* S^n *is given by*

$$C_a(S^n) = \sum_{k=1}^{n-1} C_a(S_k^n, S_{k+1}^n). \tag{3.34}$$

We have proposed root squared differences against absolute value differences because of their much greater robustness.

In flatland, both definitions coincide (taking into account the corresponding semantics in each dimension). In the expansion of its expressions, §2.6.2 should be considered and, therefore, the $\{\ell_i\}$ and $\{\ell_i F_{ij}^{2D}\}$ probability distributions.

Euclidean Distance

Starting from the same idea on which the C_a is based, we can consider a non-information-theoretic measure, Euclidean distance. We obtain the two following analogous definitions:

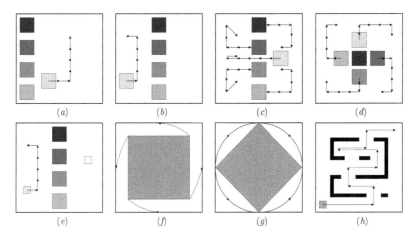

Figure 3.7: Set of S^n scenes with a vectorial representation of movement. All the patches of each scene have the same length.

Definition 41 *The Euclidean distance between two frames $k, k' \in \{1, \ldots, n\}$ of an animation S^n, not necessarily consecutive, is given by*

$$D_{\mathrm{e}}(S_k^n, S_{k'}^n) = \sqrt{\sum_{i \in S} \sum_{j \in S} \left(a_i^k F_{ij}^k - a_i^{k'} F_{ij}^{k'}\right)^2}$$

$$= \sqrt{\sum_{i \in S} a_i \sum_{j \in S} \left(F_{ij}^k - F_{ij}^{k'}\right)^2}, \tag{3.35}$$

where $\{a_i^k F_{ij}^k\}$ is the probability distribution of frame k.

In the last equivalence we have considered $a_i^k = a_i^{k'} = a_i$ because the discretisation of all the frames is the same. It vanishes when $k = k'$. With the sum of the complexities between two successive frames we can define

Definition 42 *The Euclidean distance of an animation S^n is given by*

$$D_{\mathrm{e}}(S^n) = \sum_{k=1}^{n-1} D_{\mathrm{e}}(S_k^n, S_{k+1}^n). \tag{3.36}$$

As we will see in the next section, this measure exhibits a very similar behaviour to C_{a}, and thus could be considered a cheaper computational alternative to this one.

The same considerations for the flatland made for C_{a} are valid for D_{e}.

3.2.2 Results

In order to illustrate the feasibility of the animation complexity measure, we compute C_{a} and D_{e} for eight sequences of frames in flatland (Fig. 3.7) whose values are contained in Table 3.1.

For each sequence of frames, 10^5 global lines have been cast to obtain an approximated Monte Carlo solution for the form factors [195], by counting the number of intersections between pairs of segments which are visible.

S	frames	$|S|$	I_p^c	$C_a(S^n)$	$D_e(S^n)$
a	7	176	[1.573, 1.659]	0.126	0.030
b	7	176	[1.239, 1.309]	0.241	0.048
c	7	176	[1.124, 1.546]	0.748	0.129
d	7	176	[1.087, 1.647]	0.710	0.121
e	7	176	[1.192, 1.227]	0.133	0.032
f	10	200	[1.567, 1.833]	0.501	0.085
g	2	200	1.825	0.139	0.028
h	75	234	[1.833, 1.889]	2.227	0.373

Table 3.1:   The scene, the number of frames and patches, the I_p^c range, and the C_a and D_e values for the S^n scenes in Fig. 3.7 are shown. A total of 10^5 global lines were used to obtain these values.

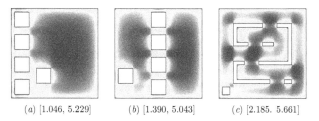

(a) [1.046, 5.229]   (b) [1.390, 5.043]   (c) [2.185. 5.661]

Figure 3.8:   Complexity field maps and ranges corresponding to S_1^n in Figs. 3.7.$\{a, b, h\}$, respectively. The computation has been carried out by casting 10^3 lines from a grid of 96×96.

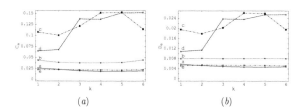

(a)   (b)

Figure 3.9:   Evolution from Figs. 3.7.a–e of (a) $C_a(S_k^n, S_{k+1}^n)$ and (b) $D_e(S_k^n, S_{k+1}^n)$.

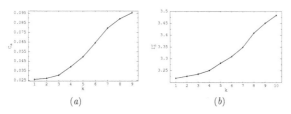

Figure 3.10: Evolution from Fig. 3.7.f of (a) $C_a(S_k^n, S_{k+1}^n)$ and (b) $I_s^c(\mathcal{S})$.

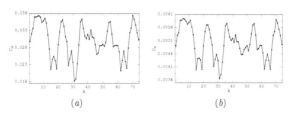

Figure 3.11: Evolution from Fig. 3.7.h of (a) $C_a(S_k^n, S_{k+1}^n)$ and (b) $D_e(S_k^n, S_{k+1}^n)$.

The first two sequences (Figs. 3.7.a–b) show a moving square following two different paths. Animation in Fig. 3.7.b is more complex than in Fig. 3.7.a because the movement is produced in a more complex region (between the wall and four objects). This can be seen in Figs. 3.8.a–b where we show the complexity field maps (§3.1.3), computed with (3.25), corresponding to both sequences in Figs. 3.7.a–b, respectively. It is interesting to remark that in the sequence from Fig. 3.7.b, the scene complexity I_s^c is lower than in the other one where the four objects are placed near one edge (Fig. 3.7.a).

In Figs. 3.7.c–d all the objects are moved simultaneously. As we might expect, the animation complexity increases dramatically.

In Fig. 3.7.e, the decrease in size of the moving square implies a decrease in animation complexity. Fig. 3.9 collects the first five sequences together (Figs. 3.7.a–e) and shows the animation complexity and the Euclidean distance of each step. An almost identical behaviour can be observed from both graphs.

In Fig. 3.7.f, an interior square rotates (5 degrees on each step) in a square enclosure from a position with parallel sides to a position where the vertexes of the interior square almost touch the enclosure. In this case, the animation complexity increases at each step (Fig. 3.10.a), similarly to the scene complexity I_s^c (Fig. 3.10.b).

Fig. 3.7.g simply represents a rotation of 90 degrees. In this case, the animation complexity is high because the variation of the relationship between the patches has been important.

Finally, in the labyrinth scene (Fig. 3.7.h), the high complexity is due to the large number of frames. In Fig. 3.8.c we show the corresponding complexity field map and in Fig. 3.11 we again observe a very similar evolution of C_a and D_e.

Now, in the first scene (Fig. 3.7.a) we have two alternative animations (Fig. 3.12). From its complexity field map (Fig. 3.8.a), we expect that the animation represented by a continuous line is more complex because it crosses a more complex region. If we measure the complexity of these two animations, we observe the concordance between this measure and the complexity field map: C_a values are 0.241 for the continuous line and 0.126 for the dashed line. Crossing complex regions will yield a higher value in the animation complexity measure.

From all these experiments, we conclude:

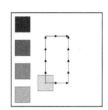

Figure 3.12: Animation complexity versus complexity field. Two alternative animations are represented by a continuous line and a dashed line with C_a equal to 0.241 and 0.126, respectively. The complexity field map is shown in Fig. 3.8.a. The cost of the animation which crosses a higher complexity field is higher.

- Both measures, C_a and D_e, capture the complexity of the animation well, exhibiting very similar behaviour.

- The animation will be more complex if it is produced in regions with a higher complexity field.

- The increase in the number of moving objects increases the animation complexity.

- Given a moving object, the bigger its size relative to the scene, the higher the animation complexity.

3.3   Region Complexity

As we have seen, the mutual information measure is used to quantify the average information shared in a scene (2.90), the correlation between all their patches (2.89), the complexity at a point (3.9), or the complexity of an animation (3.34). In this section, the mutual information is used to study the complexity of a region of a scene.

On the one hand, we study the complexity generated between the surfaces which delimit a region (§3.3.1) and, on the other hand, the complexity of a region of the interior space of a scene (§3.3.2). Some potential applications of these measures are determining how difficult it is to recompute the visibility for an animation or to obtain the complexity of the movement of a robot. They could also be applied in parallel computation (e.g., by obtaining an optimal load balancing by dividing the geometry into equal complexity regions).

3.3.1   Surface-to-Surface Complexity

In order not to introduce a specific notation for the region, we consider it to be a subscene $s \subseteq S \wedge s \neq \emptyset$. Below we define the complexity of the region s from the geometric interaction established between the surfaces (3D) or lengths (2D) which make it up. Our starting point is the scene complexity (§2.6).

Continuous Scene

From (2.90), considering the property of additivity in integration, we can define

Definition 43 *The continuous scene mutual information or surface-to-surface complexity of a region* $s \subseteq S$ *is given by*

$$I_s^c(S, s) = \int_{A_s} \int_{A_S} \frac{1}{A_T} F_{x \leftrightarrow y} \log(A_T F_{x \leftrightarrow y}) \mathrm{d}A_y \mathrm{d}A_x, \tag{3.37}$$

where A_s *is the area of the region* s.

It can be interpreted as the total information transferred by this subscene or its contribution to the global complexity. Clearly, $I_s^c(S, s) = I_s^c(S)$ when $s = S$. If we apply the same property to the interior integral, we obtain

Definition 44 *The continuous scene mutual information or surface-to-surface complexity between two regions $s, s' \subseteq S$ is given by*

$$I_s^c(S, s, s') = \int_{A_s} \int_{A_{s'}} \frac{1}{A_T} F_{x \leftrightarrow y} \log(A_T F_{x \leftrightarrow y}) \mathrm{d}A_y \mathrm{d}A_x, \qquad (3.38)$$

where A_s and $A_{s'}$ are the areas of regions s and s', respectively.

It can be interpreted as the total information transferred between two subscenes or its contribution to the global complexity. A particular case is $I_s^c(S, s, s)$, which expresses the interaction inside the subscene itself. Obviously, $I_s^c(S, s, s') = I_s^c(S, s)$ when $s' = S$ and $I_s^c(S, s, s') = I_s^c(S)$ when, moreover, $s = S$.

According to (2.91), the scene complexity can be approximately computed by casting uniformly distributed global lines. Analogously, the surface-to-surface complexity of s can be obtained by the same process, but now we need only to consider the segments related to A_s. Thus,

$$I_s^c(S, s) \approx \frac{1}{|\mathcal{G}_{S^2}|} \sum_{(x,y) \in \mathcal{G}_{A_s \times S}} \log(A_T F_{x \leftrightarrow y}), \qquad (3.39)$$

where the pdf is $\frac{1}{A_T} F_{x \leftrightarrow y}$, $\mathcal{G}_{S^2}$ is the set of all global segments in S, and $\mathcal{G}_{A_s \times S} = \{(x, y) \in \mathcal{G}_{S^2} \mid x \in A_s \vee y \in A_s\}$ (§2.2.2). The global segment set $\mathcal{G}_{A_s \times A_{s'}} = \mathcal{G}_{A_s \times S} \cap \mathcal{G}_{A_{s'} \times S}$ will be used to calculate the surface-to-surface complexity between s and s':

$$I_s^c(S, s, s') \approx \frac{1}{|\mathcal{G}_{S^2}|} \sum_{(x,y) \in \mathcal{G}_{A_s \times A_{s'}}} \log(A_T F_{x \leftrightarrow y}), \qquad (3.40)$$

Conceptually, in expression (3.39) each term $\log(A_T F_{x \leftrightarrow y})$ can be interpreted as the information transfer between the points x and y. Note that this expression has the same structure as the global segment generated by the random line used in point complexity calculation (3.10): $\log(A_T F_{x \leftrightarrow y})$. Both expressions play the role of a *complexity segment*. The distance and orientation components are also present in them (§3.1.1). Note that $\mathcal{G}_{A_s \times S}$ and $\mathcal{P}_{x \times S}$ refer to segments between points of $A_S \times A_S$ and $\mathcal{I}_S \times A_S$, respectively.

Considering the relation $\mathcal{G}_{A_s \times A_{s'}} \subseteq \mathcal{G}_{A_s \times S} \cup \mathcal{G}_{A_{s'} \times S} \subseteq \mathcal{G}_{S^2}$, it can be seen that the precision of results will decrease in the same measure as do the relative areas since the number of complexity segments decreases. To solve this, either we increase the number of global lines, or we use the local lines strategy (§2.2.2).

As we already know §3.1.2, the adaptation to flatland requires only changing the concept of areas by lengths and using the corresponding new form factors. Thus, the previous concepts are the same and the two basic definitions are:

Definition 45 *The continuous scene mutual information or length-to-length complexity of a 2D-region $s \subseteq S$ is given by*

$$I_s^c(S, s) = \int_{L_s} \int_{L_S} \frac{1}{L_T} F_{x \leftrightarrow y}^{2D} \log(L_T F_{x \leftrightarrow y}^{2D}) \mathrm{d}L_y \mathrm{d}L_x, \qquad (3.41)$$

where L_s is the length of the region.

Definition 46 *The continuous scene mutual information or length-to-length complexity between two 2D-regions $s, s' \subseteq S$ is given by*

$$I_s^c(S, s, s') = \int_{L_s} \int_{L_{s'}} \frac{1}{L_T} F_{x \leftrightarrow y}^{2D} \log(L_T F_{x \leftrightarrow y}^{2D}) \mathrm{d}L_y \mathrm{d}L_x, \qquad (3.42)$$

where L_s and $L_{s'}$ are the lengths of regions s and s', respectively.

The calculation via complexity lines is identical to 3D considering the 2D term: $\log\left(L_T F_{x \leftrightarrow y}^{2D}\right)$.

Discrete Scene

If we take the discretised scene, the subscene $s \subseteq S$ which defines the region consists of a nonempty set of patches. This allows us to consider the kind of subscenes of minimum cardinality: a single patch (i.e., $|s| = 1$). Any other subscene is the union of a subset of a sole patch. Analogously to the continuous case, where we split the integration domain at area level, now we can split the discrete sums at patch level.

From (§2.6.1), we can define I_s (2.89) in terms of a symmetric mutual information matrix $I^{N_P \times N_P}$:

- $I_{ij}(S) = a_i F_{ij} \log \frac{F_{ij}}{a_j}$ (2.93)

- $I_i(S) = a_i \sum_{j \in S} F_{ij} \log \frac{F_{ij}}{a_j}$ (2.94)

- $I_s(S) = \sum_{i \in S} I_i(S) = \sum_{i \in S} \sum_{j \in S} I_{ij}(S)$ (2.95)

where each of them represents the corresponding level of complexity (i.e., discrete visibility information transfer) between the elements involved. From this perspective, we can consider

Definition 47 *The discrete scene mutual information or surface-to-surface complexity of a region $s \subseteq S$ is given by*

$$I_s(S, s) = \sum_{i \in s} I_i(S). \tag{3.43}$$

It expresses the information transferred by s (i.e., its contribution to the total complexity). For the particular cases of the minimum ($s = \{i\}$) and the maximum ($s = S$) subscene, we have $I_s(S, s) = I_i(S)$ and $I_s(S, s) = I_s(S)$, respectively.

As in the continuous case, we can define

Definition 48 *The discrete scene mutual information or surface-to-surface complexity between two regions $s, s' \subseteq S$ is given by*

$$I_s(S, s, s') = \sum_{i \in s} \sum_{j \in s'} I_{ij}(S). \tag{3.44}$$

It can be interpreted as the total information transferred between two subscenes (i.e., its contribution to the total complexity). A particular case is $I_s^c(S, s, s)$, which expresses the interaction inside the subscene itself. Now the simplest case appears when both subscenes are made of a sole patch ($s = \{i\}$ and $s' = \{j\}$) and we have $I_s(S, s, s') = I_{ij}(S)$. Obviously, the most complex case appears when $s = s' = S$ obtaining $I_s(S, s, s') = I_s(S)$.

The adaptation to flatland is straightforward: only the areas and form factors needs to be changed, by lengths and 2D form factors, respectively, in order to obtain the *segment-to-segment complexity*. Thus, the previous concepts are the same in 2D and the two basic definitions, Def. 47 and Def. 48, remain syntactically equal but considering the matrix term $I_{ij}(S) = \ell_i F_{ij}^{2D} \log \frac{F_{ij}^{2D}}{\ell_j}$.

Example

s	1	2	3	4	$I_s^c(\mathcal{S}, s)$	%	$\imath_c(\mathcal{S}, s)$
1	0.110	0.058	0.013	0.089	0.270	10.74	0.688
2	0.058	0.371	0.037	0.051	0.517	20.53	2.541
3	0.013	0.037	0.752	0.162	0.964	38.28	3.547
4	0.089	0.051	0.162	0.464	0.766	30.45	1.536
					2.517	100.00	

Table 3.2: Surface-to-surface complexities from Fig. 3.13, their contributions to the global complexity I_s^c, and their indexes of clustering $\imath_c$.

In order to illustrate the behaviour of the measures introduced, we show in Table 3.2 the values obtained for a simple 2D-scene, with a rectangle and a square in its interior, which has been partitioned into four regions (Fig. 3.13). We can see that region 3 has a higher complexity with an important contribution to the interaction between the patches of this region and the scene. In contrast, in region 1, the complexity is lowest and the total contribution of the interaction with the other regions is more important than the interaction inside the region itself.

Figure 3.13: Four regions have been labelled in this basic scene. Its surface-to-surface complexities are in Table 3.2.

In neuroscience studies, mutual information has been used to analyse the brain complexity. A subset of regions that are much more highly interactive among themselves than with the rest of the brain is called a functional cluster. Tononi et al. [230] measure the functionality of a cluster with the *cluster index*, obtained by dividing the statistical dependence within the subset by that between the subset and rest of the brain. A cluster index value nearly 1 indicates a homogeneous system, while a high cluster index indicates that a subset of brain regions forms a distinct functional cluster (i.e., an area that is mutually highly statistically dependent while at the same time independent from the rest of the system). This measure is applied to multidimensional data sets from computer simulations as well as from neurophysiology or neuroimaging. In a similar way, we can consider instead of the neuronal complex graph the graph formed by the surfaces of the scene and their geometric visibility relationship. Then,

Definition 49 *The cluster index of a region $s \subseteq \mathcal{S}$ is given by*

$$\imath_c(\mathcal{S}, s) = \frac{I_s^c(\mathcal{S}, s, s)}{I_s^c(\mathcal{S}, s, \mathcal{S} - s)} = \frac{I_s^c(\mathcal{S}, s, s)}{I_s^c(\mathcal{S}, s) - I_s^c(\mathcal{S}, s, s)}. \tag{3.45}$$

It can be interpreted as the degree of internal versus external dependence, between the surfaces of the region and the rest of the scene, respectively. This measure is applicable as much to the continuous case as to the discrete one. In Table 3.2, we have included this measure. Observe how the minimum value corresponds to region 1, due to the fact that the weak internal complexity is surpassed by the also small relation with the rest of the regions. The maximum is in region 3, where its high internal complexity widely surpasses its dependence of the rest of regions.

3.3.2 Spatial Complexity

In this section, we present a measure for the complexity of a region s defined as a subset of the interior points $\mathcal{I}_S$ ($\mathcal{I}_S^{2D}$ in 2D). The basic concept used will be point complexity (3.9).

3D-Scene

The idea is to capture all the average information transfer intensity inside a spatial region. Given that we can compute the field intensity at a point (§3.1.1), we can consider the complexity of a region as the average of its complexity fields. That is,

Definition 50 *The spatial complexity of a region $s \subseteq \mathcal{I}_{\mathcal{S}}$ is given by*

$$C_r(\mathcal{S}, s) = \frac{1}{V_s} \int_s I_p^c(\mathcal{S}, x) dx, \tag{3.46}$$

where V_s is the volume of s.

This value can be obtained by computing[9] the complexity of (ideally) all the points in s. In practise, we compute an approximation from the information which the corresponding complexity field map of the region provides us with. This is the equivalent of a uniform sampling of the function based on the 3D uniform grid associated with the complexity map (Fig. 3.2.a). With this set of sampling points s^d, the set of complexity segments $\mathcal{P}_{x \times \mathcal{S}}$ of each of them (of the Monte Carlo integration for point complexity), and the application of (3.12) we can compute

$$C_r(\mathcal{S}, s) \approx \frac{1}{|s^d|} \sum_{x \in s^d} I_p^c(\mathcal{S}, x)$$

$$\approx \frac{1}{|s^d|} \sum_{x \in s^d} \left(\frac{1}{|\mathcal{P}_{x \times \mathcal{S}}|} \sum_{y \in \mathcal{P}_{x \times \mathcal{S}}} I_p^c(\mathcal{S}, x, y) \right)$$

$$= \frac{1}{|s^d| N} \sum_{x \in s^d} \sum_{y \in \mathcal{P}_{x \times \mathcal{S}}} \log \frac{A_T \cos \theta_{n_y}^{\overline{yx}}}{4 \pi r_{xy}^2}, \tag{3.47}$$

where we consider the same number of complexity lines per point in the last expression: $\forall x \in s^d. |\mathcal{P}_{x \times \mathcal{S}}| = N$.

This measure associates a quantitative value of complexity to a spatial region of a scene. Presented together with the corresponding field map and with its range, they characterise the complexity in a univocal way (§3.1.3). As it will be seen later on (Table 3.3), in a more complex region it will be more costly to insert an object than in a less complex one confirming an earlier result: the more complex the region the more complex the animation in this region (§3.2.2).

2D-Scene

The spatial complexity in flatland is straightforward considering the usual changes (§3.1.2). The measure of volume is replaced by the area in Def. 50 and, for the approximate computation of complexity, we obtain

$$C_r(\mathcal{S}, s) \approx \frac{1}{|s^d| N} \sum_{x \in s^d} \sum_{y \in \mathcal{P}_{x \times \mathcal{S}}} \log \frac{L_T \cos \theta_{n_y}^{\overline{yx}}}{2 \pi r_{xy}}, \tag{3.48}$$

where $s \subseteq \mathcal{I}_{\mathcal{S}}^{2D}$ and taking into account the same considerations as in (3.47).

Example

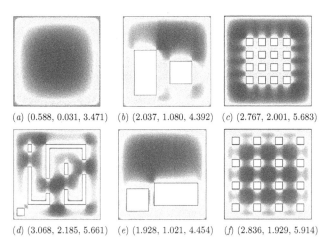

(a) (0.588, 0.031, 3.471)   (b) (2.037, 1.080, 4.392)   (c) (2.767, 2.001, 5.683)

(d) (3.068, 2.185, 5.661)   (e) (1.928, 1.021, 4.454)   (f) (2.836, 1.929, 5.914)

Figure 3.15: Spatial complexity and complexity field map for six regions ($s = \mathcal{S}$): (C_r, $\min\{I_p^c\}$, $\max\{I_p^c\}$). Different grids have been used with 10^3 lines cast from each $x \in s^d$.

In order to analyse the spatial complexity of a region, without loss of generality, we consider the defined region as the main scene ($s = \mathcal{S}$) and compute C_r in six different 2D-scenes (Fig. 3.15). For each scene we show the complexity field map which illustrates the field intensity of each region. In these figures we specify the range of complexity obtained in each scene. As we already knew about complexity at a point (§3.1.2), the highest complexity is found near the objects, the walls, in the corners, and especially in the narrow spaces.

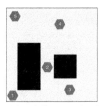

Figure 3.14: A hexagon is situated in Fig. 3.15.b in five different places. The scene complexity value for each position is shown in Table 3.3.

An experiment is designed to test the increase in scene complexity I_s^c when we insert an object in a region. In Fig. 3.14, a hexagon is placed in five different places corresponding to five different area complexities of a region (Fig. 3.15.b). In Table 3.3, we observe the perfect concordance between the two measures: the higher the area complexity of a region the higher the increase in scene complexity.

---

[9] We consider s such that integral (3.46) exists.

case	$I_s^c(\mathcal{S})$	Δ	%
0	2.517	0	0
1	2.860	0.343	13.62
2	2.795	0.278	11.06
3	2.733	0.216	8.58
4	2.663	0.146	5.79
5	2.763	0.245	9.75

Table 3.3: I_s^c values from Fig. 3.14 where an hexagon is situated in five different positions. The increase in scene complexity is shown in each case [1..5] with respect to the reference scene in Fig. 3.15.b.

Summary

We have presented a set of information-theoretic tools to deal with the *geometric visibility* of a scene (3D/2D) using the entropy and mutual information. From them, three types of complexity are defined.

Firstly, we define a new form factor formalism for an interior point of a scene from where, interpreting the scene as an information channel and carrying out a physical analogy with the concepts of *interaction* and *field*, the measures of discrete entropy fields, discrete mutual information field, and continuous mutual information field at an interior point are defined. The *discrete entropy field* represents the information content that all the patches create at a point while the *mutual information field* is interpreted as the information transfer which exists at the point due to the patches (discrete scene) or to all the surface points (continuous scene). The continuous mutual information field is considered to be *point complexity*. The discrete entropy and discrete mutual information fields are related through the *discrete cross entropy field*. From the calculation of the complexity at an interior point using random lines, the concept of *complexity segment* appears as the basic element for the calculation of the transference of geometric information. The *field maps*, based on the range of intensities of the field, are employed to represent the influence of these measures on the scene. These measures can be applied in areas such as rendering, computer vision, robot motion, object recognition, architecture, design, crowd rendering and simulation, and visualisation.

Secondly, in the field of animation, we present a study of several measures to evaluate the complexity of a sequence of 3D/2D animated discrete scenes. Two measures showed a good behaviour: the *animation complexity* and the *Euclidean distance*. The first consists in the accumulation of the differences of information exchange, due to the movement, which the patches of the two consecutive frames present. The other is based on the accumulation of the differences between the form factors of the patches which make up the frames. Both present similar results which are coherent with the measures of the scene and point complexities (e.g., the movement is more costly in regions of high complexity).

And thirdly, the complexity of a region has been studied from two perspectives. From the geometry of the surfaces which delimit a region, *surface-to-surface complexity* (*segment-to-segment complexity* in 2D), and from the interior space defined by a region, *spatial complexity* (3D/2D). For the surface-to-surface complexity, the measure is obtained from the continuous scene mutual information between the region and the scene. It expresses the information transfer between their respective surfaces. The measure is also defined between two regions and for the discrete cases (using the discrete scene mutual information). For the spatial complexity of a region, we define the average of the transference of existing information between all the points of the interior space which makes up the region itself. Its calculation therefore is based on the complexity at a point. We compute both complexity measures using complexity segments. The results allow us to obtain the contribution of the complexity of a region to the complexity of a scene (considering surface or volume). Direct applications of these measures are to look for an optimal load balancing in a parallel computation and to evaluate the information in fields such as neuroimaging and image registration.

Chapter 4

Entropy-Based Sampling for Ray-Tracing

Although ray-tracing is a straightforward and powerful image synthesis technique, it usually requires many rays per pixel to eliminate the aliasing or noise in the final image (§2.1.1). However, not all the pixels in the image require the same number of rays. The edge of an object, the contour of a shadow, and a high illumination gradient will require a much better treatment than a region with almost uniform illumination. To this effect, many pixel supersampling refinement criteria have been defined in the literature (§2.1.4).

The measures used in these criteria are based on intensities (image space) and also on geometry (object space). They are also useful for an adaptive subdivision of image space for progressive refinement [151]. Some of them have been applied in the image based rendering field for weighting pixel colour for reconstruction [168] and adaptive sampling strategies [45, 46], and creating a priority scheme for sampling in interactive rendering [216]. The final objective is always to find the best final-image quality with a reasonable cost (1.1). In order to do this, we have to sample each pixel of the image plane carefully. It is essential to have a quantitative measure in order to evaluate when there is sufficient information about the pixel.

The data of a sample set through the pixel can be used to calculate a pixel homogeneity measure from two different points of view: *radiance* and *visibility*. The information which we will manipulate will be exclusively colour (radiance) and geometry (visibility), essential parameters for deciding on the "quality" of a pixel. In this context, the Shannon entropy will be interpreted as a measure of the degree of homogeneity of a pixel in the sense that the more heterogeneous the pixel, the more difficult it is to obtain its actual value. From it, we associate homogeneity with quality, so that the need for pixel refinement is proportional to the lack of quality (i.e., heterogeneity of the samples). The idea behind the new scheme is to obtain sufficient information in the refinement algorithm in order to find out the sampling needs (§2.1.4).

Consequently, in this chapter we present a framework for entropy-based sampling applied to ray-tracing methods. First, definitions of new measures of *pixel quality* based on entropy are presented (§4.1). Next, we present the pixel quality as a measure of *pixel contrast* (§4.2). Then, this contrast is applied to classic *supersampling* ray-tracing (§4.3) and *adaptive sampling* (§4.4). This framework is easily adaptable to other stochastic processes which require measures of quality in order to reach decisions.

4.1 Pixel Quality

In this section we introduce a new pixel quality measure, the *pixel entropy*. This measure will be defined from the information provided by set of samples on the image plane. We use the following sets:

- Let P be the set of pixels of the image plane with $|P| = N_p > 0$.
- Let S_p be the set of samples of a pixel $p \in P$ with $|S_p| = N_s^p > 1$.

∘ Let S_P be the set of samples of the image plane where $S_\mathsf{P} = \cup_{\mathsf{p}\in\mathsf{P}}S_\mathsf{p}$ with $|S_\mathsf{P}| = N_\mathrm{s}^\mathsf{P} = \sum_{\mathsf{p}\in\mathsf{P}} N_\mathrm{s}^\mathsf{p}$.

The implementation of a sample consists in casting a ray r_v^Θ from a scene viewpoint v through the image plane and, in particular, through a pixel: $\Theta \in \Omega_{v\to\mathsf{p}}$. Let us consider that each sample $s \in S_\mathsf{P}$ that hits a scene surface gives us information about the colour, distance and orientation of the hit point with respect to the viewpoint.

The definition of entropy (2.72)

$$H(X) = -\sum_{i=1}^{n} p_i \log p_i, \tag{4.1}$$

measures the expectation of the surprise of the distribution p and it can be considered also to be a measure of its homogeneity (§2.5.1). From the sample set and from the entropy, two different quality measures are defined, *pixel colour entropy* and *pixel geometry entropy*, based on the colour and geometry respectively. These concepts are in agreement with the considerations made in §2.1.4 with respect to a clear signal (homogeneity) and to the classification of the refinement criteria in image-space (colour) and object-space (geometry).

4.1.1   Pixel Colour Entropy

Our first objective is to define the pixel colour entropy. We start with a global definition of entropy concerning all the samples passing through the image plane. We consider that the colour belongs to a colour system **c** structured in components called *colour channels*[1]. Without loss of generality, in the majority of cases our colour measures will refer to a single channel $c \in \mathbf{c}$, $c(s)$ being the colour channel data of a sample $s \in S$ (e.g., radiance, luminance, and RGB values).

Let us consider the probability of each image plane sample as its colour channel contribution relative to the whole of the image plane sample set. Thus,

Definition 51 *The image plane channel entropy of a channel c is given by*

$$H^c(\mathsf{P}) = -\sum_{i=1}^{N_\mathrm{s}^\mathsf{P}} r_i \log r_i \qquad r_i = \frac{c(s_i)}{\sum_{j=1}^{N_\mathrm{s}^\mathsf{P}} c(s_j)}, \tag{4.2}$$

where r_i represents the channel colour fraction of sample $s_i \in S_\mathsf{P}$.

This measure can be interpreted as the colour channel homogeneity of the samples passing through the image plane (§2.5.1). Analogously, at the pixel level, we consider the probability of each pixel sample as its colour channel contribution relative to the whole of the pixel sample set. Then,

Definition 52 *The pixel channel entropy of a channel c is given by*

$$H^c(\mathsf{p}) = -\sum_{i=1}^{N_\mathrm{s}^\mathsf{p}} p_i \log p_i \qquad p_i = \frac{c(s_i)}{\sum_{j=1}^{N_\mathrm{s}^\mathsf{p}} c(s_j)}, \tag{4.3}$$

where p_i represents the channel colour fraction of sample $s_i \in S_\mathsf{p}$.

From the properties of the entropy (§2.5.1), the image plane channel entropy ranges from 0 to $\log N_\mathrm{s}^\mathsf{P}$ and the pixel channel from 0 to $\log N_\mathrm{s}^\mathsf{p}$. The maximum values are obtained when the channel colour of all the samples is the same (i.e., we have an uniform probability distribution). Using the grouping property (2.74) it is easy to see that image plane and pixel channel entropies can be related in the following way:

$$H^c(\mathsf{P}) = \sum_{i=1}^{N_\mathsf{p}} q_i H^c(\mathsf{p}_i) - \sum_{i=1}^{N_\mathsf{p}} q_i \log q_i = \sum_{i=1}^{N_\mathsf{p}} q_i H^c(\mathsf{p}_i) + H_\mathrm{I}^c(\mathsf{P}), \tag{4.4}$$

---

[1] Or simply *channel* throughout this chapter. This name has been chosen because the colour information captured by an observer is due to the information which three nerves, or channels, transmit from the eye to the brain. These channels carry information which is derived from the three retinal photoreceptors. It is for this reason that the majority of colour systems are based on tristimulus values (§2.2.4).

where $q_i = \sum_{j=1}^{N_s^{p_i}} r_j$ is the *importance* (sum of probabilities) of pixel p_i, $H^c(\mathsf{p}_i)$ is the channel entropy of pixel p_i, and $H_I^c(\mathsf{P}) = -\sum_{i=1}^{N_p} q_i \log q_i$ is the *importance entropy* of the image plane calculated from the importance of each pixel. Thus, the global entropy of the image plane is the sum of all the pixel entropies, weighted by the importance of each pixel, and the importance entropy obtained from the importance of each pixel.

The image plane and pixel entropies can be interpreted as the colour *homogeneity* or *uniformity* measured by its sample set and thus can be considered measures of the *quality* of the colour channel (i.e., lack of heterogeneity and noise). We can also observe that the entropy increases with the number of samples. In order to give a pixel quality measure between 0 and 1, the pixel channel entropy can be normalised with $\log N_s^p$. Thus,

Definition 53 *The pixel channel quality of a channel c is given by*

$$Q^c(\mathsf{p}) = \frac{H^c(\mathsf{p})}{\log N_s^p}. \tag{4.5}$$

If we want to consider the global quality of a pixel, we need only mix its set of channels. Then,

Definition 54 *The pixel colour quality of a colour system* **c** *is given by the weighting of its pixel channel qualities:*

$$\mathbf{Q^c}(\mathsf{p}) = \frac{\sum_{c \in \mathbf{c}} w^c Q^c(\mathsf{p})}{\sum_{c \in \mathbf{c}} w^c}, \tag{4.6}$$

where w^c is the weight of channel c.

The weighted values depend on each colour system. Without a priori information, the same weight per channel can be considered, otherwise a weight based on human perception[2]. This measure will enable us to define a new colour contrast measure for pixel sampling (§4.2.1). Note that the larger the number of samples the more accurate the quality measure.

In Fig. 4.1.b, we present a *colour quality map* to show the colour quality of all the pixels from Fig. 4.1.a using an sRGB colour system with the same weight by channel. The colour scale used corresponds to Fig. 3.2.c where the minimum quality corresponds to the blue and the maximum to the red[3]. A low quality in shadow areas and edges can be observed.

4.1.2 Pixel Geometry Entropy

Similar concepts introduced in the above section can be defined in this one with respect to a geometric measure. If $x = \Lambda(v, \Theta)$ is the hitpoint of a sample ray $s = r_v^\Theta$, the geometric information of each sample is given by $\theta_{n_x}^{-\Theta}$ (i.e., the angle of the normal at the hit point) and by the distance r_{vx} between this point and the origin of the ray (i.e., ray length). We take

$$g(s) = \frac{\cos \theta_{n_x}^{-\Theta}}{r_{vx}^2} \tag{4.7}$$

as a geometry factor of a sample. This value provides a quality measure of visibility of a scene point from the observer's point of view. Note that this factor is directly proportional to the point-to-differential form factor at an interior point of a scene (3.1). Given that $x = \Lambda(v, \Theta) \Rightarrow V(v, x) = 1$, we have $g(s) = 4\pi F_{v \to dA_x}$.

Let us define the probability of each image plane sample as its relative geometric contribution to the whole image plane sample set.

---

[2] For an sRGB system, $w^R = 0.2126$, $w^G = 0.7152$, and $w^B = 0.0722$ (2.53).

[3] In order to observe more details in the colour quality maps, the *outliers* are reduced to the borders of the interval $[-k\sigma, k\sigma]$ where σ is the standard deviation of the results and k is a parameter that modulates the width of the interval.

(a) Reference   (b) $\mathbf{Q^c}$ (c) Q^g

Figure 4.1: Colour and geometry quality maps. (a) Reference image obtained with $N_s^p = 8$. (b) Pixel colour quality $\mathbf{Q^{sRGB}}$ with the same weight per channel. (c) Pixel geometry quality Q^g.

Definition 55 *The image plane geometry entropy is given by*

$$H^g(\mathsf{P}) = -\sum_{i=1}^{N_s^p} r_i \log r_i \qquad r_i = \frac{g(s_i)}{\sum_{j=1}^{N_s^p} g(s_j)}, \tag{4.8}$$

where r_i represents the geometry fraction of sample $s_i \in S_{\mathsf{P}}$.

Considering the probability of each pixel sample as its relative geometrical contribution to the whole of the pixel sample set we have

Definition 56 *The pixel geometry entropy is given by*

$$H^g(\mathsf{p}) = -\sum_{i=1}^{N_s^p} p_i \log p_i \qquad p_i = \frac{g(s_i)}{\sum_{j=1}^{N_s^p} g(s_j)}, \tag{4.9}$$

where p_i represents the geometry fraction of sample $s_i \in S_{\mathsf{p}}$.

Analogously to the pixel colour entropy (4.4), an identical relation can be established between the geometric entropies of the image plane and the pixel. We can also normalise the pixel geometry entropy and therefore,

Definition 57 *The pixel geometry quality is given by*

$$Q^g(\mathsf{p}) = \frac{H^g(\mathsf{p})}{\log N_s^p}. \tag{4.10}$$

In Fig. 4.1.c we show the *geometry quality map* from Fig. 4.1.a based on a grey scale. The lowest entropy corresponds to the darkest part, the highest entropy to the lightest[4]. Observe that the edges have a very low entropy and are very clearly emphasised.

4.2   Pixel Contrast

In this section we present new pixel contrast measures based on pixel entropy (§4.1). As the entropy represents the homogeneity of the information brought back by the samples (i.e., rays crossing a pixel), we can define a simple measure which expresses the diversity or contrast of a pixel.

---

[4] The outliers have the same treatment as in the colour quality maps.

4.2.1 Pixel Colour Contrast

In the colour theory, the *colour contrast* is the phenomenon that alters the observation of the colours depending on their surroundings[5] [74]. We use the same words to express the degree of heterogeneity of the colour in the region defined by a pixel given that this value depends directly on the colours that are around it. As we have seen, $H^c(\mathbf{p})$ represents the entropy or the degree of colour homogeneity of pixel $\mathbf{p}$. From this measure,

Definition 58 *The pixel channel contrast of a channel c is given by*

$$C^c(\mathbf{p}) = 1 - Q^c(\mathbf{p}) = 1 - \frac{H^c(\mathbf{p})}{\log N_s^{\mathbf{p}}}. \tag{4.11}$$

It represents the colour channel heterogeneity or contrast of a pixel with a range of $[0, 1]$. We can also introduce the pixel binary contrast from minimum and maximum colour channel probabilities captured by this pixel. This measure is obtained from the binary entropy of these values (2.73). Thus,

Definition 59 *The pixel channel binary contrast of a channel c is given by*

$$C_b^c(\mathbf{p}) = 1 - H_b^c(\mathbf{p}) \qquad H_b^c(\mathbf{p}) = H(\{\frac{p_{\min}}{p_{\min} + p_{\max}}, \frac{p_{\max}}{p_{\min} + p_{\max}}\}), \tag{4.12}$$

where $H_b^c(\mathbf{p})$ is the binary entropy of the minimum and maximum channel colour probabilities, $p_{\min}$ and $p_{\max}$, respectively.

Both measures, $H_b^c(\mathbf{p})$ and $C_b^c(\mathbf{p})$, range also between 0 and 1 due to the fact that, in this case, only two values are taken into account. As we will see in our experiments, this binary measure yields more radical contrast than $C^c(\mathbf{p})$.

Similarly to previous works [135, 74, 216] (§2.1.4), we can obtain the colour contrast of a pixel by averaging all the colour channel contrasts weighted by their respective importances (colour channel average). This avoids oversampling on the areas with small colour values. Then, considering all the colour channels,

Definition 60 *The pixel colour contrast of a colour system **c** is given by the weighting of its pixel channel contrasts:*

$$\mathbf{C}^{\mathbf{c}}(\mathbf{p}) = \frac{\sum_{c \in \mathbf{c}} w^c \overline{c} \, C^c(\mathbf{p})}{\sum_{c \in \mathbf{c}} w^c \overline{c}} \qquad \overline{c} = \frac{1}{N_s^{\mathbf{p}}} \sum_{i=1}^{N_s^{\mathbf{p}}} c(s_i), \tag{4.13}$$

where the channel contrasts are weighted by perceptual coefficients w^c, and $\overline{c}$ is the colour average in channel c of all $s \in S_{\mathbf{p}}$.

Definition 61 *The pixel colour binary contrast of a colour system **c** is given by*

$$\mathbf{C}_b^{\mathbf{c}}(\mathbf{p}) = \frac{\sum_{c \in \mathbf{c}} w^c \overline{c} \, C_b^c(\mathbf{p})}{\sum_{c \in \mathbf{c}} w^c \overline{c}}. \tag{4.14}$$

In an sRGB system, the colour contrast measures ($\mathbf{C}^{\mathbf{sRGB}}$ and $\mathbf{C}_b^{\mathbf{sRGB}}$) have three channels with coefficients w^R, w^G, and w^B. These values depend on the specific use of contrast, but in general they can take the values proposed in the pixel colour quality (4.6), or also, for a perceptual balance of the channels, they can take those of the thresholds proposed in [135, 216]: 0.4, 0.3, and 0.6, respectively (§2.1.4).

This last option is chosen in the next examples where a *colour contrast map* is used as a visual representation of the contrast measures in the same way that the quality map is used for the quality measures. Thus, in Fig. 4.2 we show different colour contrast maps to compare the heuristic (2.7), p_c (Fig. 4.2.*b*), with measures $\mathbf{C}^{\mathbf{c}}$ (Fig. 4.2.*c*), and $\mathbf{C}_b^{\mathbf{c}}$ (Fig. 4.2.*d*). Another comparison is shown in Fig. 4.3 with a more complex scene. We can observe how these measures present a very good behaviour in critical areas (represented by warm colours) such as object edges and shadow contours. With respect to Fig. 4.2.*b* and Fig. 4.3.*b*, our measures are more discriminating, especially the binary contrast.

---

[5] The origin of the colour contrast is the way in which the information is transmitted from the retinal photoreceptors to the brain. The name of this study is the *colour opponency* theory.

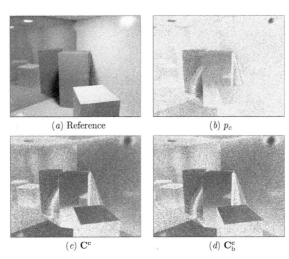

Figure 4.2: Colour contrast maps. (a) Reference image obtained with $N_s^p = 8$. (b) Pixel colour contrast p_c (2.7). (c) Pixel colour contrast $\mathbf{C}^c$. (d) Pixel colour binary contrast $\mathbf{C}_b^c$.

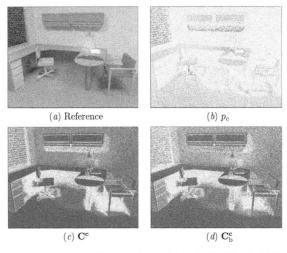

Figure 4.3: Colour contrast maps. (a) Reference image obtained with $N_s^p = 8$. (b) Pixel colour contrast p_c (2.7). (c) Pixel colour contrast $\mathbf{C}^c$. (d) Pixel colour binary contrast $\mathbf{C}_b^c$.
Credit: Modelled by Gregory J. Ward, Albany (CA), USA.

4.2.2 Pixel Geometry Contrast

As we have seen in (4.9), H^g represents the entropy or the degree of geometric homogeneity of a pixel. From this measure,

Definition 62 *The pixel geometry contrast is given by*

$$C^g(\mathbf{p}) = 1 - Q^g(\mathbf{p}) = 1 - \frac{H^g(\mathbf{p})}{\log N_s^g}. \qquad (4.15)$$

Similarly to the above section, we introduce the pixel binary contrast from minimum and maximum geometry factor probabilities of this pixel. Thus,

Definition 63 *The pixel geometry binary contrast is given by*

$$C_b^g(\mathbf{p}) = 1 - H_b^g(\mathbf{p}) \qquad H_b^g(\mathbf{p}) = H(\{\frac{p_{\min}}{p_{\min} + p_{\max}}, \frac{p_{\max}}{p_{\min} + p_{\max}}\}), \qquad (4.16)$$

where $H_b^g(\mathbf{p})$ is the binary entropy of the minimum and maximum geometry factor probabilities, $p_{\min}$ and $p_{\max}$ respectively.

A third case can also be considered:

Definition 64 *The pixel logarithmic-difference contrast is given by*

$$C_{\log}^g(\mathbf{p}) = \log p_{\max} - \log p_{\min} = \log \frac{p_{\max}}{p_{\min}}. \qquad (4.17)$$

This measure, introduced in Rigau et al. [173], is based on the gradient between the minimum and maximum complexity segments (3.12). As we will see, $C_{\log}^g(\mathbf{p})$ also shows a good behaviour.

For the previous reference scene in Fig. 4.2.a, we now show the geometry contrast measures using the corresponding maps in Figs. 4.4.a–c. These maps are compared with the map in Fig. 4.4.d, created using the depth difference heuristic p_d (2.14). The same comparison is carried out for the reference scene Fig. 4.3.a in Fig. 4.5. It can be seen that our measures capture the majority of edges because we take into account two components: distance and orientation. These geometry contrast maps have been generated by using the representation scale of the colour contrast maps in order to be able to compare, visually with each other, how the two types of contrast, colour (Fig. 4.3) and geometry (Fig. 4.5), work. The specialisation of each of the contrasts is evident: colour maps show the heterogeneity of regions while geometric maps identify edges.

4.2.3 Pixel Colour-Geometry Contrast

Finally, a combination of colour and geometry contrasts is considered. This combination enables us to graduate, with a coefficient δ between 0 and 1, the influence of both measures. Then,

Definition 65 *The pixel contrast of colour system $\mathbf{c}$ is given by*

$$C^\mathbf{c}(\mathbf{p}) = \delta\mathbf{C}^\mathbf{c}(\mathbf{p}) + (1-\delta)C^g(\mathbf{p}). \qquad (4.18)$$

This combination can be made with any type of pixel colour contrast and geometry contrast. In general, good behaviour has been shown with binary contrasts (colour and geometry), and $\delta \in [0.8, 0.95]$.

We show for another scene, Fig. 4.6, two different lineal combinations. On the one hand, in Fig. 4.6.a we use the priority-value combination p_v (2.15), made up also of colour, p_c (2.7), and geometry, p_d (2.14). And, on the other hand, in Fig. 4.6.b we combine our measures $\mathbf{C}_b^c$ (4.14) and C^g (4.15). The same values $N_s^p = 4$ and $\delta = 0.9$ are used in both cases. A significant difference is observed: our combination tends to obtain more radical contrasts (highly or less complex cases) as opposed to the other option which takes values in a far more homogeneous interval. The explanation lies in the behaviour of the binary colour contrast which works exclusively with the extreme data.

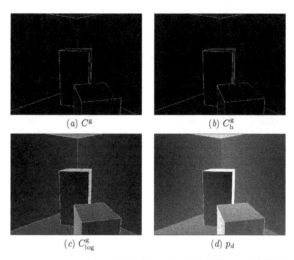

Figure 4.4: Geometry contrast maps from Fig. 4.2.a obtained with $N_s^p = 8$. (a) Pixel geometry contrast C^g. (b) Pixel geometry binary contrast C_b^g. (c) Pixel logarithmic-difference contrast $C_{\log}^g$. (d) Pixel depth difference p_d.

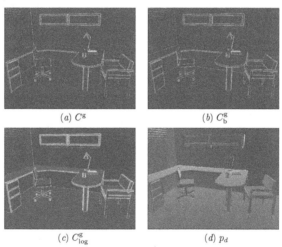

Figure 4.5: Geometry contrast maps from Fig. 4.3.a obtained with $N_s^p = 8$. For a visual comparison between the geometry and colour contrast in Fig. 4.3, the thermic scale is used. (a) Pixel geometry contrast C^g. (b) Pixel geometry binary contrast C_b^g. (c) Pixel logarithmic-difference contrast $C_{\log}^g$. (d) Pixel depth difference p_d.
Credit: Modelled by Gregory J. Ward, Albany (CA), USA.

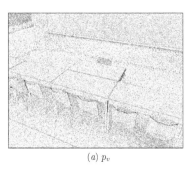 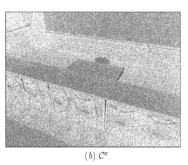

$(a)\ p_v$ $\qquad\qquad\qquad\qquad\qquad\qquad\qquad (b)\ \mathcal{C}^{c}$

Figure 4.6: Pixel contrast obtained with $N_s^p = 4$ and a lineal combination with $\delta = 0.9$. (a) Pixel priority-value p_v (2.15). (b) Pixel contrast $\mathcal{C}^c$ using $\mathbf{C}_b^c$ and C^g.
Credit: Model included in RenderPark [33], Computer Graphics Research Group, Department of Computer Science, Katholieke Universiteit Leuven, Leuven, Belgium.

4.3 Entropy-Based Supersampling

In this section, we apply the newly defined contrast measures to supersampling (§2.1.2) in a stochastic ray-tracing implementation (§2.3.2).

4.3.1 Method

Ray-tracing is a point-sampling-based technique for image synthesis (§2.3). Rays are traced from the camera through a pixel to sample radiance at the hitpoint in the scene, where radiance is usually computed by a random walk method (§2.3.2 and §2.3.3). Since a finite set of samples is used, some of the information in the scene is lost. Thus, aliasing errors are unavoidable [49]. These errors can be reduced by using extra sampling, called *supersampling*, in regions where the sample values vary most (§2.1.2).

In order to obtain reliable data to achieve photo-realistic effects (e.g., diffuse and specular interreflections, shadow and penumbra, depth of field, motion blur, and translucency), the regions of the scene with the most complex illumination would need a more intensive treatment than a region with almost uniform illumination. This way of supersampling is called *adaptive sampling* [49, 151] (§2.1.3). A pixel is first sampled at a relatively low density. From this set of samples, a *refinement criterion* is used to decide whether more sampling is required or not. Finally, all the samples are used to obtain the final pixel colour values. We can consider two kinds of adaptive sampling: first, when the refinement criterion plays the role of an oracle which decides the place and the quantity of supersampling necessary in one evaluation of the initial sampling only and, second, when the refinement criterion constantly evaluates the information received because of a supersampling and acts in consequence until it becomes satisfied. In this work we use the term *supersampling* exclusively for the first case and *adaptive sampling* for the second (§4.4).

We implement a simple supersampling technique: the sample set S will be proportionally distributed over the image plane with respect to the contrast $\mathcal{C}^c$ estimated in each $\mathsf{p} \in \mathsf{P}$. This is equivalent to the use of the *pixel contrast* as an oracle. For definition of the measure itself (§4.2), the cost in samples is controlled by the diversity of colour and geometry in the pixel (i.e., low quality). Given that a high contrast is synonymous of low pixel quality and low contrast of high quality pixel, the measure adapts the densities of sampling to the necessity of improvement in pixel quality. Remembering the importance of each one of the samples (1.1) and without more prior information, this system will improve, on average, the pixel quality in particular and the image in general. The generic procedure is made up of three sequentially quite different phases:

Oracle A pixel contrast is selected as oracle and a first estimate of actual contrast per pixel is obtained using an initial stratified sampling against the image plane (§2.1.3). Usual values are 2, 4, and 8 (n_s^p). If we consider that the total number of samples N_s^P destined for the image is prefixed, the final value of the average of samples per pixel is $N_s^p = \frac{N_s^P}{N_p}$ and then, $1 < n_s^p \ll \lfloor N_s^p \rfloor$ where the left side inequality is due to the definition of the measure of contrast and the right side inequality to being able to carry out supersampling. The result of this phase is the answer from the oracle: the contrast map.

Sampling The unused samples in the calculation of the contrast, $N_p(N_s^p - n_s^p)$, are proportionally distributed to the values of contrast obtained per pixel. In each one of them, the sampling is also carried out with stratification. The distribution of the new set of samples gathers information from the scene in the regions of more diversity, with a proportional effort on this. The result of this phase is a supersampling directed exclusively by the contrast map generated in the previous phase.

Reconstruction The colour information gathered in the previous phase is put together with that obtained in the initial phase. Its evaluation allows us to achieve a more precise vision of the contents of the pixel and as a result an improvement in its quality. It only remains for the signal to be recuperated and to carry out the resampling process for each one of the pixels $\mathsf{p} \in \mathsf{P}$ with any of the reconstruction methods applicable to the sampling system used (§2.1.6). The result of this phase is the solution for the image plane thanks to the assignment of the final colour to all of its pixels.

This proceeding is adaptable in any of its phases (e.g., stochastic ray-tracing method, pattern of initial sampling, supersampling method, and filters).

4.3.2   Results

Here, we show an example of our contrast measure $\mathcal{C}^c$ (4.18) used as a supersampling oracle in path-tracing (§2.3.2).

In Fig. 4.7.$a.i$ we show a supersampling image obtained with $N_s^p = 32$ in the following way. First, a uniform stratified sampling with $n_s^p = 8$ has been made in order to obtain the contrast map in Fig. 4.7.$a.ii$. Secondly, this map has been used in the supersampling process with an average of 24 rays per pixel. And thirdly, in order to analyse the behaviour of the contrast, the signal reconstruction in the last phase is carried out by a piece-wise continuous reconstruction (2.16) using a box filter (2.1). The final pixel value corresponds to its signal average. The contrast measure used is a colour and geometry combination with $\delta = 0.5$ based on binary contrasts $\mathbf{C}_b^c$ (4.14) and C_b^g (4.16). This means that the more critical the area, the more supersampled it is (warm colours), and the less critical, the more undersampled it is (cool colours, with a minimum of 8 rays per pixel). Two detailed regions are compared from the supersampling image (Figs. 4.7.b–$c.i$) and a similar image obtained by uniform stratified sampling with $N_s^p = 32$ (Figs. 4.7.b–$c.ii$). We can observe a decrease in noise in the supersampled regions, and a better representation of shadow contour and edges.

4.4   Entropy-Based Adaptive Sampling

In (4.4) we have seen that image plane and pixel channel entropies are related thanks to the grouping property (2.74). It is important to note that this kind of decomposition can be applied recursively if the pixels are recursively subdivided. We will show in this section that this recursive decomposition provides us with a natural method of dealing with an adaptive sampling technique (§2.1.3). Our scheme, valid for any pixel sampling and ray-tracing method, is applied to stochastic ray-tracing (§2.3.2) and compared with other options.

4.4.1   Adaptive Sampling

In previous sections (i.e., §2.1.1, §2.1.2, §2.1.3, and §4.3.1) it has been explained that, in order to obtain a realistic image, the aliasing has to be reduced by adapting the density sampling to the complexity of the region aiming at a good balance between cost and quality (1.1).

(a.i) Supersampling image

(a.ii) Oracle $\mathcal{C}^{\mathrm{c}}$ for (a.i)

(b.ii) Close-up from (a.i)

(b.ii) Close-up from uniform sampling

(c.i) Close-up from (a.i)

(c.ii) Close-up from uniform sampling

Figure 4.7: Entropy-based supersampling versus uniform sampling. (a.i) Supersampling with an $N_{\mathrm{s}}^{\mathrm{p}} = 32$. (a.ii) Binary contrast map $\mathcal{C}^{\mathrm{c}}$ used as oracle to obtain (a.i). It has been calculated with $n_{\mathrm{s}}^{\mathrm{p}} = 8$, $\mathbf{C}_{\mathrm{b}}^{\mathrm{c}}$, $C_{\mathrm{b}}^{\mathrm{g}}$, and $\delta = 0.5$. Close-up details from (a.i) are shown in (b-c.i). They are compared with the same regions, (b-c.ii) respectively, taken from a uniform stratified sampling image with $N_{\mathrm{s}}^{\mathrm{p}} = 32$.

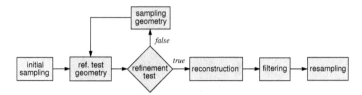

Figure 4.8: Adaptive sampling process with three phases: initial sampling (blue), refinement tree (gold), and image reconstruction (green).

We consider three phases in order to describe a generic process of adaptive sampling [74] (Fig. 4.8, §1.1.1, and §2.1.3), for which the scheme used in the supersampling procedure of §4.3.1 is a particular case:

Initial sampling An *initial sampling* pattern at a predetermined density is established. Normally, in order to choose its density we assume that the signal has a Nyquist rate (§2.1.1) similar to the frequency of the reconstruction samples (e.g., one sample per pixel[6]). It is also usual for this density to be constant across the space, even though in the next phase, it should be increased locally if necessary.

Refinement tree The image space is divided up into regions (e.g., pixels). For each one of them, a *refinement test geometry* selects a subset of samples for evaluation. A *refinement test* is a criterion used for the evaluation of one or more characteristics which estimate the good quality of the current density. If the result is negative, a new set of samples are generated at the points indicated by the new *sampling geometry* and the process goes back to the refinement test geometry until the refinement criterion decides that the density of sampling in the region is accurate enough. The result of this process is a *refinement tree* of the image space where every node is a region with a density of sampling adapted to its own signal. In order to control extreme cases, it is usual to dispose of other criteria to finish the recursion (e.g., minimum area of the regions and/or maximum depth of tree).

Reconstruction The information of the signal collected at every region is unified by a *reconstruction* process and, if necessary, sent to a *filtering* process. Finally, a *resampling* process (e.g., centre of pixel) determines the final values for each of the pixels on the image plane (§2.1.6).

Note that however much we increase the density of sampling locally, given that the signal is not usually band-limited, the sampling theory tell us that we can never capture it correctly (§2.1.1). Thus, fine details of edges, shadings, textures, and others will hardly have enough quality in the final image. The approximation done by the method consists in looking for the minimum set of samples which estimates the signal locally accurately enough (1.1). A critical subproblem appears in each of its phases [151] and many approaches are found to deal with them:

- *Efficient sample generation.* Different nonuniform pixel sampling methods have been introduced (§2.1.3).

- *Control of the sampling rate.* Diverse refinement criteria for adaptive sampling, based on image and/or object space, can be found to control the sampling rate (§2.1.4).

- *Filtering.* A great variety of filter shapes are used in image reconstruction (§2.1.6).

We focus our attention on obtaining an adaptive algorithm centred mainly on the refinement tree phase bringing a new perspective to the subproblem of controlling the sampling rate (new refinement criterion).

---

[6] The minimum number of samples per pixel fulfils $N_s^p > 1$ (§4.1).

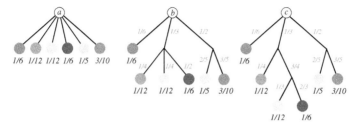

Figure 4.9: Grouping property of entropy. The entropy of probability distributions of ⓐ is $H(\{\frac{1}{6}, \frac{1}{12}, \frac{1}{12}, \frac{1}{6}, \frac{1}{5}, \frac{3}{10}\})$, of ⓑ is $H(\{\frac{1}{6}, \frac{1}{3}, \frac{1}{2}\}) + \frac{1}{3}H(\{\frac{1}{4}, \frac{1}{4}, \frac{1}{2}\}) + \frac{1}{2}H(\{\frac{2}{5}, \frac{3}{5}\})$, and of ⓒ is $H(\{\frac{1}{6}, \frac{1}{3}, \frac{1}{2}\}) + \frac{1}{3}(H(\{\frac{1}{4}, \frac{3}{4}\}) + \frac{3}{4}H(\{\frac{1}{3}, \frac{2}{3}\})) + \frac{1}{2}H(\{\frac{2}{5}, \frac{3}{5}\})$. Accordingly to (4.19), they all have the same value: $H(a) = H(b) = H(c) = 2.445$.

4.4.2 Recursive Entropy Tree

The natural way to represent information is by entropy (§2.5.1), which in our context is interpreted as a measure of the degree of homogeneity of a region. Thus, using an entropy criterion means to evaluate the homogeneity (§4.1) or heterogeneity (§4.2) on a pixel. The fundamental idea behind our scheme is to capture the information in the refinement tree which results from the recursive decomposition of the entropy.

Generalising the grouping property (2.74), the entropy can be recursively decomposed in the following way: Let X be a discrete random variable over the set $\mathcal{X} = \{x_1, \ldots, x_n\}$ with probability distribution $p = \{p_1, \ldots, p_n\}$ (§B). Let us consider a partition of the set $\mathcal{X}$ in m-disjoint sets $\mathcal{Y} = \{\mathcal{Y}_1, \ldots, \mathcal{Y}_m\}$ where $|\mathcal{Y}_j| = n_j$. Let us associate the discrete random variable Y to $\mathcal{Y}$ with probability distribution $q = \{q_1, \ldots, q_m\}$ where $q_j = \sum_{k=1}^{n_j} p_{j_k}$ ($j_k \in \{1, \ldots, n\}$), and a new discrete random variable Y_j to each set $\mathcal{Y}_j$ with probability distribution $r_j = \{r_{j_1}, \ldots, r_{j_{n_j}}\}$ where $r_{j_k} = \frac{p_{j_k}}{q_j}$. Then

$$H(X) = \sum_{j=1}^{m} q_j H(Y_j) - \sum_{j=1}^{m} q_j \log q_j. \tag{4.19}$$

This formula can be written as $H(X) = H_{\text{in}}(\mathcal{Y}) + H_{\text{out}}(\mathcal{Y})$ where $H_{\text{in}}(\mathcal{Y}) = \sum_{j=1}^{m} q_j H(Y_j)$ and $H_{\text{out}}(\mathcal{Y}) = H(Y) = -\sum_{j=1}^{m} q_j \log q_j$ represent, respectively, the hidden information (pending to be discovered) and the information already acquired in the descent of the tree created from an $\mathcal{Y}$ partition (Fig. 4.9).

In our case, (4.19) can also be interpreted taking into account only one colour channel (4.3) in the following way:

- $H(X)$ represents the entropy of the image plane.

- $H(Y_j)$ represents the entropy of each root pixel.

- Probability q_j is the proportion between the channel colour of pixel j and the sum of the channel colour of all pixels. It can be considered the "importance" of pixel j.

The decomposition of entropy can be recursively extended to the subpixels. This interpretation can also be applied to geometry entropy (4.9).

In our approach, probabilities are obtained by stochastic sampling. From the definition of entropy, we can see that when the number of samples tends to infinity, entropy also goes to infinity (§2.5.1). In fact, we can consider that the original continuous scene contains infinite information. The following sampling algorithm will extract more information from the regions with more sample variation.

4.4.3   Algorithm

We present a new adaptive scheme for adaptive sampling, complementary to the entropy-based super-sampling method (§4.3.1), with the important feature that it is based on the recursive expression of the Shannon entropy (i.e., the entropy tree). For the sake of simplicity, in the following analysis we only consider the colour information of one channel, although in the final algorithm we will take the combination of colour and geometry contrasts into account (4.18).

A general description of our algorithm is as follows: On the image plane we sample each pixel to capture the colour of hitpoints and thus evaluate the information content (entropy) from the colour probability distribution. If the information of a pixel is high enough (i.e., the rays provide us with sufficient colour homogeneity on that pixel), refinement is not made, and the colour reconstruction of this pixel is done. When the information is not high enough, this pixel is subdivided into regions and we proceed in the same way for each region (subpixel). *"The approach will be to make sure that all the samples in a given region are similar in some specified way, so we can feel that we have captured what is happening in a region of the signal"* [74].

This recursive process defines a tree with two well-separated phases for a pixel:

○ *Pixel refinement.* Until enough information is extracted (tree descent).

○ *Pixel colour.* Computation of the final colour (tree ascent).

The descent in the refinement tree can be interpreted as a progressive gain in information. The information acquired at each level is added together so that, at the end of the refinement process, the total information from the tree is the sum of the information obtained over all the branches (4.19). The measure used to capture the information will be the pixel contrast (§4.2).

Before introducing the algorithm we will give the definitions of the data used in it. Concerning the tree data structure, n represents the tree level where

○ $n = 0$ is the image level (root).

○ $n = 1$ is the pixel level (composed of $N_{\mathbf{p}}$ pixels of the image).

○ $n > 1$ is the subpixel level.

We consider an n-node at any node of the tree with a level of $n > 0$ (i.e., no root). The set of data is described in Table 4.1. To compute the final colour of a pixel, we follow a path through the tree (Fig. 4.10). In the analysis below, we focus our attention on the tree-path k of length m going from pixel k_0 to subpixel k_{m-1}. In this path, p_n represents the probability of the tree-branch at level n and q_n the *importance* of the n-node. In our algorithm, this quantity appears naturally due to recursive decomposition of the entropy (see (4.19), Fig. 4.9, and Fig. 4.10). The value of importance is given by the probability of the n-node:

$$q_n = \begin{cases} 1, & \text{if } n = 0, \\ p_0 \cdots p_{n-1} = \dfrac{\bar{c}_{0,k_0}}{\sum_{i \in R_0} \bar{c}_{0,i}} \prod_{\ell=1}^{n-1} p_\ell, & \text{if } n > 0. \end{cases} \tag{4.20}$$

For our purposes, q_n does not need to be normalised, thus we omit the normalisation constant $\sum_{i \in R_0} \bar{c}_{0,i}$ and we take $q_n = \bar{c}_{0,k_0} \prod_{\ell=1}^{n-1} p_\ell$.

Proposition 3 *The computation of q_n can be simplified to*[7]

$$q_n \approx \frac{\bar{c}_n}{N_{\mathrm{r}}^{n-1}}. \tag{4.21}$$

Observe first that for a given path and $n > 0$, the colour $\bar{c}_n$ of an n-node is more accurate than the colour average of its respective region, k_{n-1}, in the preceding level. Thus, the accuracy of p_n, and at the same time of q_n, can be increased by substituting $\bar{c}_{n-1,k_{n-1}}$ for $\bar{c}_n$. Let us prove now (4.21) by induction.

---

[7] In an abuse of notation, all the superindexes corresponding to arithmetic expressions must be interpreted as a power.

id	description	asserts
N_r	Number of regions in which an n-node can potentially be subdivided.	$N_r > 1 \wedge A_{1 \leq i \leq N_r} = \frac{A_{n-node}}{N_r}$
N_s^r	Number of samples of an n-node.	$N_s^r \geq N_r \wedge N_s^r \in N_r \mathbb{N}^+$
R_n	Set of regions of an n-node.	$|R_0| = N_p \wedge \forall_{n>0}. |R_n| = N_r$
S_n	Set of samples of an n-node.	$|S_0| = N_s^r N_p \wedge \forall_{n>0}. |S_n| = N_s^r$
$S_{n,i}$	Set of samples of an n-node region $i \in R_n$.	$S_n = \bigcup_{i \in R_n} S_{n,i}$ $|S_{n,i}| = \frac{|S_n|}{|R_n|} = \frac{N_s^r}{N_r}$
k	Path-tree $k = (k_0, \ldots, k_{m-1})$ where k_n is the region chosen at level n.	$m > 0 \wedge \forall_{n<m}. k_n \in R_n$
$\bar{c}_n$	Average colour channel data in an n-node.	$\bar{c}_n = \frac{1}{|S_n|} \sum_{s \in S_n} c(s)$
$\bar{c}_{n,i}$	Average colour in an n-node region $i \in R_n$.	$\bar{c}_{n,i} = \frac{1}{|S_{n,i}|} \sum_{s \in S_{n,i}} c(s)$ $\bar{c}_n = \frac{1}{|R_n|} \sum_{i \in R_n} \bar{c}_{n,i}$
p_n	Probability of region k_n of an n-node in a path k.	$p_n = \frac{\sum_{s \in S_{n,k_n}} c(s)}{\sum_{s \in S_n} c(s)} = \frac{\bar{c}_{n,k_n}}{\sum_{i \in R_n} \bar{c}_{n,i}}$
q_n	Probability of an n-node in a path k.	$q_n = \prod_{\ell=0}^{n-1} p_\ell$

Table 4.1: Description of the data set of the refinement phase of entropy-based adaptive sampling in an image plane of N_p pixels. An n-node is a node of level $n > 0$ in the refinement-tree.

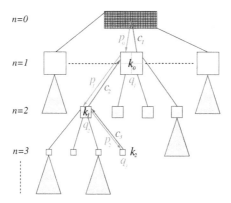

Figure 4.10: A refinement-tree-path $k = (k_0, k_1, k_2)$ of length $m = 3$ of entropy-based sampling. The number of regions of an n-node is $N_r = 4$. We show the computation of the k_0-pixel colour: $c_{0,k_0} = c_1$ from the refinement (red) and reconstruction (blue) phases. The probabilities p_n and importances q_n are computed in the refinement phase to evaluate the entropy contrast (4.18).

Proof: For $n = 1$,

$$q_n = \overline{c}_{0,k_0} \approx \overline{c}_1 = \frac{\overline{c}_1}{N_r^0} = \frac{\overline{c}_n}{N_r^{n-1}}.$$

Hypothesis: $\forall_{0 < \ell < n}. q_\ell = \frac{\overline{c}_\ell}{N_r^{\ell-1}}$. Then, for $n > 1$

$$q_n = \overline{c}_{0,k_0} \prod_{\ell=1}^{n-1} p_\ell = q_{n-1} p_{n-1}$$

$$= \frac{\overline{c}_{n-1}}{N_r^{n-2}} \frac{\overline{c}_{n-1,k_{n-1}}}{\sum_{i \in R_{n-1}} \overline{c}_{n-1,i}}$$

$$\approx \frac{\overline{c}_{n-1}}{N_r^{n-2}} \frac{\overline{c}_n}{\overline{c}_{n-1} N_r} = \frac{\overline{c}_n}{N_r^{n-1}}. \quad \square$$

Now we can proceed to explain the algorithm. In the descent phase we sample an n-node and compute the contrast using expression $\mathcal{C}^c$ (4.18). In (4.13) we must substitute the channel importance $\overline{c}$ by q_n and, according to §4.2, for a sRGB colour system (§2.2.4) we can take the perceptual coefficients $w^R = 0.2126$, $w^G = 0.7152$ and $w^B = 0.0722$ which capture the sensitivity of human colour perception [32] (2.53).

Thus, for each n-node, the colour contrast (4.13) converts into

$$\mathbf{C}_n^c = \sum_{c \in \mathbf{c}} w^c C_n^c q_n^c \tag{4.22}$$

and the colour and geometry combination (4.18) will be

$$\mathcal{C}_n^c = \delta \mathbf{C}_n^c + (1 - \delta) C_n^g. \tag{4.23}$$

Note that this expression could also be calculated from the respective binary versions of colour and geometry contrasts (§4.2).

In the algorithm, we subdivide the pixel or subpixel when the contrast of an n-node is not less than a given threshold ($\mathcal{C}_n^c \geq \epsilon$). Thus, the phase of ascent begins when the test fails ($\mathcal{C}_n^c < \epsilon$). This happens because either the contrast (which represents the colour heterogeneity) or the importance ($q_n \to 0$ for growing n) are low. In this phase, each n-node in the path provides its colour estimation $\widehat{c}_n$ from the signal reconstructed for each $c(s)$ where $s \in S_n$.

The final colour of an n-node is given by

$$c_n = \begin{cases} \widehat{c}_n, & \text{if } \mathcal{C}_n^c < \epsilon, \\ \sum_{i \in R_n} c_{n,i}, & \text{otherwise,} \end{cases} \tag{4.24}$$

where $c_{n,i}$ is the final colour of i-region of the n-node. Finally, we get c_1 for the colour of the pixels (or equivalently c_{0,k_0} in the path considered). An example of this process is shown in Fig. 4.10.

Observe that importance sampling is naturally integrated in the algorithm. Following importance sampling criteria a function should be sampled proportionally to its value which is what we obtain with our adaptive descent.

4.4.4   Implementation

The only precondition to implementing the entropy-based adaptive algorithm is to have at our disposal a method that gives us back the colour and geometry data from any sample in the image plane. We can also trade aliasing for noise using stochastic ray-tracing, as the human visual system is more sensitive to structured aliasing artifacts than to noise (§2.1.3). In particular, we use the path-tracing method (§2.3.2). With respect to the three subproblems of an adaptive sampling scheme (§4.4.1), we should consider the following:

Sampling Generation

A usual implementation of adaptive sampling consists in an adaptive subdivision of the sampling region in a predetermined way. This subdivision generally corresponds to a split into k equal subregions. Then, the data is stored in a k-tree, usually a binary-tree or quad-tree [248, 106, 151] (§2.1.5). We use this last option.

For each region, we choose an *adaptive stratified sampling* [74]. As its name indicates, it is a hybrid of both stratified sampling and adaptive sampling (§2.1.3). Stratified sampling is not very practical when it is not known in advance how many samples can be employed. In adaptive sampling, we want to start with a sparse sampling density and gradually increase it. For this situation, the adaptive strategy is joined together with the stratified sampling method. The basic idea is to start with an initial stratification of the domain (as sparse as desired), and if we want to take one more sample, then we can choose a stratum and split it. One of the two new strata does not have any samples and it is there where the new sample will fall. The process can be repeated until the refinement criteria indicate that it is enough. The critical issues in this method are choosing which stratum to split, how to split it, and how to store the strata.

We use this approach and, in order to simplify the implementation, the stratification is adapted to the number of subregions and samples. This makes the re-use of the samples at every new level of subdivision easier while it also offers the answers to the previous issues: the strata to split are all those which belong to the region selected by the refinement criterion, the split is done in k equal regions, and the strata data is stored in the k-tree.

Sampling Rate

The refinement criteria is essential in any scheme of adaptive sampling (§2.1.3). Our scheme used the entropy from the pixel contrast $\mathcal{C}^c$ (4.18) in any of its variants (e.g., binary contrast).

The entropy-based refinement tree built in §4.4.3 enables us to evaluate the information from the signal in order to adapt the density of sampling. The structure implements an importance sampling approach (contrast-based) directed towards the complex regions (heterogeneity in colour and geometry). For extreme situations, the refinement criterion evaluates additional parameters of stop, independent of the signal sampled, as those already mentioned in §4.4.1. When this is the case, the stop criterion used will be indicated. Note that the controls for depth of the refinement-tree and for minimum area are equivalent when the subdivision produces equal regions[8].

Filtering

The same considerations made in supersampling are valid (§4.3.1). Due to the stratified system, we use the piecewise-continuous image reconstruction (2.16) method using a box filter (2.1) directly incorporated into the colour computation phase (tree ascent). For this case, the final colour is equivalent to adding each one of the $s \in S_p$ weighted by the area of its corresponding stratum (2.3). Other local filters can be applied in this context (§2.1.6). The resampling is replaced by the reconstructed signal averaged in the whole domain of the pixel. Note that, from the perspective of the signal space domain, the task of the refinement criterion consists precisely in "conducting" the sampling, with the maximum possible precision, towards the most complex regions of the space. In consequence, at the lowest level, the precision of the tiling achieved (strata of the leaves of the refinement-tree) is what determines the quality of the final image.

In conclusion, respect to the presented method (Fig. 4.8), we have:

- Initial sampling: stratified ($N_s^r N_p$ samples).
- Refinement test geometry: true (S_n).
- Refinement test criterion: pixel contrast ($\mathcal{C}_n^c < \epsilon$).
- Sampling geometry: quad-tree ($k = 4$).
- Reconstruction: piecewise-continuous image (2.16).

---

[8] We assume the same area for all the pixels.

 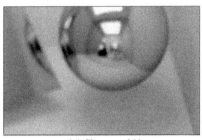

(*i*) General view   (*ii*) Close-up of (*i*)

Figure 4.11: Reference image used in the test in Fig. 4.12: (*i*) general view and (*ii*) close-up of (*i*). The image has been obtained with a path-tracing algorithm with 1,024 samples per pixel in a stratified way.

○ Filtering: box filter (2.1).
○ Resampling: any (signal average at pixel domain).

4.4.5   Results

For the purpose of comparison, in Fig. 4.12 we present the results for different techniques for the test scene in Fig. 4.11. We compare the following methods:

- *Classic contrast* (CC): A recursive adaptive sampling scheme based on contrast by channel (2.6) (with thresholds proportional to the visual system) weighted by its respective channel colour average [74, 216]. The maximum recursive level has been limited to 4 (Fig. 4.12.*a*).

- *Importance-weighted contrast* (IC): The same as in CC but each channel contrast is weighted with the respective importance q (4.21), as in our approach (Fig. 4.12.*b*).

- *Confidence test* (CT): Statistical approach based on a confidence interval (2.11) with a confidence level of $\alpha = 0.1$ and a tolerance $t = 0.025$ (§C) (Fig. 4.12.*c*).

- *Entropy-based contrast* (EC): Our approach (4.24) taking only colour contrast, $\delta = 1$ in (4.23) (Fig. 4.12.*d*).

Observe that the EC approach can be easily implemented on any standard hierarchical algorithm, using importance (4.21) and the new refinement criterion (4.23), with negligible additional cost.

In CC, IC, and EC, the number of subdivisions is $N_r = 4$ and the number of samples is $N_s^r = 8$. To compute the contrast measures for the refinement decision, the samples have been cast in a stratified way at each n-node (i.e., pixel or subpixel) and re-used at the next levels in the tree. In CT, groups of 8 samples were added in a stratified way until meeting the condition of the criterion. An implementation of classic path-tracing with next event estimator was used to compute all images (§2.3.2). The parameters were tuned so that all four test images were obtained with a similar average number of rays per pixel ($N_s^p = 60$) and computational cost. The resulting images are shown in Figs. 4.12.*.i* with close-ups in Figs. 4.12.*.ii*. A sampling density map[9] (SDM) for each one is given in Figs. 4.12.*.iii*.

The overall aspect of the images in Figs. 4.12.*.i* shows that our supersampling scheme performs best. Observe, for instance, the reduced noise in the shadows cast by the objects. This is further checked in the close-up images in Figs. 4.12.*.ii*. Observe also the detail of the sphere shadow reflected on the pyramid. It is important to note that we managed to improve the classic contrast approach in CC greatly by including the importance used in our scheme (compare results in Fig. 4.12.*a* with Fig. 4.12.*b*). A

---

[9] Generated under the same conditions as the quality (§4.1) and contrast (§4.2) maps. According to the scale in Fig. 3.2.*c*, warm colours correspond to the highest sampling rate and cold colours to the lowest.

oracle	general view				close-up			
	RMSE$_a$	RMSE$_p$	PSNR$_a$	PSNR$_p$	RMSE$_a$	RMSE$_p$	PSNR$_a$	PSNR$_p$
CC	13,727	13,599	25,379	25,461	20,276	20,024	21,991	22,100
IC	8,124	8,110	29,935	29,951	13,751	13,568	25,364	25,481
CT	5,194	5,174	33,822	33,855	8,407	8,338	29,638	29,710
EC	6,937	7,018	31,308	31,207	9,886	9,933	28,231	28,189

Table 4.2: The RMSE and PSNR of CC, IC, CT, and EC oracles applied to the general view (Fig. 4.11.i) and close-up (Fig. 4.11.ii) of the test scene. The average number of rays per pixel is $N_s^p = 60$ in all methods.

comparison of the SDMs shows a better discrimination of complex regions of the scene in the entropy case against the classic contrast case. This explains the better results obtained by our approach. Moreover, the confidence test approach CT (Fig. 4.12.c) also performs better than the classic contrast-based methods CC (Fig. 4.12.a) and IC (Fig. 4.12.b). The SDM of CT also explains why it performs better. However, it is unable to render the reflected shadows under the mirrored pyramid and sphere with precision (see close-up in Fig. 4.12.$c.ii$).

In Table 4.2 we show two measures (error and quality) obtained in Figs. 4.12.$*.i$–ii with respect to the test scene in Figs. 4.11.i–ii, respectively. We select the root of the mean square error[10] (RMSE) and the peak signal to noise ratio[11] (PSNR) to evaluate the results. For each one, we consider a weight balanced by every colour channel (RMSE$_a$ and PSNR$_a$) and a perceptual one (RMSE$_p$ and PSNR$_p$) in accordance with the sRGB system[12]. These measures reflect the good behaviour mentioned in CT and EC oracles (i.e., low RMSEs and high PSNRs). Although the error obtained using our approach is bigger than that with CT method, the visual results are better in the EC case (observe Figs. 4.12.c–d). This is due to the fact that the measures do not manage to reflect exactly the perceptual quality of the image. The EC images look better because the oracle distributes the samples in the perceptual critical regions more accurately (see SDMs).

Now, we present a test using the geometry component with $1 - \delta = 0.1$ in (4.23) and, at the same time, the binary contrast in colour and geometry. To do this, our approach is compared with the priority-value combination (2.15) made up of a colour contrast of the CC type and also by an usual geometry factor. Perceptual coefficients are taken equal as in our approach in both cases (§4.4.3). The tree depth level is set to 4 and the N_s^r is reduced by half (i.e., 4 samples) but maintaining the average per pixel (i.e., $N_s^p = 60$).

The images obtained are shown in Fig. 4.13. In Fig. 4.13.a, the entropy-contrast $\mathcal{C}_n^c$ (4.23) with $\mathbf{C}^c$ (4.13) and C^g (4.15). In Fig. 4.13.b, the binary-entropy contrast: $\mathcal{C}_n^c$ using $\mathbf{C}_b^c$ (4.14) and C_b^g (4.16). And, in Fig. 4.13.c, the priority-value approach p_v (2.15) with p_c (2.7) and p_d (2.14). The respective SDMs from Figs. 4.13.$*.i$ are shown in Figs. 4.13.$*.ii$.

We see from comparing the images that the entropy contrast is much better than the classic contrast used here. Observe for instance the ceiling, the shadows and the mirroring wall. A drawback of our approach is the peaks of high radiance that we observe on the right wall because this region is under-sampled in our method. However, this effect can be easily solved by a filtering technique (§2.1.6). The comparison of the SDMs shows a better discrimination of complex regions of the scene in the entropy case (Figs. 4.13.a–$b.ii$) against the priority-value contrast case (Fig. 4.13.$c.ii$). This explains the better results obtained with our approach.

Finally, in Fig. 4.14.a we show another scene obtained with our approach using an average of $N_s^p = 200$ and $\delta = 0.95$. Observe, in Fig. 4.14.b, how well the SDM works out both the geometry and colour details as in the shadow contours on the walls[13].

---

[10] It is calculated from the MSE (B.3) of each colour channel.

[11] Measure of the quality of a reconstructed image compared with an original image computing the ratio between the maximum possible power of a signal and the power of corrupting noise that affects the fidelity of its representation. Because many signals have a very wide dynamic range, it is usually expressed in terms of the logarithmic decibel scale: $10 \log_{10}(I_{\max}^2 / MSE)$ dB.

[12] $w^R = 0.2126$, $w^G = 0.7152$, and $w^B = 0.0722$ (2.53).

[13] The remaining spiked noise could easily be eliminated by filtering with an image smoothing method.

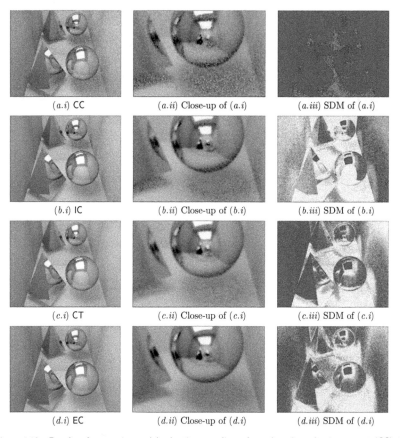

Figure 4.12: Results of comparisons: (a) adaptive sampling scheme based on classic contrast (CC), (b) importance-weighted contrast (IC), same as in (a) but weighting with importance q (4.21), (c) confidence test method (CT), and (d) entropy-based method (EC) with colour contrast only ($\delta = 1$). By columns: (i) shows the resulting images, (ii) close-up of regions of (i), and (iii) the sampling density maps of (i). The average number of rays per pixel is $N_{\mathrm{s}}^{\mathrm{p}} = 60$ in all methods, with a similar computational cost.

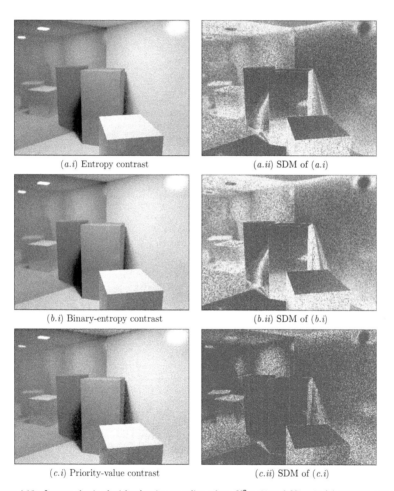

(a.i) Entropy contrast   (a.ii) SDM of (a.i)

(b.i) Binary-entropy contrast   (b.ii) SDM of (b.i)

(c.i) Priority-value contrast   (c.ii) SDM of (c.i)

Figure 4.13: Images obtained with adaptive sampling where $N_{\overline{s}}^{p} = 60$ and $N_s^r = 4$: (a) entropy contrast, (b) binary-entropy contrast, and (c) priority-value contrast. By columns: (i) Image sampled and (ii) sampling density map of (i).

(a) Entropy-based contrast   (b) SDM of (a)

Figure 4.14: Image obtained with entropy-based adaptive sampling where $N_s^p = 200$ and $\delta = 0.95$. (a) Sampled image. (b) Sampling density map of (a).

Summary

We present a set of entropy-based measures to evaluate the pixel quality. The interpretation of quality corresponds to the idea that the colour assigned to a pixel is more exact the more homogeneous the signal of the scene sampled through the pixel is. The entropy is chosen to express the level of homogeneity of the information extracted from a region. Two types of data are obtained by sampling the image plane: colour and geometry.

With respect to colour, the measures are defined by a colour system based on channels or components. From the application of the entropy to the information provided by sampling on the image plane, we obtain the *image plane channel entropy* and the *pixel channel entropy*. The normalisation of the value of homogeneity brought by the entropy allows us to define the *pixel channel quality* which duly weighted by each of the channels becomes the *pixel colour quality* corresponding to the colour system. A set of analogue measures are defined by using the geometric information contributed by samples: orientation and distance. The *image plane geometry entropy*, *pixel geometry entropy*, and *pixel geometry quality* measures are obtained.

Complementary to the concept of pixel quality, the *pixel contrast* (heterogeneity) is defined. For each of the measures of quality we obtain a contrast measure as well as a binary variant for the colour (*pixel channel binary contrast* and *pixel colour binary contrast*) and two for the geometry (*pixel geometry binary contrast* and *pixel logarithmic-difference contrast*). A linear combination of both perspectives, colour and geometry, is used to define a global *pixel contrast*. Assigning more weight to one option than the other, the aspects of colour (e.g., shadows) or geometry (e.g., edges) stand out. The measures of quality and contrast can be extended to any process that requires an evaluation of these types of characteristics, simply adapting the probability distributions to the kind of relevant information.

Two applications of the pixel contrast are presented as refinement criteria in adaptive sampling methods used in ray-tracing techniques. On the one hand, a method of supersampling based on a refinement criterion of one sole level of analysis is shown: *entropy-based supersampling*. The supersampling of each pixel is carried out directly proportional to its contrast. On the other hand, the same measure is applied in a recursive adaptive sampling scheme. Taking advantage of the recursive property of the entropy, an entropy-tree is generated bringing about the adaptive refinement-tree. This allows the measure of contrast to be naturally incorporated into the method and a new *entropy-based adaptive sampling* is presented. It works by locally adapting the density of sampling to the contrast of the region being evaluated until a sufficiently low predetermined contrast is attained. Examples and comparisons with other usual methods of contrast accompany both applications, showing how well the entropy-based approach behaves.

Chapter 5

Oracles Based on Generalised Entropy for Hierarchical Radiosity

In the previous chapter we have observed how the application of entropy measures to refinement criteria has given good results in the ray-tracing technique (pixel-driven approach). Now, we consider the application of new information-theoretic measures to hierarchical radiosity (object-space approach).

The radiosity method solves the problem of illumination in an environment with diffuse surfaces by using a finite element approach (§2.4). The scene discretisation has to represent the illumination accurately by trying to avoid unnecessary subdivisions that would increase the computation time. The two most important problems are [12]:

- *Meshing* (accuracy). Meshing largely determines the accuracy of the solution that can be obtained. The mesh should be fine enough to capture smooth illumination variations accurately, as well as illumination discontinuities such as at shadow boundaries.

- *Form factor computation* (speed and storage). The number of form factors is the square of the number of mesh elements., and, for each form factor, a difficult integral needs to be solved.

A good meshing strategy will balance the requirements of accuracy and computational cost. In the hierarchical radiosity algorithms the mesh is generated adaptively (§2.4.3): when the constant radiosity assumption on a patch is not valid for the radiosity received from another patch, the refinement algorithm will refine it in a set of subpatches or elements. A refinement criterion, usually called *oracle* in hierarchical radiosity, informs us if a subdivision of the surfaces is needed, bearing in mind that its cost should remain acceptable (§2.4.4). The difficulty in obtaining a precise solution to the global illumination mainly depends on the degree of dependence between all the elements of the adaptive mesh. This dependence can be quantified by the mutual information, which is a measure of the information transfer between the different parts of a scene (§2.6). In addition, the mutual information was used in Feixas et al. [63] to obtain a refinement criterion for the hierarchical radiosity algorithm (§2.4.4). The results motivated us further to try new information-theoretic oracles based on entropy measures.

In this chapter, we tackle the radiosity problem from the perspective of generalised information-theoretic measures. Because of its good properties and recent applications in physical problems, we analyse the behaviour of the *generalised entropy of Harvda-Charvát-Tsallis*, or HCT entropy, and the *generalised mutual information* (§5.1). Their use in hierarchical radiosity is based on the information content and information transfer between two elements of the mesh, from a geometric visibility perspective. Thus, new information-theoretic oracles are defined in hierarchical radiosity (§5.2) —based on transported information (§5.3), information smoothness (§5.4), and mutual information (§5.5)— to look for a correspondence with the classic oracles —based on transported power, kernel smoothness, and smoothness of received radiosity (§2.4.4)—. The results obtained show that the new oracles improve on their classic counterparts confirming the usefulness of the information-theoretic approach in dealing with the radiosity problem. The oracle based on mutual information stands out among them (§5.6).

5.1   HCT Entropy

As a previous step in defining the oracles of hierarchical radiosity, we present the HCT generalised entropy together with some of its properties (§5.1.1), and its associated relative entropy and mutual information (§5.1.2). The historical origins and evolution of these measures can be found in Taneja [227, 228]. Currently, they are frequently applied in the statistical mechanics field thanks to the works of Tsallis [233, 234, 235].

5.1.1   Generalised Entropies

Since Rudolph Clausius coined the word *entropy* (1865), different scientists have reformulated the concept several times. Ludwing Boltzmann and Josiah W. Gibbs introduced entropy in terms of microscopic quantities (1867, see also §2.5.1). John von Neumann presented the quantum entropy (1927). Shannon defined a new entropy expression and interpreted it in terms of information and communication theory [200] (1948, §2.5). In 1957, Jaynes reformulated statistical mechanics in terms of probability distributions derived from the use of the principle of maximum entropy, contributing with a very practical general vision [100, 101]. New and different entropic forms appeared in various fields (e.g., information theory, complexity, and nonlinear dynamical systems). Among them, a group of parametrised entropies called generalised entropies.

It was in 1960 when Rényi [172] proposed a generalised entropy[1], which recovers the Shannon entropy as a special case[2]. In 1963, Aczél and Daróczy [1] presented a generalisation that includes the Rény entropy. In 1967, Harvda and Charvát [88] introduced a new generalised definition of entropy. Afterwards, in 1970 Daróczy [44] gave an alternative approach for it. In 1975, Sharma and Mittal [202], and Sharma and Taneja [203] introduced two-parameter entropies where Rényi and Harvda-Charvát entropies are particular cases. Tsallis, in 1988 [233], used the Harvda-Charvát entropy again[3], in order to generalise the Boltzmann-Gibbs entropy in statistical mechanics.

Definition 66 *The Harvda-Charvát-Tsallis entropy of a discrete random variable X, with $|X| = n$ and p_X as a probability distribution, is given by*

$$H_\alpha(X) = k \frac{1 - \sum_{i=1}^n p_i^\alpha}{\alpha - 1}, \tag{5.1}$$

where k is a conventional positive constant and $\alpha \in \mathbb{R}\backslash\{1\}$.

The transition to continuous measures is straightforward. In Fig. 5.1.a we show its behaviour for some α values[4]. This entropy recovers the Boltzmann-Gibbs-Shannon discrete entropy (§2.5.1) when $\alpha \to 1$:

$$\begin{aligned} H_1(X) &\equiv \lim_{\alpha \to 1} H_\alpha = \lim_{\alpha \to 1} k \frac{1 - \sum_{i=1}^n p_i e^{(\alpha-1)\ln p_i}}{\alpha - 1} \\ &= \lim_{\alpha \to 1} k \frac{1 - \sum_{i=1}^n p_i(1 + (\alpha-1)\ln p_i)}{\alpha - 1} = -k \sum_{i=1}^n p_i \ln p_i. \end{aligned} \tag{5.2}$$

The HCT entropy exhibits notable properties. We list some of them below [163, 235]:

---

[1] According to Csiszar's survey [42], it seems that this was a rediscovery of a former work by Paul-Marcel Schutzenberg in 1954.

[2] In the limit when $\alpha \to 1$.

[3] He was only aware at that moment of Rényi's entropy [235]. The origins of the Tsallis' measures are detailed specifically in Taneja [228]. In this context, the classical physical system Σ with W possible microscopic configurations and p_i the probability of finding the system in the configuration i, is replaced by the discrete random variable $X = (\mathcal{X}, p_X)$, where $|\mathcal{X}| = n$ (§B). Finally, recall that all the superindexes corresponding to arithmetic expressions must be interpreted as a power.

[4] In a scene, for $\alpha = 2$ and $k = 1$, we obtain the trace of the covariance matrix (i.e., sum of variances) of a multinomial distribution defined by estimating all form factors. For each patch i, and $j \in \{1, \ldots, N_p\}$, we have $\sum_j F_{ij}(1 - F_{ij}) = 1 - \sum_j F_{ij}^2 = H_2(\{F_{ij}\})$, using local or global lines (§2.2.2). As form factors represent visibility, this value gives the expected error in visibility for the primary estimator.

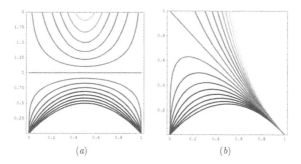

(a) (b)

Figure 5.1: HCT entropy for $\alpha = \frac{i}{4}$, $i \in \{-8,\ldots,8\}$ (green to blue, through red, respectively), and $k = 1$. (a) Case of $n = 2$ (5.1) and (b) the contribution of an event to the entropy (5.12).

Non-negativity From (5.1), $H_\alpha \geq 0$. The equality holds whenever there is a unique $p_i = 1$.

Boundaries A global absolute maximum $(\alpha > 0)$ or minimum $(\alpha < 0)$ is obtained in the case of equiprobability (i.e., $p_i = \frac{1}{n}$): $H_\alpha = k\frac{n^{1-\alpha}-1}{1-\alpha}$. In the limit $\alpha \to 1$, the Boltzmann expression is obtained: $H_1 = k\ln n$.

Concavity The functional H_α is (§D)

  ◦ Concave: $\alpha > 0$
  ◦ Constant: $\alpha = 0$ $(H_0(X) = n - 1)$
  ◦ Convex: $\alpha < 0$

Grouping If the N_X states of a system X, with probability distribution p_X, are divided into two subsystems Y and Z with N_Y and N_Z states respectively (i.e., $N_Y + N_Z = N_X$), we can define $p_y = \sum_{i \in Y} p_i$ and $p_z = \sum_{i \in Z} p_i$ (i.e., $p_y + p_z = 1$). Then,

$$H_\alpha(p_X) = H_\alpha(\{p_y, p_z\}) + p_y^\alpha H_\alpha\left(\frac{p_Y}{p_y}\right) + p_z^\alpha H_\alpha\left(\frac{p_Z}{p_z}\right), \tag{5.3}$$

where $\frac{p_W}{p_w} = \{\frac{p_i}{p_w} \mid p_i \in p_W\}$. Note that this expression is a generalisation of Shannon's grouping property for the particular case of bipartition (2.74).

5.1.2 Entropic Index

A number of entropy-like quantities have appeared in the scientific literature sharing some properties with the Boltzmann-Gibbs-Shannon entropy [7, 227]. Taneja [226] unifies some of the generalised entropies and presents a complete study in [227]. The HCT entropy[5] is currently considered to be one of the most important examples of generalised entropies. It is suitable for dealing with nonextensive settings [235]:

Definition 67 *If two systems X and Y, with respective marginal probabilities p_X and q_Y, are independent in the sense of the theory of probabilities (i.e., $p_{XY} = p_X q_Y$, §B), then*

$$H_\alpha(X,Y) = H_\alpha(X) + H_\alpha(Y) + (1-\alpha)H_\alpha(X)H_\alpha(Y), \tag{5.4}$$

where superextensivity, extensivity or subextensivity occurs when $\alpha < 1$, $\alpha = 1$, and $\alpha > 1$, respectively.

---

[5] Without loss of generality, we assume from now on $k = 1$.

From the good results obtained by Tsallis, H_α is being applied to many different areas of research. Important applications have been developed in thermodynamics and more recent examples include [163, 235]: self-gravitating systems, two dimensional pure electron plasma, solar neutrino problems, cosmology, chaotic systems, the n-body gravitational problem, etc. This last case [164] has a clear correspondence with the hierarchical radiosity (§2.4.3). Tsallis' attempt to develop a complete thermostatically formalism on the basis of a nonlogarithmic entropy function has raised many interesting issues related both to the mathematical structure and the physical implications. Many scientists refer to the α parameter as the *entropic index* or the nonextensive index (5.4). It appears to be a simple and efficient manner to characterise what is currently referred to as *complexity*, or at least some types of complexity [78]. The case of $\alpha = 2$ becomes the *Gini-Simpson index* of diversity which has been widely used in learning (e.g., Elomaa and Rousu [56]).

Analogously to the Kullback-Leibler divergence (2.77), Tsallis proposed in [234] a generalised divergence associated with Harvda-Charvát-Tsallis entropy that was presented years ago by Rathie and Kannappan [170]:

Definition 68 *The directed divergence or relative entropy of type-α between probability distributions p_X and q_X is given by*

$$D_\alpha(p,q) = \frac{1}{1-\alpha}\left(1 - \sum_{i=1}^n \frac{p_i^\alpha}{q_i^{\alpha-1}}\right),\qquad(5.5)$$

with $\alpha \in \mathbb{R}\backslash\{1\}$.

When $\alpha \to 1$, the Kullback-Leibler divergence is obtained[6]. It benefits from the good properties derived from the HCT entropy (see [234, 69]) and it is applied, also with good results, outside physics (e.g., image registration [130]). From this divergence, Tsallis [234] defined the corresponding mutual information, previously proposed by Taneja [225, 226] (§2.5.2):

Definition 69 *The generalised mutual information between two discrete random variables (X, Y), with $|X| = n$, $|Y| = m$, joint probability distribution p_{XY}, and marginal probability distributions p_X and q_Y, is defined as the directed divergence between p_{XY} and $p_X q_Y$:*

$$I_\alpha(X,Y) = D_\alpha(p_{XY}, p_X q_Y) = \frac{1}{1-\alpha}\left(1 - \sum_{i=1}^n \sum_{j=1}^m \frac{p_{ij}^\alpha}{p_i^{\alpha-1} q_j^{\alpha-1}}\right).\qquad(5.6)$$

An alternative form of (5.6) using entropies is given by

$$I_\alpha(X,Y) = H_\alpha(X) + H_\alpha(Y) - (1-\alpha)H_\alpha(X)H_\alpha(Y) - H_\alpha(X,Y).\qquad(5.7)$$

Shannon mutual information (§2.5.2) is obtained with $\alpha \to 1$. Some alternative ways for the generalised mutual information can be seen in [226]. The transition to continuous measures is straightforward.

5.2   Towards the Information-Theoretic Oracles

Our objective is to study the behaviour of three information-theoretic oracles for hierarchical radiosity based on the HCT generalised entropy in correspondence with the three classic oracles reviewed in §2.4.4. Once introduced H_α (5.1), we set up the common framework.

As we have seen, the radiosity method uses a finite element approach, discretising the diffuse environment into patches and considering the radiosities, emissivities and reflectances constant over them (§2.4). With these assumptions, the discrete radiosity equation is given by (2.62):

$$B_i = E_i + \rho_i \sum_{j \in S} F_{ij} B_j,\qquad(5.8)$$

---

[6] The $D_\alpha(p,q)$ can be expressed also as $-\sum_{i=1}^n p_i \ln_\alpha \frac{q_i}{p_i}$, where $\ln_\alpha(x) \equiv \frac{x^{\alpha-1}-1}{1-\alpha}$ with the convention $0\ln_\alpha(\cdot) \equiv 0$. This form reminds of the usual Kullback-Leibler divergence.

where B_i, E_i, and ρ_i, are respectively the radiosity, emissivity, and reflectance of patch i, B_j is the radiosity of patch j, and F_{ij} is the patch-to-patch form factor. The matrix element F_{ij} is given by (2.25):

$$F_{ij} = \frac{1}{A_i} \int_{A_i} \int_{A_j} F_{dA_x \leftrightarrow dA_y} dA_y dA_x, \tag{5.9}$$

where $F_{dA_x \leftrightarrow dA_y}$ (2.23) corresponds to the point-to-point form factor ($F_{x \leftrightarrow y}$, §2.2.2). From (2.32), F_{ij} can be calculated using an area-to-area sampling:

$$F_{ij} \approx A_j \frac{1}{|\mathcal{S}_{i \times j}|} \sum_{(x,y) \in \mathcal{S}_{i \times j}} F_{x \leftrightarrow y}, \tag{5.10}$$

where the computation accuracy depends on the number of random segments between i and j ($|\mathcal{S}_{i \times j}|$). To solve the system (5.8), a hierarchical refinement algorithm is used (§2.4.3). The application of a good refinement criterion is fundamental for its efficiency. In the classic oracles (§2.4.4), the form factor plays an important role. It appears with different expressions in the three kernels weighted by the reflectance of patch i and the radiosity of patch j. Similarly to the radiosity equation, where we observe that the contribution of patch j to the radiosity of patch i is given by $\rho_i F_{ij} B_j$, we can consider these oracles under the form

$$\rho_i \tau B_j < \epsilon, \tag{5.11}$$

where τ is a specific kernel function for every approach and the inequality is understood as referring to current discretisation S.

For each of the classic methods, we will obtain a similar oracle within the context of information theory, using the HCT entropy. The use of this measure is justified by the good results obtained in other areas with nonnegative entropic indexes[7]. Thus, within the hierarchical radiosity context, we will interpret the scene as an information channel (§2.6) and we will use the HCT entropy to substitute for the Shannon entropy (§2.5.1).

The application of the HCT entropy introduces the concepts[8] of α-*information content* and α-*information transfer* between the elements of a hierarchical mesh. In the following new oracles, as in the classic cases, we will weight the corresponding α-information kernel by the factor $\rho_i B_j$ to obtain the oracle (5.11). Thus, we will convert kernels based on *geometric data* into kernels based on *geometric α-information*. In the rest of this chapter, we refer to the generalised α-information simply as *information*.

5.3 Transported Information

As we know from §2.4.4, the classic transported power oracle is based on the energy transported between the patches (2.66):

$$\rho_i A_i F_{ij} B_j < \epsilon. \tag{TP}$$

From (5.11), we have[9] $\tau = A_i F_{ij}$. Now, we want to replace this geometric kernel by an information-theoretic kernel based on the information content between two patches.

5.3.1 Concept

From (5.1), an individual term of HCT entropy is given by

$$h_\alpha(p) = \frac{1}{\alpha - 1}(p - p^\alpha). \tag{5.12}$$

It expresses the contribution of an event with probability p into the system entropy[10] (Fig. 5.1.b). Thus, we can rewrite (5.1) as $H_\alpha(X) = \sum_{i=1}^{n} h_\alpha(p_i)$ and, from the discrete scene entropy (2.87), we have

---

[7] For values of $\alpha < 0$, the values of the HCT entropy are unbounded and grow with $-\alpha$ (Fig. 5.1.b).
[8] The word α-*information* is used to denote the generalisation of the Shannon information introduced by the Harvda-Charvát-Tsallis entropy.
[9] It gives the measure of lines between i and j.
[10] For $\alpha = 2$, it represents a term of the trace as commented in footnote 5.

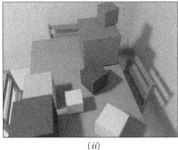

(i)   (ii)

Figure 5.2: Test scene: (i) view$_1$ and (ii) view$_2$. The image has been obtained with a path-tracing algorithm with 1,024 samples per pixel in a stratified way.

Definition 70 *The discrete scene HCT entropy of S is given by*

$$H_\alpha(S) = \sum_{i \in S} a_i \sum_{j \in S} h_\alpha(F_{ij}) = \sum_{i \in S} \sum_{j \in S} H_{\alpha_{ij}}(S), \qquad (5.13)$$

where the term $H_{\alpha_{ij}}(S) = a_i h_\alpha(F_{ij})$ is an element of the discrete scene HCT entropy matrix.

The H_α value gives the average information content[11] of S and is equivalent to the Shannon information content (2.87) when $\alpha \to 1$. It is always nonnegative and, in general, $H_{\alpha_{ij}} \neq H_{\alpha_{ji}}$. It represents the degree of information content between two surfaces i and j from the perspective of i ($i \to j$). In the hierarchical radiosity context, the event represents the emission of energy from the element j and the reception on i. Thus, while the energy transported is evaluated from $j \to i$, the information content is obtained from the visibility from $i \to j$.

We build the new oracle by replacing τ in (5.11) with $H_{\alpha_{ij}}$. In order to standardise the shape of its expression, we multiply the inequality by the constant A_T ($a_i = \frac{A_i}{A_\text{T}}$) and we have:

Definition 71 *The oracle for S in hierarchical radiosity based on transported information is given by*

$$\rho_i A_i h_\alpha(F_{ij}) B_j < \epsilon. \qquad \text{(TI)}$$

This new oracle is proportional to the geometric information content between two elements of the hierarchical mesh and to the area of the receiver element. The cost of this oracle does not change with respect to the classic version: it depends on the accuracy which is desired in the estimate of the form factor (5.10).

5.3.2   Results

---

[11] For $\alpha = 2$, it represents the visibility scene error when computing the form factors (see footnotes 10 and 5).

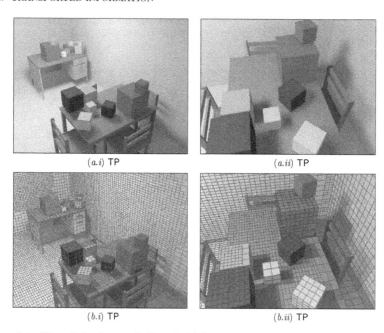

(*a.i*) TP   (*a.ii*) TP

(*b.i*) TP   (*b.ii*) TP

Figure 5.4: TP oracle for the scene in Fig. 5.2: (*a*) Gouraud shaded solution and (*b*) its final adaptive mesh. By columns, (*i*) view₁ and (*ii*) view₂ are shown. The oracle has been evaluated by using only one line as a cheap form factor estimator.

The classic and information-theoretic oracles have been implemented on top of the hierarchical Monte Carlo radiosity method and we show the results obtained for Fig. 5.2 and Fig. 5.3 (scenes used as a common test throughout this chapter). It should be noted here that our oracles can be used with any hierarchical radiosity method. Both oracles (TP and TI) have been evaluated with only one line as a cheap form factor estimator.

With respect to Fig. 5.2, around 2,684,000 rays are cast in order to distribute the power and a final mesh of approximately 19,000 patches is obtained for each oracle. For comparison purposes, these values are kept for all the oracles on this scene. In Fig. 5.4 we show the results for the TP oracle with a Gouraud shaded solution and its adaptive mesh. In Fig. 5.5 we present the behaviour of the TI oracle for three entropic indexes: a superextensivity of 0.5, the extensivity, and a subextensivity of 1.5. The final meshes corresponding to Fig. 5.5 are mapped to Fig. 5.6. In Table 5.1 we show the measures of RMSE and PSNR for the mentioned images and for two entropic indexes more ($\alpha \in \{0.75, 1.25\}$).

Figure 5.3: Test scene. The image has been obtained with a path-tracing algorithm with 1,024 samples per pixel in a stratified way.

We proceed in the same way for the scene in Fig. 5.3, where for each oracle, only 129,000 rays are cast to distribute the power and around 1,000 patches are obtained for each mesh. These values are also kept for all the oracles on this scene. In Fig. 5.7 we show the images for the TP and TI oracles with

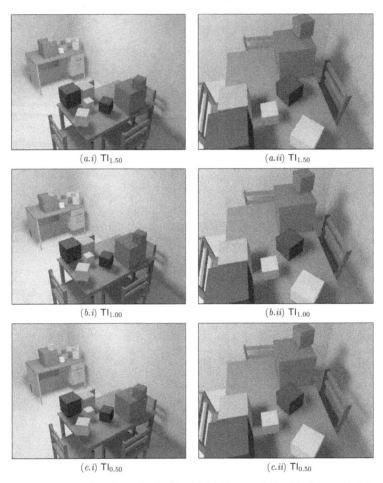

$(a.i)$ $\mathsf{TI}_{1.50}$ $(a.ii)$ $\mathsf{TI}_{1.50}$

$(b.i)$ $\mathsf{TI}_{1.00}$ $(b.ii)$ $\mathsf{TI}_{1.00}$

$(c.i)$ $\mathsf{TI}_{0.50}$ $(c.ii)$ $\mathsf{TI}_{0.50}$

Figure 5.5: Gouraud shaded solution for the TI oracle for the scene in Fig. 5.2. An entropic index of (a) 1.5, (b) 1, and (c) 0.5 has been used. By columns, (i) view$_1$ and (ii) view$_2$ are shown. The respective meshes are shown in Fig. 5.6. The oracles have been evaluated by using only one line as a cheap form factor estimator.

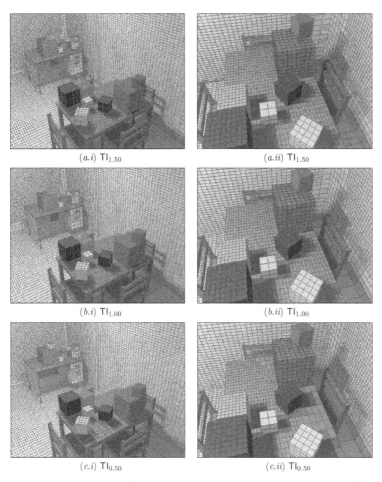

Figure 5.6: Adaptive mesh for the TI oracle for the scene in Fig. 5.2. An entropic index of (a) 1.5, (b) 1, and (c) 0.5 has been used. By columns, (i) view$_1$ and (ii) view$_2$ are shown. The respective Gouraud shaded solutions are shown in Fig. 5.5. The oracles have been evaluated by using only one line as a cheap form factor estimator.

oracle	view₁				view₂			
	RMSE$_a$	RMSE$_p$	PSNR$_a$	PSNR$_p$	RMSE$_a$	RMSE$_p$	PSNR$_a$	PSNR$_p$
TP	9.836	9.064	28.275	28.984	10.670	10.005	27.567	28.127
TI$_{1.50}$	9.717	8.924	28.380	29.120	10.579	9.785	27.642	28.320
TI$_{1.25}$	9.685	8.916	28.409	29.127	10.459	9.753	27.741	28.348
TI$_{1.00}$	9.675	8.884	28.418	29.158	10.316	9.605	27.860	28.481
TI$_{0.75}$	9.847	9.058	28.265	28.990	10.489	9.747	27.716	28.354
TI$_{0.50}$	10.154	9.390	27.998	28.678	10.603	9.880	27.622	28.236

Table 5.1:   The RMSE and PSNR measures of the TP and TI$_\alpha$ oracles applied to Fig. 5.2. The images for the TP and TI$_\alpha$ for $\alpha \in \{0.5, 1, 1.5\}$ oracles are shown in Fig. 5.4 and Fig. 5.5, respectively. The oracles have been evaluated with one line only as a cheap form factor estimator.

oracle	RMSE$_a$	RMSE$_p$	PSNR$_a$	PSNR$_p$
TP	11.301	11.198	27.068	27.148
TI$_{1.50}$	11.369	11.358	27.016	27.025
TI$_{1.25}$	11.332	11.231	27.045	27.123
TI$_{1.00}$	11.186	11.062	27.157	27.254
TI$_{0.75}$	11.472	11.414	26.938	26.982
TI$_{0.50}$	11.649	11.682	26.805	26.780

Table 5.2:   The RMSE and PSNR measures of the TP and TI$_\alpha$ oracles applied to Fig. 5.3. The images for the TP and TI$_\alpha$ for $\alpha \in \{0.5, 1, 1.5\}$ oracles are shown in Fig. 5.7. The oracles have been evaluated with one line only as a cheap form factor estimator.

a Gouraud shaded solution (Figs. 5.7.$*.i$) and their respective meshes (Figs. 5.7.$*.ii$). In Table 5.2, we show the measures of RMSE and PSNR for a set of results obtained with these oracles, including the previously mentioned images.

For the visual and quantitative results for the scenes tested, the quality of the new oracle with respect to its classic counterpart is similar with slight improvements over TP without being able to establish a firm conclusion about an optimal value of α. The best case occurs when $\alpha = 1$, where we find the lowest RMSEs, and in consequence, the highest PSNRs.

5.4   Information Smoothness

The kernel smoothness-based oracles are defined from the "variation" of the radiosity kernel between a pair of elements in order to improve on power-based refinement (§2.4.4). In particular, the oracle proposed by Gortler et al. [76] is given by (2.68)

$$\rho_i \max\{F_{ij}^{\mathrm{max}} - F_{ij}^{\mathrm{avg}}, F_{ij}^{\mathrm{avg}} - F_{ij}^{\mathrm{min}}\}A_j B_j < \epsilon, \tag{KS}$$

where the kernel is a difference of form factors created from the maximum and minimum values computed between pairs of random points on both elements: $\tau = \max\{F_{ij}^{\mathrm{max}} - F_{ij}^{\mathrm{avg}}, F_{ij}^{\mathrm{avg}} - F_{ij}^{\mathrm{min}}\}A_j$, where $F_{ij}^{\mathrm{avg}} = \frac{F_{ij}}{A_j}$ (5.10) is the average of the point-to-point form factors between elements i and j. In this section, this oracle is taken as the reference for a new oracle based on the variation of information content between these elements.

5.4.1   Concept

As we have seen in §5.3.1, the information content between two elements i and j of a scene is given by $H_{\alpha_{ij}}(S) = a_i h_\alpha(F_{ij})$ (5.13). The same uniform area-to-area sampling employed for the estimate of F_{ij} provides us with the minimum and maximum point-to-point form factor between the elements i and j:

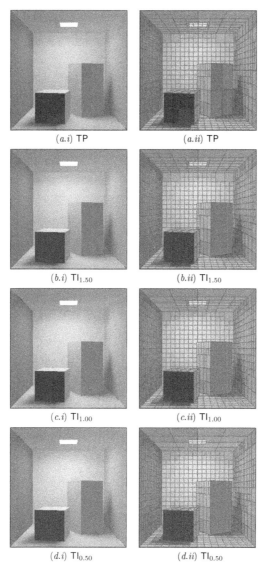

Figure 5.7: TP and $\text{TI}_{\alpha \in \{0.5,1,1.5\}}$ oracles for the scene in Fig. 5.3. By columns, (*i*) Gouraud shaded solution and (*ii*) its final adaptive mesh are shown. The oracles have been evaluated by using only one line as a cheap form factor estimator.

oracle	view$_1$				view$_2$			
	RMSE$_a$	RMSE$_p$	PSNR$_a$	PSNR$_p$	RMSE$_a$	RMSE$_p$	PSNR$_a$	PSNR$_p$
KS	13.791	13.128	25.339	25.767	15.167	14.354	24.513	24.991
IS$_{1.50}$	9.983	9.218	28.146	28.838	10.212	9.497	27.948	28.579
IS$_{1.25}$	9.957	9.193	28.168	28.862	10.189	9.502	27.968	28.575
IS$_{1.00}$	9.905	9.144	28.213	28.908	10.210	9.501	27.950	28.576
IS$_{0.75}$	9.793	9.017	28.312	29.029	10.131	9.394	28.018	28.674
IS$_{0.50}$	9.712	8.931	28.384	29.113	9.930	9.162	28.192	28.891

Table 5.3: The RMSE and PSNR measures of the KS and IS$_\alpha$ oracles applied to Fig. 5.2. The images for the KS and IS$_\alpha$ for $\alpha \in \{0.5, 1, 1.5\}$ oracles are shown in Fig. 5.8 and Fig. 5.9, respectively. The oracles have been evaluated with 10 random lines between elements.

$F_{ij}^{\min}$ and $F_{ij}^{\max}$, respectively. We consider their corresponding information terms:

$$H_{\alpha_{ij}}^{\min}(S) = a_i h_\alpha(F_{ij}^{\min}) = a_i(F_{ij}^{\min} - (F_{ij}^{\min})^\alpha)(\alpha - 1)^{-1} \tag{5.14}$$

$$H_{\alpha_{ij}}^{\max}(S) = a_i h_\alpha(F_{ij}^{\max}) = a_i(F_{ij}^{\max} - (F_{ij}^{\max})^\alpha)(\alpha - 1)^{-1}. \tag{5.15}$$

From these expressions[12], analogously to the KS, we can consider the difference between the information values corresponding to minimum and maximum point-to-point form factors with respect to that obtained on the estimate of the form factor. Then, taking the maximum variation of information content of $i \rightarrow j$, we can obtain the new kernel on S as

$$\tau = \max\{|H_{\alpha_{ij}} - H_{\alpha_{ij}}^{\min}|, |H_{\alpha_{ij}}^{\max} - H_{\alpha_{ij}}|\}$$
$$= a_i \max\{|h_\alpha(F_{ij}) - h_\alpha(F_{ij}^{\min})|, |h_\alpha(F_{ij}^{\max}) - h_\alpha(F_{ij})|\}. \tag{5.16}$$

The oracle is obtained by applying (5.11) and, to standardise the shape of its expression, we multiply the inequality by the constant A_T:

Definition 72 *The oracle for S in hierarchical radiosity based on information smoothness is given by*

$$\rho_i A_i \max\{|h_\alpha(F_{ij}) - h_\alpha(F_{ij}^{\min})|, |h_\alpha(F_{ij}^{\max}) - h_\alpha(F_{ij})|\}B_j < \epsilon. \tag{IS}$$

Thus, this new oracle is proportional to the maximum variation in the geometric information content between two elements of the hierarchical mesh and to the area of the receiver element. Like the TI oracle (§5.3), the cost of the IS oracle does not change with respect to its classic counterpart KS, and continues to be determined by the desired accuracy in the calculation of the form factor.

5.4.2 Results

The same setting presented for the test scenes Fig. 5.2 and Fig. 5.3, in the previous TP and TI oracles (§5.3.2), is now presented for KS and IS ones. For the sake of comparison, adaptive meshes of identical size have been generated with the same cost for the power distribution. With regard to the estimate of the form factor, the number of random lines has been increased to 10 ($|S_{i \times j}|$) since we require more information to be able to carry out the smoothing process.

For the scene in Fig. 5.2, the mesh and power distribution is made up of approximately 19,000 patches and 2,684,000 rays, respectively. In Fig. 5.8 we show the results obtained for the KS oracle with a Gouraud shaded solution and its final adaptive mesh. In Fig. 5.9 we present the behaviour of the IS oracle for the three entropic indexes of 0.5, 1, and 1.5. The final meshes of these results are mapped to Fig. 5.10. In Table 5.3, we show the results for the RMSE and PSNR measures and the entropic index set used in Table 5.1, with respect to images obtained with the KS and IS oracles.

Analogously, we present the results for the scene in Fig. 5.3, where 129,000 rays are cast to distribute the power and approximately 1,000 patches are obtained for each mesh. In Fig. 5.11 we show the images

---

[12] Observe that in general, for a sampling between i and j, $H_{\alpha_{ij}}^{\min} \neq \min\{H_{\alpha_{ij}}\}$ and $H_{\alpha_{ij}}^{\max} \neq \max\{H_{\alpha_{ij}}\}$.

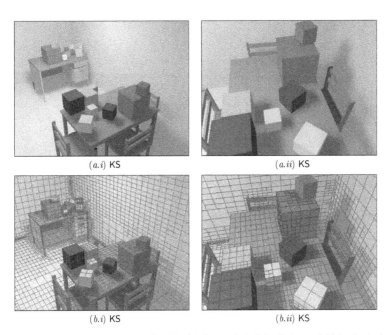

Figure 5.8: KS oracle for the scene in Fig. 5.2: (a) Gouraud shaded solution and (b) its final adaptive mesh. By columns, (i) view$_1$ and (ii) view$_2$ are shown. The oracle has been evaluated with 10 random lines between elements.

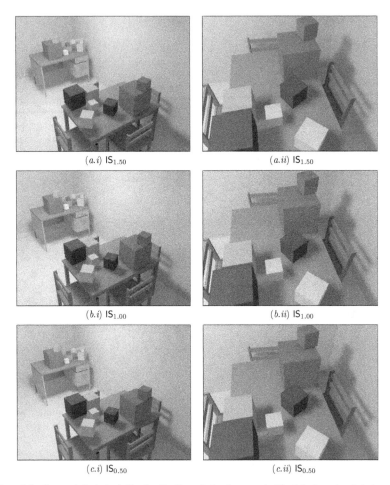

$(a.i)$ $\mathsf{IS}_{1.50}$ $(a.ii)$ $\mathsf{IS}_{1.50}$

$(b.i)$ $\mathsf{IS}_{1.00}$ $(b.ii)$ $\mathsf{IS}_{1.00}$

$(c.i)$ $\mathsf{IS}_{0.50}$ $(c.ii)$ $\mathsf{IS}_{0.50}$

Figure 5.9: Gouraud shaded solution for the IS oracle for the scene in Fig. 5.2. An entropic index of (a) 1.5, (b) 1, and (c) 0.5 has been used. By columns, (i) view$_1$ and (ii) view$_2$ are shown. The respective meshes are shown in Fig. 5.10. The oracles have been evaluated with 10 random lines between elements.

$(a.i)$ $\mathsf{IS}_{1.50}$ $(a.ii)$ $\mathsf{IS}_{1.50}$

$(b.i)$ $\mathsf{IS}_{1.00}$ $(b.ii)$ $\mathsf{IS}_{1.00}$

$(c.i)$ $\mathsf{IS}_{0.50}$ $(c.ii)$ $\mathsf{IS}_{0.50}$

Figure 5.10: Adaptive mesh for the IS oracle for the scene in Fig. 5.2. An entropic index of (a) 1.5, (b) 1, and (c) 0.5 has been used. By columns, (i) view$_1$ and (ii) view$_2$ are shown. The respective Gouraud shaded solutions are shown in Fig. 5.9. The oracles have been evaluated with 10 random lines between elements.

oracle	RMSE$_a$	RMSE$_p$	PSNR$_a$	PSNR$_p$
KS	13.531	13.520	25.504	25.511
IS$_{1.50}$	10.978	10.899	27.321	27.383
IS$_{1.25}$	10.989	10.909	27.311	27.375
IS$_{1.00}$	11.086	10.977	27.235	27.321
IS$_{0.75}$	11.126	11.019	27.204	27.288
IS$_{0.50}$	11.220	11.224	27.131	27.128

Table 5.4: The RMSE and PSNR measures of the KS and IS$_\alpha$ oracles applied to Fig. 5.3. The images for the KS and IS$_\alpha$ for $\alpha \in \{0.5, 1, 1.5\}$ oracles are shown in Fig. 5.11. The oracles have been evaluated with 10 random lines between elements.

for the KS and IS oracles with Gouraud shaded solutions (Figs. 5.11.*.i) and their respective meshes (Figs. 5.11.*.ii). In Table 5.4, we show the measures of RMSE and PSNR for a set of results obtained with these oracles, including the previously mentioned images.

The results obtained for the scenes tested present an improvement against the classic version but, as in the the case of the TI, we cannot establish a predefined behaviour for the entropic index. For the scenes shown, the tendency is subextensive for Fig. 5.2 and superextensive for Fig. 5.3. The better results are for an index of 0.50 and 1.50, respectively.

5.5 Mutual Information

We consider now a classical oracle based on the smoothness of received radiosity, where an optimal refinement can be expected by directly estimating how well the radiosity $B_j(x)$, received at $x \in A_i$ from A_j, is approximated by a linear combination of the basis functions on A_i. This is achieved by estimating the discretisation error (§2.4.4). Specifically, we select the oracle (2.69) proposed by Lischinski et al. [124]:

$$\rho_i \max\{F_{ij} - \min_{x \in A_i}\{F_{x \to j}\}, \max_{x \in A_i}\{F_{x \to j}\} - F_{ij}\}B_j < \epsilon. \qquad \text{(RS)}$$

The cheapest and most frequently used oracle has been the TP oracle. However, its use results in sub-optimal shadow boundaries and excessive refinement in smoothly illuminated areas receiving a lot of power. The KS and RS oracles were proposed as an alternative for solving this problem. However, the oracle based on kernel smoothness has the problem of unnecessary subdivisions where the kernel is unbounded, and the one based on received radiosity relies on a costly accurate computation of form factors. All in all, the additional cost invested in both smoothness-based oracles, mainly through visibility computations, may not be balanced by the improvements obtained. We will see below how the generalised mutual information can be introduced in this oracle scheme obtaining good results with regard to quality versus cost.

5.5.1 Concept

In the previous TP and KS oracles we have directly applied the HCT entropy in order to obtain kernels based purely on the geometric information content. In order to approximate a good balance between cost and results, now our strategy will be based on the estimate of the discretisation error taking the difference between the continuous and discrete information transfer, or mutual information (5.6), between two elements of the adaptive mesh. The scene discretisation error based on Shannon mutual information has been introduced by Feixas et al. [63] (§2.6.1) and applied to hierarchical radiosity with very good results (2.70).

First of all, analogously to how we proceeded with the previous oracles based on the information content, we need to rewrite the generalised mutual information in order to be able to work at patch level. Let us consider the expression

$$\imath_\alpha(p, q) = \frac{1}{1 - \alpha} \frac{q^\alpha - p^\alpha}{q^{\alpha - 1}}. \qquad (5.17)$$

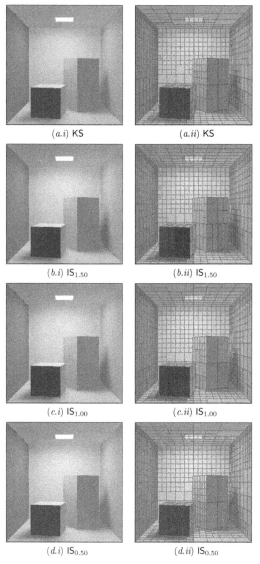

$(a.i)$ KS $\qquad$ $(a.ii)$ KS

$(b.i)$ IS$_{1.50}$ $\qquad$ $(b.ii)$ IS$_{1.50}$

$(c.i)$ IS$_{1.00}$ $\qquad$ $(c.ii)$ IS$_{1.00}$

$(d.i)$ IS$_{0.50}$ $\qquad$ $(d.ii)$ IS$_{0.50}$

Figure 5.11: KS and IS$_{\alpha \in \{0.5,1,1.5\}}$ oracles for the scene in Fig. 5.3. By columns, (i) Gouraud shaded solution and (ii) its final adaptive mesh are shown. The oracles have been evaluated with 10 random lines between elements.

Then, the discrete directed divergence (5.5) can be expressed as $D_\alpha(p,q) = \sum_{i=1}^n \imath_\alpha(p_i, q_i)$ and, consequently, the discrete generalised mutual information (5.6) can be rewritten as

$$I_\alpha(X, Y) = D_\alpha(p_{XY}, p_X q_Y) = \sum_{i=1}^n \sum_{j=1}^m \imath_\alpha(p_{ij}, p_i q_j). \tag{5.18}$$

The transition to continuous measures is straightforward. In the context of a discrete scene information channel (§2.6), the marginal probabilities are $p_X = q_Y = \{a_i\}$ (i.e., relative area) and the conditional $p_{XY} = \{a_i F_{ij}\}$. Then, from (5.18):

Definition 73 *The discrete scene generalised mutual information of S is given by*

$$I_\alpha(S) = \sum_{i \in S} \sum_{j \in S} \imath_\alpha(a_i F_{ij}, a_i a_j). \tag{5.19}$$

It is defined as a measure of the average information transfer in a discrete scene. The term $\imath_\alpha(a_i F_{ij}, a_i a_j)$ can be considered as an element of the symmetric scene generalised mutual information matrix I_α, representing the information transfer between patches i and j.

To compute I_α, the area-to-area sampling (5.10) is used obtaining for each pair of elements

$$\begin{aligned}
I_{\alpha_{ij}}(S) &= \imath_\alpha(a_i F_{ij}, a_i a_j) \\
&= \frac{1}{1-\alpha} \frac{a_i^\alpha a_j^\alpha - a_i^\alpha F_{ij}^\alpha}{a_i^{\alpha-1} a_j^{\alpha-1}} \\
&= \frac{1}{1-\alpha} \left(a_i a_j - a_i \frac{F_{ij}^\alpha}{a_j^{\alpha-1}} \right) \\
&= \frac{1}{1-\alpha} \left(\frac{A_i}{A_\mathrm{T}} \frac{A_j}{A_\mathrm{T}} - \frac{A_i}{A_\mathrm{T}} \frac{A_j}{A_\mathrm{T}} A_\mathrm{T}^\alpha \left(\frac{F_{ij}}{A_j} \right)^\alpha \right) \\
&\approx \frac{1}{1-\alpha} \frac{A_i}{A_\mathrm{T}} \frac{A_j}{A_\mathrm{T}} \left(1 - A_\mathrm{T}^\alpha \left(\frac{1}{|\mathcal{S}_{i \times j}|} \sum_{(x,y) \in \mathcal{S}_{i \times j}} F_{x \leftrightarrow y} \right)^\alpha \right).
\end{aligned} \tag{5.20}$$

This information transfer between two patches can be obtained more accurately with the continuous generalised mutual information between them. The pdfs are $p(x) = q(y) = \frac{1}{A_\mathrm{T}}$ and $p(x,y) = \frac{1}{A_\mathrm{T}} F_{x \leftrightarrow y}$ and, from the discrete form (5.19), we have

Definition 74 *The continuous scene generalised mutual information of S is given by*

$$I_\alpha^\mathrm{c}(S) = \int_A \int_A \imath_\alpha \left(\frac{1}{A_\mathrm{T}} F_{x \leftrightarrow y}, \frac{1}{A_\mathrm{T}^2} \right) \mathrm{d}A_y \mathrm{d}A_x. \tag{5.21}$$

This represents the global information transfer in the continuous scene. We can split the integration domain and for two surface elements i and j we have

$$I_{\alpha_{ij}}^\mathrm{c}(S) = \int_{A_i} \int_{A_j} \imath_\alpha \left(\frac{1}{A_\mathrm{T}} F_{x \leftrightarrow y}, \frac{1}{A_\mathrm{T}^2} \right) \mathrm{d}A_y \mathrm{d}A_x \tag{5.22}$$

that, analogously to the discrete case, expresses the partial contribution of information shared between two patches.

Both continuous expressions, (5.21) and (5.22), can be solved by Monte Carlo integration (§2.2.1).

Thus, taking as pdf $\frac{1}{A_i A_j}$, the last expression (5.22) can be approximated by

$$
\begin{aligned}
I_{\alpha_{ij}}^c(S) &\approx A_i A_j \frac{1}{|\mathcal{S}_{i \times j}|} \sum_{(x,y) \in \mathcal{S}_{i \times j}} \imath_\alpha \left(\frac{1}{A_{\mathrm{T}}} F_{x \leftrightarrow y}, \frac{1}{A_{\mathrm{T}}^2} \right) \\
&= A_i A_j \frac{1}{1-\alpha} \frac{1}{|\mathcal{S}_{i \times j}|} \sum_{(x,y) \in \mathcal{S}_{i \times j}} \left(\frac{1}{A_{\mathrm{T}}^2} - \frac{F_{x \leftrightarrow y}^\alpha}{A_{\mathrm{T}}^{2-\alpha}} \right) \\
&= A_i A_j \frac{1}{A_{\mathrm{T}}^2} \frac{1}{1-\alpha} \left(\left(\frac{1}{|\mathcal{S}_{i \times j}|} \sum_{(x,y) \in \mathcal{S}_{i \times j}} 1 \right) - \left(A_{\mathrm{T}}^\alpha \frac{1}{|\mathcal{S}_{i \times j}|} \sum_{(x,y) \in \mathcal{S}_{i \times j}} F_{x \leftrightarrow y}^\alpha \right) \right) \\
&= \frac{A_i}{A_{\mathrm{T}}} \frac{A_j}{A_{\mathrm{T}}} \frac{1}{1-\alpha} \left(1 - A_{\mathrm{T}}^\alpha \left(\frac{1}{|\mathcal{S}_{i \times j}|} \sum_{(x,y) \in \mathcal{S}_{i \times j}} F_{x \leftrightarrow y}^\alpha \right) \right).
\end{aligned} \tag{5.23}
$$

At this point, we have the discrete and continuous generalised mutual information of the scene, as much global as partial between two surfaces. Both measures, for a determinate entropic index α, can be considered as geometric visibility complexity measures of a scene (§2.7). These mutual information complexity measures are interpreted as the difficulty of discretising a scene: the higher the continuous mutual information, the more difficult it is to obtain an accurate discretisation and probably more refinements are necessary to achieve a predefined precision (§2.6.1).

Definition 75 *The generalised discretisation error of S is given by*

$$
\Delta_\alpha(S) = I_\alpha^c(S) - I_\alpha(S) = \sum_{i \in S} \sum_{j \in S} \Delta_{\alpha_{ij}}(S), \tag{5.24}
$$

where $\Delta_{\alpha_{ij}}(S) = I_{\alpha_{ij}}^c(S) - I_{\alpha_{ij}}(S)$.

This expresses the loss of information transfer in a scene due to the discretisation. The term $\Delta_{\alpha_{ij}}$ gives us the loss of information transfer or the maximum potential gain of information transfer between the elements i and j. Hence this difference can be interpreted as the benefit to be gained by refining and can be used as a decision criterion. It also represents the variation of the radiosity kernel and constitutes the base of the new oracle.

Using (5.20) and (5.23), we obtain

$$
\begin{aligned}
\Delta_{\alpha_{ij}}(S) &\approx \frac{A_i}{A_{\mathrm{T}}} \frac{A_j}{A_{\mathrm{T}}} \frac{1}{1-\alpha} \left(1 - A_{\mathrm{T}}^\alpha \left(\frac{1}{|\mathcal{S}_{i \times j}|} \sum_{(x,y) \in \mathcal{S}_{i \times j}} F_{x \leftrightarrow y}^\alpha \right) \right) \\
&\quad - \frac{A_i}{A_{\mathrm{T}}} \frac{A_j}{A_{\mathrm{T}}} \frac{1}{1-\alpha} \left(1 - A_{\mathrm{T}}^\alpha \left(\frac{1}{|\mathcal{S}_{i \times j}|} \sum_{(x,y) \in \mathcal{S}_{i \times j}} F_{x \leftrightarrow y} \right)^\alpha \right) \\
&= A_i A_j A_{\mathrm{T}}^{\alpha-2} \frac{1}{1-\alpha} \delta_{\alpha_{ij}}(S),
\end{aligned} \tag{5.25}
$$

where

$$
\delta_{\alpha_{ij}}(S) = \left(\frac{1}{|\mathcal{S}_{i \times j}|} \sum_{(x,y) \in \mathcal{S}_{i \times j}} F_{x \leftrightarrow y} \right)^\alpha - \frac{1}{|\mathcal{S}_{i \times j}|} \sum_{(x,y) \in \mathcal{S}_{i \times j}} F_{x \leftrightarrow y}^\alpha. \tag{5.26}
$$

The expression $\Delta_{\alpha_{ij}}$ is nonnegative and, therefore, Δ_α also. The function $f(x^\alpha)$ is convex for $\alpha > 1$ (§D) and using Jensen's inequality (D.3), $\delta_{\alpha_{ij}} \le 0$ but $\Delta_{\alpha_{ij}} \ge 0$ thanks to the factor $1-\alpha$. When $\alpha < 1$, the previous inequalities are reversed and they keep the non-negativity. Observe that $\Delta_{\alpha_{ij}}$ is symmetric for the reciprocity property of the form factors (2.26). From these values, the global discretisation error Δ_α can be computed (5.24). For $\alpha \to 1$, we obtain the particular case of Shannon mutual information

oracle	$view_1$				$view_2$			
	$RMSE_a$	$RMSE_p$	$PSNR_a$	$PSNR_p$	$RMSE_a$	$RMSE_p$	$PSNR_a$	$PSNR_p$
RS	14.925	14.144	24.653	25.119	14.254	13.845	25.052	25.305
$MI_{1.50}$	11.889	11.280	26.628	27.084	13.046	12.473	25.821	26.211
$MI_{1.25}$	10.872	10.173	27.405	27.982	11.903	11.279	26.618	27.086
$MI_{1.00}$	9.998	9.232	28.133	28.825	10.438	9.709	27.758	28.387
$MI_{0.75}$	9.555	8.786	28.526	29.254	10.010	9.257	28.122	28.801
$MI_{0.50}$	9.370	8.568	28.696	29.473	9.548	8.740	28.533	29.300

Table 5.5: The RMSE and PSNR measures of the RS and MI_α oracles applied to Fig. 5.2. The images for the RS and MI_α for $\alpha \in \{0.5, 1, 1.5\}$ oracles are shown in Fig. 5.12 and Fig. 5.13, respectively. The RS and MI oracles have been evaluated with 100 and 10 random lines between elements, respectively.

commented on in §2.6.1 and used in the hierarchical radiosity oracle (2.70). Note the conceptual similarity between $\delta_{\alpha_{ij}}$ (5.26) and δ_{ij} (2.71).

Taking the generalised discretisation error between two patches as the new kernel for our smoothness-based oracle, we have $\tau = \Delta_{\alpha_{ij}}$. To standardise the shape of its expression, we multiply the inequality by the constant $A_T{}^{2-\alpha}(1-\alpha)$:

Definition 76 *The oracle for S in hierarchical radiosity based on generalised mutual information is given by*

$$\rho_i A_i A_j \delta_{\alpha_{ij}} B_j < \epsilon.$$ (MI)

The critical factor is the continuous versus discrete error of information transfer which represents a loss of information due to the discretisation and which must be minimised. The oracle works in this direction looking for an optimum adaptive mesh from the point of view of geometric visibility α-information.

5.5.2   Results

Finally, the setting for the scenes in Fig. 5.2 and Fig. 5.3 of the previous oracles is shown by both RS and MI oracles. We continue to keep the same size for the adaptive mesh and the same cost for the power distribution. As we have said previously (§5.5.1), MI focuses on the calculation of the kernel of the smoothness of received radiosity from another point of view, in order to reduce the cost of RS. Thus, RS has been calculated using 100 lines (10 point-to-patch form factors have been computed with 10 random lines for each one), while MI has been evaluated using only 10 random lines between two elements (for the sake of comparison with IS).

We recall that for Fig. 5.2, we use around 19,000 patches and 2,684,000 rays for the mesh and power distribution, respectively. In Fig. 5.12 we show the results obtained for the RS oracle with a Gouraud shaded solution and with a final adaptive mesh. In Fig. 5.13 we present the behaviour of the MI oracle for the three entropic indexes of 0.5, 1, and 1.5. The final meshes of these results are mapped to Fig. 5.14. As in the previous oracles, in Table 5.5 we show the measures of RMSE and PSNR for these previous images and other entropic indexes with respect to the scene in Fig. 5.2.

Differing from the TI and IS information-theoretic oracles, the improvement of the MI is significantly important with respect to the classic version. Moreover, the behaviour of MI, which is based on generalised discretisation error, denotes a tendency to improve towards the entropic subextensive indexes. It is necessary to take also into account, that the cost for the calculation of the new oracle with respect to RS is one tenth. In fact, for the same cost, the images improve as against any of the previous oracles. Within the values analysed, the best result is obtained for $\alpha = 0.5$ but if the size of the mesh increases (19,875 patches with 6,711,250 rays to distribute the power) and also the accuracy of the calculation of the oracle (20 random lines), the index decreases to 0.25 obtaining a better quantitative and visual result: $(RMSE_a, RMSE_p, PSNR_a, PSNR_p)$ is equal to (8.719, 7,836, 29.322, 30.249) and (8.618, 7,704, 29.423, 30.397) for $view_1$ and $view_2$, respectively (see Fig. 5.15).

With regard to Fig. 5.3, we keep the 129,000 rays for the power distribution and around 1,000 patches for mesh. Similarly to the previous oracles, in Fig. 5.16 we show the images for the RS and MI oracles

Figure 5.12: RS oracle for the test scene in Fig. 5.2: (a) Gouraud shaded solution and (b) its final adaptive mesh. By columns, (i) view$_1$ and (ii) view$_2$ are shown. The oracle has been evaluated with 100 random lines between elements.

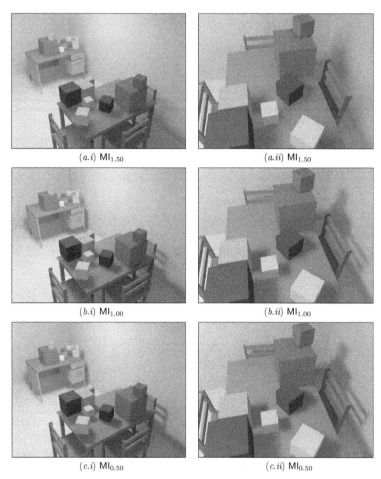

$(a.i)$ $\mathsf{MI}_{1.50}$ $(a.ii)$ $\mathsf{MI}_{1.50}$

$(b.i)$ $\mathsf{MI}_{1.00}$ $(b.ii)$ $\mathsf{MI}_{1.00}$

$(c.i)$ $\mathsf{MI}_{0.50}$ $(c.ii)$ $\mathsf{MI}_{0.50}$

Figure 5.13: Gouraud shaded solution for the MI oracle for the scene in Fig. 5.2. An entropic index of (a) 1.5, (b) 1, and (c) 0.5 has been used. By columns, (i) view$_1$ and (ii) view$_2$ are shown. The respective meshes are shown in Fig. 5.14. The oracle has been evaluated with 10 random lines between elements.

$(a.i)$ MI$_{1.50}$ $(a.ii)$ MI$_{1.50}$

$(b.i)$ MI$_{1.00}$ $(b.ii)$ MI$_{1.00}$

$(c.i)$ MI$_{0.50}$ $(c.ii)$ MI$_{0.50}$

Figure 5.14: Adaptive mesh for the MI oracle for the scene in Fig. 5.2. An entropic index of (a) 1.5, (b) 1, and (c) 0.5 has been used. By columns, (i) view$_1$ and (ii) view$_2$ are shown. The respective Gouraud shaded solutions are shown in Fig. 5.13. The oracle has been evaluated with 10 random lines between elements.

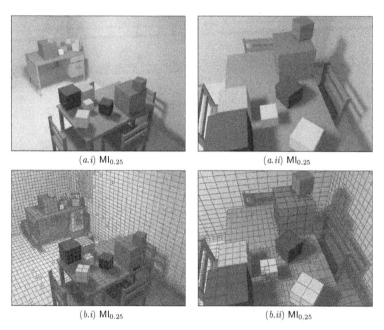

$(a.i)$ $\mathsf{MI}_{0.25}$ $(a.ii)$ $\mathsf{MI}_{0.25}$

$(b.i)$ $\mathsf{MI}_{0.25}$ $(b.ii)$ $\mathsf{MI}_{0.25}$

Figure 5.15: $\mathsf{MI}_{0.25}$ oracle for the scene in Fig. 5.2: (a) Gouraud shaded solution and (b) its final adaptive mesh. By columns, (i) view$_1$ and (ii) view$_2$ are shown. The data (RMSE$_a$, RMSE$_p$, PSNR$_a$, PSNR$_p$) are equal to (i) (8.719, 7,836, 29.322, 30.249) and (ii) (8.618, 7,704, 29.423, 30.397). The oracle has been evaluated with 20 random lines between elements.

oracle	RMSE$_a$	RMSE$_p$	PSNR$_a$	PSNR$_p$
RS	13.198	13.171	25.721	25.738
MI$_{1.50}$	13.162	13.178	25.745	25.734
MI$_{1.25}$	12.011	11.943	26.539	26.588
MI$_{1.00}$	11.175	11.109	27.166	27.217
MI$_{0.75}$	10.810	10.745	27.454	27.507
MI$_{0.50}$	10.361	10.344	27.823	27.837

Table 5.6: The RMSE and PSNR measures of the RS and MI$_\alpha$ oracles applied to Fig. 5.3. The images for the RS and MI$_\alpha$ for $\alpha \in \{0.5, 1, 1.5\}$ oracles are shown in Fig. 5.16. The RS and MI oracles have been evaluated with 100 and 10 random lines between elements, respectively.

oracle	RMSE$_a$	RMSE$_p$	PSNR$_a$	PSNR$_p$
RS	14.768	13.909	24.744	25.265
MI$_{1.50}$	16.529	15.530	23.766	24.307
MI$_{1.25}$	15.199	14.145	24.494	25.119
MI$_{1.00}$	14.958	13.844	24.633	25.306
MI$_{0.75}$	14.802	13.683	24.724	25.407
MI$_{0.50}$	14.679	13.573	24.797	25.477

Table 5.7: The RMSE and PSNR measures of the MI$_\alpha$ oracle applied to Fig. 5.17.a. The image for MI$_{0.5}$ oracle is shown in Fig. 5.17.b. The oracle has been evaluated with 10 random lines between elements.

with Gouraud shaded solutions (Figs. 5.16.$*.i$) and their respective meshes (Figs. 5.16.$*.ii$). In Table 5.6, we show the measures of RMSE and PSNR for a set of results obtained with these oracles, including the previously mentioned images.

For this oracle, in order to analyse its behaviour, we add another set of data in Table 5.7. The reference scene is in Fig. 5.17.a and the meshes are made up of 10,000 patches with 9,268,000 rays to distribute the power. We have kept the cost for the each kind of oracle: 100 and 10 random lines between elements for the RS and MI oracles, respectively. In spite of the biggest work invested by RS, similar values of error and quality are reached in MI for an entropic index of 0.5 (Figs. 5.17.b–c). Note the sequence of improvements in the table of results of each scene with respect to the subextensivity.

5.6   Back over the Information-Theoretic Oracles

At this point, a brief overview of the results is needed. In the previous sections we have presented three new information-theoretic oracles for hierarchical radiosity for solving the problem of illumination in an environment with diffuse surfaces in accordance with the general aims of §5.2 and those particular to each approach: transported information (§5.3), information smoothness (§5.4), and mutual information (§5.5). They have been compared with their classic counterparts: transported power, kernel smoothness, and received radiosity smoothness, respectively.

Observe in the view$_1$ of the test scene in Fig. 5.2, obtained by the information-theoretic oracles, the finer details of the shadow cast on the wall by the chair on the right-hand side and also, the better-defined shadow on the chair on the left-hand side and the one cast by the desk. In view$_2$ we can also see how the new oracles outperform the classic ones, especially in the much more defined shadow of the chair on the right. Note the superior quality mesh created by the smoothness information-theoretic oracles as opposed to the classic ones (e.g., on the table). Comparing our three information-theoretic oracles we conclude that TI is an effective and cheap cost oracle, and that IS gives a very good quality mesh, although they are outperformed, with the same cost, by the MI oracle. In general, we observe a better behaviour of the information-theoretic oracles towards the classic versions, especially for a specific value of entropic index.

We should point out the better behaviour of the MI oracle with respect to the other ones. For

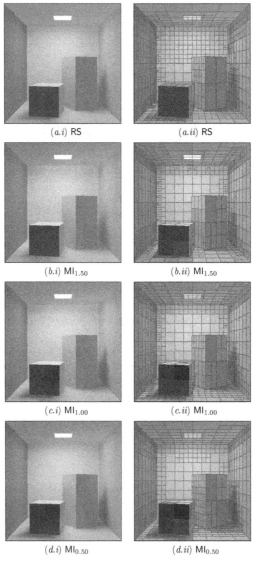

Figure 5.16: RS and $MI_{\alpha \in \{0.5, 1, 1.5\}}$ oracles for the scene in Fig. 5.3. By columns, (i) Gouraud shaded solution and (ii) its final adaptive mesh are shown. The RS and MI oracles have been evaluated with 100 and 10 random lines between elements, respectively.

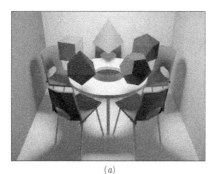

(a)

(b) MI$_{0.50}$

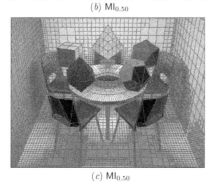

(c) MI$_{0.50}$

Figure 5.17: MI$_{0.50}$ oracle: (a) reference scene obtained with a path-tracing algorithm with 1,024 samples per pixel in a stratified way, (b) Gouraud shaded solution, and (c) its final adaptive mesh. The oracle has been evaluated with 10 random lines between elements.

subextensive indexes ($\alpha < 1$), the oracle also improves the results of its corresponding version in Shannon mutual information ($\alpha \to 1$). We consider the use of the discretisation error based on generalised mutual information instead of the generalised entropy as the key factor for the good results of this oracle. The refinement achieved using the discretisation error is much more accurate than the one obtained from the simple evaluation of the uncertainty among the elements of the mesh. This mutual information based kernel adequately directs the oracle towards the minimum loss of information in the refinement, obtaining an optimum mesh from an α-information point of view. The cost of all the oracles is similar (TI and IS) or even less (MI) than its corresponding classic ones.

The study carried out confirms the feasibility of the information-theoretic oracles, based on the HCT entropy and generalised mutual information, for dealing with the hierarchical radiosity; but it is evident that further studies are necessary to analyse possible correlations between the entropic index and the scene complexity (§2.7.3). On the other hand, characterisations could exist for the scenes (geometric and/or physical) which would enable us to associate them with a specific type of extensivity which would be applicable from the point of view of the oracles.

Summary

Three new refinement criteria based on generalised information-theoretic measures have been introduced for hierarchical radiosity. From the Harvda-Charvát-Tsallis generalised entropy (HCT entropy), the concept of α-*information* for an event appears. The α is called the *entropic index* and characterises a specific system. Associated with the HCT entropy, the generalised mutual information is reviewed.

When these generalised measures are applied to a scene as an information channel, we obtain the measures of discrete scene HCT entropy and discrete/continuous scene generalised mutual information. From the perspective of α-information, the consideration of these measures at patch level brings us the information content (entropy) and information transfer (mutual information) between two elements. When, in the hierarchical radiosity context, we consider these elements as components of an adaptive mesh involved in a transport of energy (source and receiver elements), the aforementioned measures of information make up the kernels of the new oracles. The aim is to create a correspondence between three classic typologies of oracles based on kernels of geometric data and three new kernels based on geometric α-information. The new oracles are made up proportionally to the radiosity of the source element, the reflectance of the receiver element, and the new kernel.

Firstly, we present the *transported information* oracle in correspondence with the transported power oracle. The new kernel considers the α-information content between the source and receiver elements of the hierarchical mesh and the area of the receiver element. In the tests developed, slight improvements with respect to the classic version are shown.

Secondly, we present the *information smoothness* oracle in correspondence with the smoothness-based oracle. The new kernel is based on the variation of the α-information content between the source and receiver elements of the hierarchical mesh and the area of the receiver element. The variation is obtained from the α-information values corresponding to the maximum, minimum, and average point-to-point form factors (from the source element with respect to the receiver element). The results obtained improve on the classic version in all the tests carried out.

And lastly, we present the mutual information oracle, which is based on the generalised discretisation error, in correspondence with the classic smoothness of received radiosity based oracles. This error is calculated from the difference between the continuous and discrete generalised mutual information between two elements of the adaptive mesh. This difference expresses the loss of α-information transfer in a scene due to the discretisation. The results obtained improve on the classic method significantly and become the best of the three options, being better even than the version based on the Shannon mutual information. The best entropic index is obtained with values of subextensivity in all the tests developed.

The concepts and results presented bring solidness to the applicability in hierarchical radiosity of the oracles based on generalised information-theoretic measures. The MI oracle denotes good behaviour in subextensivity and offers the best results. The cost of all the oracles is not higher than the corresponding classic ones. Further work needs to be carried out to find out more details of the relationship between the HCT entropy and the system formed by a scene.

Chapter 6

Refinement Criteria Based on f-Divergences

Just as we have seen in the previous chapters (§2.1, §4, and §5), when sampling a signal we need a criterion to decide whether to take additional samples, albeit within the original domain or within a hierarchical subdivision. The refinement criteria are mainly based on the homogeneity encountered in the samples. Heterogeneity should lead to further sampling, possibly with an adaptive subdivision of the domain. Oracles are then built based on these criteria. Examples in image synthesis of this refinement process have been applied to specific ray-tracing techniques (§4) and radiosity (§5) where, for each of them, we have incorporated new entropy-based methods.

In this chapter, we introduce new refinement criteria based on f-divergences. The introduction of these measures is motivated by the observation that the mutual information-based oracle (2.70) can be rewritten as an f-divergence. f-Divergences are a family of convex functions that possess very remarkable properties. They were introduced by Csiszár [40] and Ali and Silvey [3] as measures of discrimination or distance between probability distributions and have been successfully used in image processing and several engineering areas [150, 118, 95, 165].

Our purpose is to demonstrate the usefulness of f-divergences in computer graphics by applying them to defining new refinement criteria for the techniques of the previous chapters: hierarchical radiosity (§6.3) and adaptive sampling in ray-tracing (§6.4). We consider that some divergences are perfectly fitted as homogeneity measures, when we consider how distant the distribution of the samples is with respect to the uniform distribution. We will see how, compared with classic refinement criteria, the f-divergence-based ones give significantly better results. Previously, we give a brief introduction to divergence measures (§6.1) and in particular to the f-divergences (§6.2).

6.1 Divergence Measures

In this section, we establish the semantics of divergence measures (§6.1.1) and we present three specific types of them (§6.1.2).

6.1.1 Concept

What does "divergence" mean? One brief definition for divergence is *"a deviation from a course or standard"* [134]. In general, the difference in shades of meaning between words such as difference, dissimilarity, distance, and divergence are so subtle that we end up considering them practically synonyms in every day language. In a statistical context, the objective is to measure the level of separation between two elements of a sampling. Depending on the properties that make up the measure, it can be qualified in one sense or another [77, 23, 129].

Let X be a nonempty set and $d : X^2 \to \mathbb{R}$ a function. Then, d is a measure of

Difference If it fulfils

- ○ *Symmetry:* $d(x,y) = d(y,x) \quad \forall x, y \in X$
- ○ *Minimum difference:* $d(x,y) \geq d(x,x) \quad \forall x, y \in X$

Dissimilarity If it is a difference measure which fulfils

- ○ *Non-negativity:* $d(x,y) \geq 0 \quad \forall x, y \in X$
- ○ *Self-similarity:* $d(x,x) = 0 \quad \forall x \in X$

Distance Also called a *metric*, if it is a dissimilarity measure which fulfils

- ○ *Defined:* $d(x,y) = 0 \Rightarrow x = y \quad \forall x, y \in X$
- ○ *Triangle inequality:* $d(x,y) + d(y,z) \geq d(x,z) \quad \forall x, y, z \in X$

When the objective of the measure is to reflect the discrepancy or difference between two probability distributions, it is called divergence[1] [24]:

Definition 77 *Let $\mathcal{X}$ be a countable observation space with $n > 1$ elements and $\mathcal{P}$ the set of all the possible probability distributions of $\mathcal{X}$. Then, $D : \mathcal{P}^2 \to \mathbb{R}^+ \cup \{0\}$ is a divergence if, for all $(p,q) \in \mathcal{P}^2$, it fulfils:*

- ○ $D(\{p_1, \ldots, p_n\}, \{q_1, \ldots, q_n\})$ *is a continuous function of its $2 \cdot n$ variables.*
- ○ $D(p,q)$ *is invariant under the permutations of the pairs (p_i, q_i) for $i \in \{1, \ldots, n\}$.*
- ○ $D(\{p_1, \ldots, p_n, 0\}, \{q_1, \ldots, q_n, 0\}) = D(p,q)$.
- ○ $D(p,q) \geq 0$.
- ○ $D(p,q) = 0 \Leftrightarrow p = q$.

Note that if a divergence were symmetric it would be equivalent to a defined dissimilarity which only lacks the triangle inequality to attain the category of metric.

6.1.2   Divergence Classes

With the previous definition of divergence, it is possible to obtain a large set of divergence measures $D(p,q)$. In general, the problem consists in discerning the suitable measures for every specific case. Convexity is a desirable property (D.1). A generalisation of it, Jensen's inequality (D.2), is widely used in mathematics, information theory, and different engineering areas as a kernel of divergence measures. For example, it has been successfully applied to image registration [89] and DNA segmentation [16].

We now see particular examples of divergences (following Pardo [155]). From the perspective of information theory, the importance of the information divergence, or Kullback-Leibler distance, is objectively accepted. In mathematical statistics, the same role is played by the chi-square divergence. Also, in convex analysis, arithmetic and geometric means are used in the arithmetic-geometric divergence. In the probability theory, the Vasershtein-Ornstein divergence plays an important role together with L_α-norm divergence, which is also very useful in statistics and other mathematical areas (see Table 6.1).

These examples and many others are special cases of a kind of divergence measure which obeys the scheme[2]

$$D(p,q) = \sum_{x \in \mathcal{X}} \varphi(p(x), q(x)) \tag{6.1}$$

for a given real function $\varphi(u,v)$ of positive variables u, v. This function is assumed to be extended to $[0, \infty) \times [0, \infty)$ taking:

$$\varphi(0,0) = 0 \qquad \varphi(0,v) = \lim_{u \to 0^+} \varphi(u,v) \qquad \varphi(u,0) = \lim_{v \to 0^+} \varphi(u,v) \tag{6.2}$$

---

[1] Without loss of generality, divergences are limited to discrete probability distributions. See §B and §D for probability and convexity concepts, respectively.
[2] In this context, we keep the usual functional notation for the probability distributions.

divergence	field	definition
information	information theory	$I(p,q) = \sum_{x \in \mathcal{X}} p(x) \log \frac{p(x)}{q(x)}$
chi-squared	statistics	$\chi^2(p,q) = \sum_{x \in \mathcal{X}} \frac{(p(x)-q(x))^2}{q(x)}$
arithmetic-geometric	convex analysis	$AG(p,q) = \sum_{x \in \mathcal{X}} \ln \frac{(p(x)+q(x))/2}{\sqrt{p(x)q(x)}}$
Vasershtein-Ornstein	probability theory	$VO(p,q) = 1 - \sum_{x \in \mathcal{X}} \min\{p(x), q(x)\}$
L_α-norm	mathematics	$L_\alpha(p,q) = \sum_{x \in \mathcal{X}} |p(x) - q(x)|^\alpha \quad \alpha \in \{1, 2\}$

Table 6.1: A subset of useful divergences with its most common fields of application.

for $u, v > 0$ where the limits may be infinite.

This scheme has been introduced in information theory for some classes of functions $\varphi(u,v)$ where $(u,v) \in [0,1]^2$. An important case is the kind of divergences that can be generated with the help of a convex function $f : (0,\infty) \to (-\infty,\infty)$ (§D), extended to $[0,\infty] \to (-\infty,\infty]$ by the continuity rules:

$$f(0) = \lim_{x \to 0^+} f(x) \qquad f(\infty) = \lim_{x \to \infty} f(x). \tag{6.3}$$

Let $\mathcal{F}$ be the set of these functions f which are twice differentiable with continuous derivatives satisfying $f(1) = 0$ and $f''(1) > 0$. Using $f \in \mathcal{F}$, the following divergences are defined in accordance with (6.1):

Csiszár divergences $\varphi(u,v) = vf\left(\frac{u}{v}\right)$

Bregman divergences $\varphi(u,v) = f(u) - f(v) - f'(v)(u - v)$

Burbea-Rao divergences $\varphi(u,v) = \frac{f(u)+f(v)}{2} - f\left(\frac{u+v}{2}\right)$

These three kinds are partially overlapping [154]. We focus our attention on Csiszár divergences [40, 41], also called *f-divergences* and denoted by $D_f(p,q)$.

6.2 *f*-Divergences

f-Divergences are based on convex functions and were independently introduced by Csiszár [40], and Ali and Silvey [3]. These measures have been applied to different areas, such as medical image registration [165] and classification and retrieval [95], among others. We introduce, in this section, the definition, properties, and particular instances which we will use in the following sections [122, 147]. Accordingly §6.1.2, we take $\varphi(u,v) = vf\left(\frac{u}{v}\right)$ and

Definition 78 *Let $(p,q) \in \mathcal{P}^2$ and $f \in \mathcal{F}$. The f-divergence of the probability distributions p and q is given by*

$$D_f(p,q) = \sum_{x \in \mathcal{X}} q(x) f\left(\frac{p(x)}{q(x)}\right). \tag{6.4}$$

By extension rules (6.2), for $p, q > 0$

$$0f\left(\frac{0}{0}\right) = 0 \qquad qf\left(\frac{0}{q}\right) = qf(0) \qquad 0f\left(\frac{p}{0}\right) = p \lim_{y \to \infty} \frac{f(y)}{y}. \tag{6.5}$$

Then, $D_f(p,q)$ is well defined as a divergence measure [238]. Two important properties are:

- $D_f(p,q)$ is convex on (p,q).
  If (p,q) and (p',q') are two pairs of probability distributions, then

$$\lambda D_f(p,q) + (1-\lambda)D_f(p',q') \geq D_f(\lambda p + (1-\lambda)p', \lambda q + (1-\lambda)q'). \tag{6.6}$$

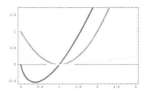

Figure 6.1:   Plot for $x \in [0,3]$ of three strictly convex functions: $u \log u$ (blue), $(u-1)^2$ (red), and $\frac{1}{2}(\sqrt{u}-1)^2$ (green). The shared intersection is $f(1) = 0$. From these functions, the Kullback-Leibler, chi-square, and the Hellinger f-divergences are obtained, respectively.

- Uniqueness.
  If $f, g \in \mathcal{F}$, then $D_f(p,q) = D_g(p,q) \Leftrightarrow \exists r \in \mathbb{R}.\ f(u) - g(u) = r(u-1)$.

f-Divergences have been studied in depth. The Research Group in Mathematical Inequalities and Applications[3] deserves a special mention since over recent years its members have made many contributions to this area [149, 50, 11, 147]. f-Divergences can be grouped together in terms of their convex functions. Considering the classification of Österreicher [147], we have the following types: χ^α-divergences, (symmetrised) dichotomy, Matusita's divergences, elementary divergences, Puri-Vincze Divergences, and Divergences of Arimoto-type. Within each type, other families of f-divergences can be created. We should mention particularly the subtype of f^α-divergences (dichotomy class) presented by Liese and Vajda [122].

Next, we select three of the most important f-divergences [50, 72, 147], called "distances" in the literature. They are built up from the convex functions in Fig. 6.1:

Kullback-Leibler $f(u) = u \log u$:

$$D_{\mathrm{KL}}(p,q) = \sum_{x \in \mathcal{X}} p(x) \log \frac{p(x)}{q(x)}. \tag{6.7}$$

Introduced by Kullback and Leibler [113], it corresponds to the relative entropy or Kullback-Leibler distance (2.77). Based on continuity arguments, $0 \log \frac{0}{q(x)} = 0$ for all $q(x)$, and $p(x) \log \frac{p(x)}{0} = \infty$ for all $p(x) > 0$ (6.2). Hence, the measure takes values in $[0, \infty]$. It is not a metric, since it is not symmetric and does not satisfy triangle inequality but, despite of this, it has many useful properties [171, 37, 72]. A square root version of Kullback-Leibler divergence has been used by Yang and Barron [253]. In Fig. $6.2.a$ we show the behaviour of this divergence by means of the contribution of a pair $(p(x), q(x))$. The maximum contribution is ∞ in $(p(x), 0)$, and the minimum is $-(e \ln 2)^{-1} \approx -0.531$ in $(\frac{1}{e}, 1)$. The contribution is null for any pair where $p(x) = 0$ or $p(x) = q(x)$. Note the relevance which the divergence takes with respect to p.

Chi-square $f(u) = (u-1)^2$:

$$D_{\chi^2}(p,q) = \sum_{x \in \mathcal{X}} \frac{(p(x) - q(x))^2}{q(x)}. \tag{6.8}$$

Defined by Pearson [160][4], this measure takes values in $[0, \infty]$ due to the limit when $q(x) = 0$ (6.2). It is not symmetric. Reiss [171] defined a divergence using the square root of D_{χ^2}. In Fig. $6.2.b$ we show the same representation as in the previous divergence. The maximum contribution is also ∞ in $(p(x), 0)$, but the minimum is 0 and it is attained in all the pairs where $p(x) = q(x)$. Observe that, even though a strong relevance with respect to p is maintained, the values of q take on more importance than in the case of D_{KL}.

---

[3] Founded in 1998 at Victoria University, Melbourne, Australia. It is chaired by professor Sever S. Dragomir and now boasts over 800 members worldwide. They publish regularly a Research Report Collection and the Journal of Inequalities in Pure and Applied Mathematics (http://rgmia.vu.edu.au).

[4] The history of this measure can be found in Liese and Vajda [122].

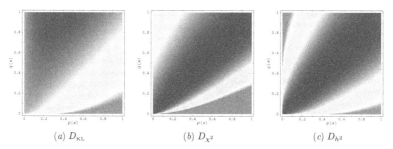

(a) D_{KL} (b) D_{χ^2} (c) D_{h^2}

Figure 6.2: Density maps of the contribution of a pair $(p(x), q(x))$ for all $x \in \mathcal{X}$: (a) D_{KL}, (b) D_{χ^2}, and (c) D_{h^2}.

Hellinger $f(u) = \frac{1}{2}(\sqrt{u} - 1)^2$:

$$D_{h^2}(p, q) = \frac{1}{2} \sum_{x \in \mathcal{X}} \left(\sqrt{p(x)} - \sqrt{q(x)} \right)^2. \tag{6.9}$$

The origins are in Hellinger [94][5]. This symmetric measure takes values in $[0, 1]$ due to the normalisation factor of $\frac{1}{2}$. If it is omitted in f, we obtain the general Hellinger form $2D_{h^2}$. The quantity $1 - D_{h^2}$ is called the Hellinger affinity, a measure popularised by Kakutani [108] who also applied the square root to the general form of Hellinger obtaining a metric [231] (the normalisation factor is $\frac{1}{\sqrt{2}}$). In Fig. 6.2.c, the contribution of each pair is shown. The maximum contribution is $\frac{1}{2}$ in $(1, 0)$ and $(0, 1)$ and the minimum is 0 when $p(x) = q(x)$. Note how the relevance between p and q has balanced out due to the symmetry.

However, none of the above f-divergences are true distances. In Österreicher [148] there is a discussion about which f-divergences have a metric behaviour. Gibbs and Su [72] provide a summary of bounds between probability metrics and distances. Three relationships between the f-divergences presented are (Fig. 6.3):

○ $D_{h^2}(p, q) \leq \frac{1}{2} D_{\mathrm{KL}}(p, q)$ [171]

○ $D_{h^2}(p, q) \leq \sqrt{D_{\chi^2}(p, q)}$ [171]

○ $D_{\mathrm{KL}}(p, q) \leq \log(1 + D_{\chi^2}(p, q))$ [72]

Figure 6.3: Bounds between D_{KL}, D_{χ^2}, and D_{h^2}, where $D_f \xrightarrow{h} D_g$ means $D_f(p, q) \leq h(D_f(p, q))$. Credit: Adapted from Gibbs and Su [72].

6.3 *f*-Divergences in Radiosity

In this section, new refinement criteria based on f-divergences are introduced for hierarchical radiosity (object-space approach). For comparison purposes, they have been applied in the same framework as in the entropy-based refinement criteria for hierarchical radiosity (§5).

6.3.1 Method

Analysing the mutual information-based oracle $\rho_i \delta_{ij} B_j < \epsilon$ (2.70) [63] we observe that it can be rewritten from a Kullback-Leibler distance. In fact, the kernel of the oracle is based on the mutual information, which at the same time is defined as a the Kullback-Leibler distance (2.79) and which, in accordance with (6.7), belongs to the f-divergences family. In order to obtain the new expression, we need to make the following considerations:

---

[5] Historical references can be found in Liese and Vajda [122] and Le Cam and Yang [115].

- Let $|\mathcal{S}_{i \times j}| = N_{\mathrm{s}}$ be the number of samples of the area sampling form factor computation.
- Let $\widehat{F} = \sum_{k=1}^{N_{\mathrm{s}}} F_{x_k \leftrightarrow y_k}$ be the form factor estimation where $(x_k, y_k) \in \mathcal{S}_{i \times j}$ ($\widehat{F} \approx \frac{F_{ji}}{A_i} = \frac{F_{ij}}{A_j}$).
- Let $p = \{ p_k = \frac{F_{x_k \leftrightarrow y_k}}{\widehat{F}} \mid 1 \le k \le N_{\mathrm{s}} \}$ be the probability distribution given for the contribution of every sample to $\widehat{F}$.

Note that $\operatorname{avg}_{1 \le k \le N_{\mathrm{s}}} \{ p_k \} = \frac{1}{N_{\mathrm{s}}}$. Then, from the discretisation error (2.71)

$$\delta_{ij} \approx \frac{A_i A_j}{A_{\mathrm{T}}} \left(\frac{1}{|\mathcal{S}_{i \times j}|} \left(\sum_{(x,y) \in \mathcal{S}_{i \times j}} F_{x \leftrightarrow y} \log F_{x \leftrightarrow y} \right) \right.$$
$$\left. - \left(\frac{1}{|\mathcal{S}_{i \times j}|} \sum_{(x,y) \in \mathcal{S}_{i \times j}} F_{x \leftrightarrow y} \right) \log \left(\frac{1}{|\mathcal{S}_{i \times j}|} \sum_{(x,y) \in \mathcal{S}_{i \times j}} F_{x \leftrightarrow y} \right) \right), \tag{6.10}$$

we can rewrite

$$\delta_{ij} \approx \frac{A_i A_j}{A_{\mathrm{T}}} \left(\operatorname{avg}_{1 \le k \le N_{\mathrm{s}}} \{ F_{x_k \leftrightarrow y_k} \log F_{x_k \leftrightarrow y_k} \} - \operatorname{avg}_{1 \le k \le N_{\mathrm{s}}} \{ F_{x_k \leftrightarrow y_k} \} \log \operatorname{avg}_{1 \le k \le N_{\mathrm{s}}} \{ F_{x_k \leftrightarrow y_k} \} \right) \tag{6.11}$$

$$= \frac{A_i A_j}{A_{\mathrm{T}}} \widehat{F} \left(\operatorname{avg}_{1 \le k \le N_{\mathrm{s}}} \{ p_k \log p_k \} - \operatorname{avg}_{1 \le k \le N_{\mathrm{s}}} \{ p_k \} \log \operatorname{avg}_{1 \le k \le N_{\mathrm{s}}} \{ p_k \} \right) \tag{6.12}$$

$$= \frac{A_i A_j}{A_{\mathrm{T}}} \widehat{F} \left(\operatorname{avg}_{1 \le k \le N_{\mathrm{s}}} p_k \log p_k - \frac{1}{N_{\mathrm{s}}} \log \frac{1}{N_{\mathrm{s}}} \right)$$

$$= \frac{A_i A_j}{A_{\mathrm{T}} N_{\mathrm{s}}} \widehat{F} \left(\left(\sum_{1 \le k \le N_{\mathrm{s}}} p_k \log p_k \right) - \log \frac{1}{N_{\mathrm{s}}} \right)$$

$$= \frac{A_i A_j}{A_{\mathrm{T}} N_{\mathrm{s}}} \widehat{F} \, D_{\mathrm{KL}}(p, q), \tag{6.13}$$

where $q = \{ q_k = \frac{1}{N_{\mathrm{s}}} \mid 1 \le k \le N_{\mathrm{s}} \}$ is the uniform distribution.

This fact suggests that we try other f-divergences in the kernel of the refinement oracle. These measures will give us the distance of the distribution of the point-to-point form factors, p, with respect to the uniform distribution, q. Thus, the Kullback-Leibler (6.7), chi-square (6.8), and Hellinger (6.9) distances have been tested. The Kullback-Leibler-based oracle has already been studied in [63, 60] from an information-theoretic perspective.

Definition 79 *Three oracles for hierarchical radiosity, based on their respective f-divergences, are given by*

- *Kullback-Leibler divergence*

$$\rho_i A_i A_j \widehat{F} \, D_{\mathrm{KL}}(p, q) B_j < \epsilon \tag{KL}$$

- *Chi-square divergence*

$$\rho_i A_i A_j \widehat{F} \, \chi^2(p, q) B_j < \epsilon \tag{CS}$$

- *Hellinger divergence*

$$\rho_i A_i A_j \widehat{F} \, D_{h^2}^2(p, q) B_j < \epsilon \tag{HL}$$

Observe that the constants $\frac{1}{A_{\mathrm{T}}}$ and $\frac{1}{N_{\mathrm{s}}}$ have been removed since they are specific constants for each scene and are implicit in the threshold.

It is important to note that the expression between parenthesis in (6.11) corresponds to Jensen's inequality (D.3) with $f(x) = x \log x$ and $x \in p$. Moreover, we can also see that expression (6.12) is equal to the first term of the log-sum inequality (D.5), taking $a_i = p_k$, $b_i = 1$, and $n = N_{\mathrm{s}}$. Thus, $\delta_{ij} \ge 0$.

(i) KL   (ii) KL

Figure 6.4: **KL** oracle for the scene in Fig. 5.2.i: (i) Gouraud shaded solution and (ii) its final adaptive mesh. The oracle has been evaluated with 10 random lines between elements.

6.3.2 Results

For comparative effects, the kernel-smoothness-based oracle,

$$\rho_i \max\{F_{ij}^{\max} - F_{ij}^{\mathrm{avg}}, F_{ij}^{\mathrm{avg}} - F_{ij}^{\min}\}A_j B_j < \epsilon, \tag{KS}$$

is chosen as a representative of the oracles which work evaluating the variation of the radiosity kernel between a pair of elements (2.68). This oracle and the f-divergence-based oracles have been implemented on top of the hierarchical Monte Carlo radiosity method (§2.4.3). It should be noted that our oracles can be used with any hierarchical radiosity method.

In Fig. 6.4 we show a general view of the test scene (Fig. 5.2.i) obtained with the **KL** oracle. The left image (i) shows the Gouraud shaded solution, while the right one (ii) corresponds to the subdivision obtained. Each oracle has been evaluated with the same general parameters that in §5: $N_s = 10$ random lines between the corresponding pair of elements; an average of 2,684,000 rays to distribute the power have been cast for each solution; and the ϵ parameter has been tuned so that the meshes obtained have approximately 19,000 patches in all the methods.

For another view of the test scene (Fig. 5.2.ii), we present the results obtained with the f-divergence-based oracles **KL**, **CS**, and **HL** (Figs. 6.5.a–c, respectively) and the **KS** oracle (Fig. 6.6.a). We can see how the f-divergence-based oracles outperform the **KS** one, working the more complex light zones better and obtaining an improved sharpness in the objects. The meshes created are of higher quality and their precision in the corners and in the transitions of light show this feature. On the other hand, comparing our three f-divergence oracles we conclude that, although they exhibit a similar quality, the **KL** one is slightly better. For instance, observe that the shadows on the table are more defined. A possible explanation for this better behaviour could be that the **KL** oracle, unlike the other ones, meets the conditions of Jensen's inequality (D.3). This confers a distinct theoretical advantage on this oracle.

From the above, one could be tempted to use Jensen's inequality alone as a kernel for a refinement oracle. We have experimented with the function $f(x) = x^2$, which when substituted in Jensen's inequality, corresponds to the variance (B.1). Thus, substituting $F_{x_k \leftrightarrow y_k} \log F_{x_k \leftrightarrow y_k}$ by $F_{x_k \leftrightarrow y_k}^2$ in (6.11), the variance-based oracle is given by

$$\rho_i A_i A_j \widehat{F}^2 V(p,q) B_j < \epsilon, \tag{VT}$$

where $V(p,q) = \mathrm{avg}_{1 \leq k \leq N_s}\{p_k^2\} - \left(\frac{1}{N_s}\right)^2$. The results obtained are presented in Fig. 6.6.b, showing the inadequacy of this function.

In Table 6.2, the results of the previous methods are evaluated with the RMSE and PSNR measures, both for the two views in Fig. 5.2. The improvement with regard to the **KS** and **VT** is reflected and the results of the **KL** oracle are noteworthy.

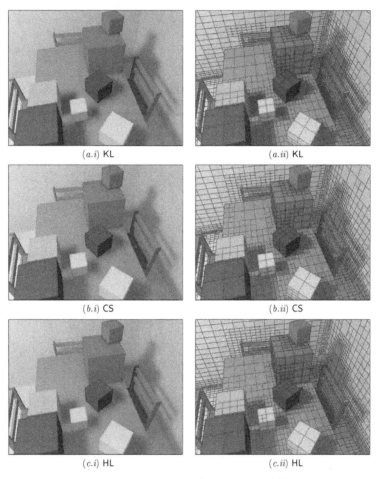

$(a.i)$ KL $(a.ii)$ KL

$(b.i)$ CS $(b.ii)$ CS

$(c.i)$ HL $(c.ii)$ HL

Figure 6.5:   The view$_2$ of the scene in Fig. 5.2.ii for comparison of f-divergence-based oracles, (a) Kullback-Leibler (KL), (b) chi-square (CS), and (c) Hellinger (HL), versus KS and VT ones (Fig. 6.6). By columns, (i) Gouraud shaded solution and (ii) its final adaptive mesh. The oracles have been evaluated with 10 random lines between elements.

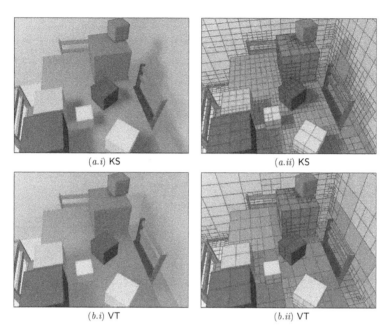

Figure 6.6: The view$_2$ of the scene in Fig. 5.2.ii for comparison of (a) kernel-smoothness-based (KS) and (b) variance-based (VT) oracles versus f-divergence-based ones (Fig. 6.5). By columns, (i) Gouraud shaded solution and (ii) its final adaptive mesh. The oracles have been evaluated with 10 random lines between elements.

oracle	view$_1$				view$_2$			
	RMSE$_a$	RMSE$_p$	PSNR$_a$	PSNR$_p$	RMSE$_a$	RMSE$_p$	PSNR$_a$	PSNR$_p$
KL	9.475	8.698	28.599	29.342	9.712	8.956	28.385	29.088
CS	10.097	9.355	28.047	28.710	10.556	9.825	27.661	28.284
HL	9.990	9.217	28.139	28.839	10.404	9.687	27.787	28.407
KS	13.791	13.128	25.339	25.767	15.167	14.354	24.513	24.991
VT	16.414	15.898	23.826	24.104	17.829	17.378	23.108	23.331

Table 6.2: The RMSE and PSNR measures of the f-divergence-based, KS, and VT oracles applied to Fig. 5.2. A set of images are shown in Fig. 6.4 (KL), Fig. 6.5 (KL, CS, and HL), and Fig. 6.6 (KS and VT). The oracles have been evaluated with 10 random lines between elements.

6.4 f-Divergences in Adaptive Sampling for Ray-Tracing

In this section, we apply the f-divergences to the refinement criteria based on ray-tracing (pixel-driven approach). To do this, we incorporate the divergences into the adaptive sampling scheme using the same basic idea as in hierarchical radiosity (§6.3) but considering the luminance information instead of the geometric information of the form factors. Therefore, we evaluate the homogeneity of a region of the image plane in accordance with the divergence between its luminance distribution and the uniform distribution. To make the comparison easier, we use the same framework as in the entropy-based refinement criteria for ray-tracing (§4).

6.4.1   Method

The f-divergences defined in §6.2 will be used to evaluate the heterogeneity of a set of samples in a region. The scheme used is the following:

1. A first batch of $N_{\mathrm{s}}^{\mathrm{p}}$ samples is cast through a pixel and the corresponding luminances $L_{i \in \{1,\ldots,N_{\mathrm{s}}^{\mathrm{p}}\}}$ are obtained. For an sRGB colour system, the luminance corresponds to the value of Y in (2.53) [32].

2. The f-divergences $D_f(p,q)$ are taken between the normalised distribution of the obtained luminances,

$$p = \{ p_i = \frac{L_i}{\sum_{j=1}^{N_{\mathrm{s}}^{\mathrm{p}}} L_j} \mid 1 \leq i \leq N_{\mathrm{s}}^{\mathrm{p}} \}, \tag{6.14}$$

and the uniform distribution $q = \{ q_i = \frac{1}{N_{\mathrm{s}}^{\mathrm{p}}} \mid 1 \leq i \leq N_{\mathrm{s}}^{\mathrm{p}} \}$.

3. The refinement criterion, given by

$$\frac{1}{N_{\mathrm{s}}^{\mathrm{p}}} \overline{L} \, D_f(p,q) < \epsilon \tag{6.15}$$

is evaluated, where D_f represents the Kullback-Leibler, chi-square, or Hellinger divergences, $\overline{L}$ is the average luminance

$$\overline{L} = \frac{1}{N_{\mathrm{s}}^{\mathrm{p}}} \sum_{i=1}^{N_{\mathrm{s}}^{\mathrm{p}}} L_i, \tag{6.16}$$

and ϵ is a predefined threshold for the refinement test. The divergence measure $D_f(p,q)$ in the kernel plays the role of a contrast. Note that to assign an importance to this value, we weight it with the average luminance (6.16), as in Glassner's version of classic contrast [74] (§2.1.4), used also in the method CC in §4.4.5. Division by the number of samples $N_{\mathrm{s}}^{\mathrm{p}}$ in (6.15) ensures that the refinement process stops.

4. Successive batches of $N_{\mathrm{s}}^{\mathrm{p}}$ rays are cast until the result of the test is true and no more refinement is necessary.

The new criteria give good visual results, but the RMSE obtained in our tests (see Table 6.3), although better than for the classic contrast, is higher than with the confidence test criterion ((2.11) and CT in §4.4.5). Our next logical step was to try the square root of Hellinger divergence, as it is a true metric. The results obtained were very encouraging and, by analogy, we extended the experimentation to the square root of the other divergences[6]. The results also improved the previous ones and were also better than in the confidence test case. The square root versions of this set of f-divergences have already been used previously in statistics. Thus,

Definition 80 *Three refinement criteria for adaptive ray-tracing, based on their respective f-divergences, are given by*

---

[6] Also used in other fields [171, 253, 231].

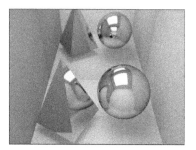

Figure 6.7: Test scene (Fig. 4.11) for the ray-tracing comparison in Fig. 6.8 and Fig. 6.9, obtained with a path-tracing algorithm with 1,024 samples per pixel in a stratified way.

- *Square root of Kullback-Leibler divergence*

$$\frac{1}{N_s^p} \overline{L} D_{\mathrm{KL}}^{\frac{1}{2}}(p,q) < \epsilon \qquad\qquad (\mathsf{KL}^{\frac{1}{2}})$$

- *Square root of chi-square divergence*

$$\frac{1}{N_s^p} \overline{L} D_{\chi^2}^{\frac{1}{2}}(p,q) < \epsilon \qquad\qquad (\mathsf{CS}^{\frac{1}{2}})$$

- *Square root of Hellinger divergence*

$$\frac{1}{N_s^p} \overline{L} D_{h^2}^{\frac{1}{2}}(p,q) < \epsilon \qquad\qquad (\mathsf{HL}^{\frac{1}{2}})$$

6.4.2   Results

In Fig. 6.8 and Fig. 6.9 we present comparative results with different techniques for the test scene in Fig. 6.7. The following two methods are compared with the three f-divergence-based criteria ($\mathsf{KL}^{\frac{1}{2}}$, $\mathsf{CS}^{\frac{1}{2}}$, and $\mathsf{HL}^{\frac{1}{2}}$ of Def. 80):

- CC: Classic contrast (2.6) of the luminance weighted with the respective importance $\overline{L}$.
- CT: Confidence test with a confidence level of $\alpha = 0.1$ and a tolerance $t = 0.025$ (see (2.11), §C, and §4.4.5).

In order to evaluate their behaviour, the images are generated by a similar process to that of adaptive sampling ray-tracing in §4.3. Clearly, all the methods are directly applicable to adaptive sampling schemes such as that presented in §4.4.1. In all the methods, 8 initial rays are cast in a stratified way at each pixel to compute the contrast measures for the refinement decision, and 8 additional rays are successively added until the condition of the criterion is met. An implementation of classic path-tracing with next event estimator was used to compute all images. The parameters were tuned so that all five test images were obtained with a similar average number of rays per pixel ($N_s^p = 60$) and a similar computational cost. The reconstruction method applied is the piecewise-continuous image (2.16) with box filter (2.1). Finally, the pixel value is the reconstructed signal average at pixel domain.

The resulting images are shown in Figs. 6.8.*.*i* (CC and CT) and Figs. 6.9.*.*i* ($\mathsf{KL}^{\frac{1}{2}}$, $\mathsf{CS}^{\frac{1}{2}}$, and $\mathsf{HL}^{\frac{1}{2}}$), with the sampling density maps in Figs. 6.8.*.*ii* and Figs. 6.9.*.*ii*, respectively. The analysis of the critical points of the images shows how our sampling scheme performs the best. Observe, for instance, the reduced noise in the shadows cast by the objects. Observe also the detail of the shadow of the sphere reflected on the pyramid.

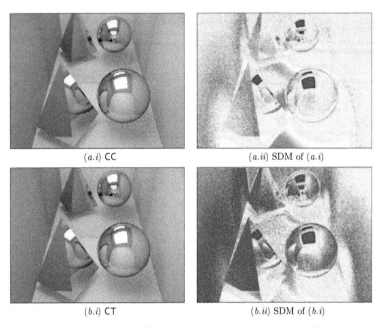

(*a.i*) CC   (*a.ii*) SDM of (*a.i*)

(*b.i*) CT   (*b.ii*) SDM of (*b.i*)

Figure 6.8: Images of the test scene (Fig. 6.7) obtained with an adaptive sampling scheme based on (*a*) classic contrast (CC) and (*b*) confidence test (CT) methods. By columns, (*i*) shows the resulting images and (*ii*) the sampling density maps of (*i*). The average number of rays per pixel is 60 in all the methods.Compare with the images in Fig. 6.9.

method	criterion	RMSE$_a$	RMSE$_p$	PSNR$_a$	PSNR$_p$
Classic	Contrast (CC)	6.157	6.126	32.344	32.387
	Confidence test (CT)	5.194	5.174	33.822	33.855
f-divergences	Kullback-Leibler (KL)	5.508	5.553	33.311	33.241
	chi-square (CS)	5.414	5.452	33.461	33.400
	Hellinger (HL)	5.807	5.862	32.852	32.770
Square root of f-divergences	Kullback-Leibler (KL$^{\frac{1}{2}}$)	4.824	4.793	34.463	34.519
	chi-square (CS$^{\frac{1}{2}}$)	4.772	4.736	34.557	34.623
	Hellinger (HL$^{\frac{1}{2}}$)	4.595	4.560	34.884	34.951

Table 6.3: The RMSE and PSNR measures of the CC, CT, and f-divergence-based refinement criteria applied to Fig. 6.7. The images for the CC and CT methods are shown in Fig. 6.8, and for the f-divergence-based ones, in Fig. 6.9. The average number of samples per pixel is 60 in all the methods.

Comparison of the SDMs shows a better discrimination of complex regions of the scene in the three divergence cases against the classic contrast and confidence test cases. This explains the better results obtained by our approach. On the other hand, the confidence test approach also performs better than the classic contrast-based method. Its SDM also explains why it performs better than the contrast-based. However, it is unable to suitably render the reflected shadows under the mirrored pyramid and sphere with precision.

In Table 6.3, we show the RMSE and PSNR of the images obtained with classic (Figs. 6.8.*.i), f-divergence, and square root of f-divergence (Figs. 6.9.*.i) methods respective to the test image in Fig. 6.7. Visual comparison is in concordance with numerical data. The f-divergence-based criteria used in our experiments (KL$^{\frac{1}{2}}$, CS$^{\frac{1}{2}}$, and HL$^{\frac{1}{2}}$) outperform both classic contrast and confidence test experiments. Finally, the better results of the HL$^{\frac{1}{2}}$ criterion could be explained by the fact that it is a true distance.

Summary

The observation that the kernel of the mutual information-based oracle of hierarchical radiosity can be rewritten as an f-divergence motivates the study of this family of divergences as refinement criteria in image synthesis. The basic idea consists in looking for the divergence between a uniform distribution (homogeneity) with respect to a defined distribution from a sample set.

We present the concept of divergence measure as against those of difference, dissimilarity, and distance. Its respective properties define its semantics unambiguously. The definition and properties for f-divergences are introduced and three particular instances of the family of Csiszár f-divergences are presented: the Kullback-Leibler, chi-square, and Hellinger divergences.

In an object-space approach, the f-divergences mentioned are analysed in the context of hierarchical radiosity. Their role as the kernel of the refinement oracle is studied starting from the mutual information based oracle (reinterpreted as the Kullback-Leibler divergence). The two distributions in play are represented, on the one hand, by the uniform distribution and, on the other one, by the distribution obtained from the normalised point-to-point form factors between two patches. The divergence between both distributions makes up the kernel of the oracle which will refine the mesh while a predetermined minimum threshold is not attained. The oracles based on the three divergences are tested against the kernel-smoothness-based and variance-based oracles showing a better behaviour.

For the pixel-driven approach, the use of the three f-divergences in the adaptive sampling technique in ray-tracing is analysed. The criterion of refinement is based on the divergence between the uniform distribution and that represented by the value of luminance of a sample with respect to the global luminance in a specific region. Until the minimum required balance, expressed by a threshold, has not been obtained, the density of the sampling is increased. The results obtained show a good behaviour of the square roots of the three divergences and particularly of the Hellinger one. Compared with the methods of classic contrast and confidence test, the measured error decreases.

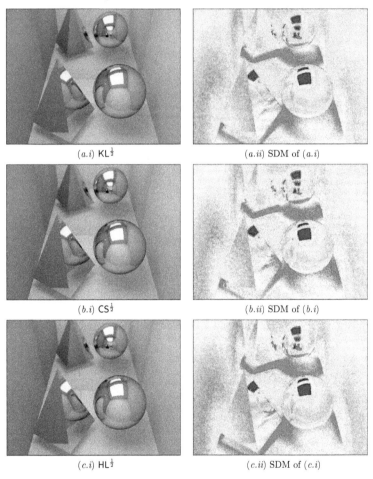

$(a.i)$ KL$^{\frac{1}{2}}$ $(a.ii)$ SDM of $(a.i)$

$(b.i)$ CS$^{\frac{1}{2}}$ $(b.ii)$ SDM of $(b.i)$

$(c.i)$ HL$^{\frac{1}{2}}$ $(c.ii)$ SDM of $(c.i)$

Figure 6.9: Images of the test scene (Fig. 6.7) obtained with an adaptive sampling scheme based on square root of (a) Kullback-Leibler (KL$^{\frac{1}{2}}$), (b) chi-square (CS$^{\frac{1}{2}}$), and (c) Hellinger (HL$^{\frac{1}{2}}$) f-divergences. By columns, (i) shows the resulting images and (ii) the sampling density maps of (i). The average number of samples per pixel is 60 in all the methods. Compare with the images in Fig. 6.8.

Chapter 7

Conclusions

In this chapter we present the conclusions (§7.1) and main contributions (§7.2) of this work as well as those publications which support it (§7.3). We also enumerate some related works with this thesis (§7.4) and some directions for future research (§7.5).

7.1 Conclusions

In this thesis we have extended the work started by Feixas et al. [61] on the application of information-theoretic tools to visibility and radiosity. Information-theoretic measures based on the Shannon and Harvda-Charvát-Tsallis entropies have been explored as divergence measures. Together with some Csiszár's f-divergences, they have been applied as refinement criteria in image synthesis, pixel-driven (ray-tracing) and object-space (hierarchical radiosity) approaches, obtaining a rich selection of efficient and discriminative measures. In addition, the concept of scene complexity, from a geometric visibility point of view, has been further explored and developed. Next, in accordance with the initial objectives (§1.2), we present the main concepts and conclusions of each chapter.

- A set of information-theoretic tools to deal with the geometric visibility information of a scene (3D/2D) have been defined. Based on mutual information, three typologies of complexity on the scene have been obtained.

  - The scene is interpreted as an information channel and, on carrying out a physical analogy with the concepts of interaction and field, new measures based on information have been defined:

    * The *discrete entropy field* represents the information content that all the patches create at a point[1].
    * The *mutual information field* represents the information transfer which exists at the point due to the patches (discrete field) or to the surface points (continuous field) of the scene.

    The continuous mutual information field is considered the *point complexity*. The discrete entropy field and discrete mutual information field are related by the *discrete cross entropy field* at a point. The concept of *complexity segment* has been defined from the calculation of these measures via random lines and this concept is the basic element of the transference of geometric visibility information. The *field map*, based on the range of intensities of a field at an interior point of a scene, is employed to represent the influence of these measures on the scene.

  - Two measures have been defined to evaluate the complexity of a sequence of animated discrete scenes:

---

[1] By default, in this context, a point belongs to the interior space of the scene $\mathcal{I}_S$ (§3.1).

  * *Animation complexity.* Based on the accumulation of the differences of information exchange due to the movement between the patches of two consecutive frames. It is computed from the scene discrete mutual information using complexity segments.

  * *Euclidean distance.* Based on the accumulation of the differences between the form factors of the patches which appear in consecutive frames.

Both present similar results which are coherent with the measures of complexity at a point: the cost of the movement is related with the complexity field of its path.

– The *region complexity* of a scene has been evaluated from two perspectives:

  * *Surface-to-surface complexity* (*segment-to-segment complexity* in 2D). Defined from the geometry of the surfaces which delimit the region. Based on the continuous (or discrete) scene mutual information between two regions of a scene.

  * *Spatial complexity.* Defined from the interior space which delimit the region. Based on the average of the complexity of all the points contained in this space.

Both measures are calculated from complexity segments. The results allow us to study the contribution of the parts of the scene to the global complexity of a scene so that they can be applied to optimal load balancing in parallel computation problems or to clustering algorithms in image processing and neuroimaging fields.

- A set of entropy-based measures to evaluate the pixel have been defined. These measures have been used in ray-tracing as refinement criteria in supersampling methods.

  – The concept of *pixel quality* has been presented from the homogeneity of the colour of the pixel. The entropy has been chosen to express the level of homogeneity of the information extracted from a region. Two types of information are obtained by sampling the image plane: colour and geometry.

    * Based on the probability distributions constructed from the information brought by the samples we have defined, for a colour system based on channels, the *image plane channel entropy*, the *pixel channel entropy*, the *image plane channel quality*, the *pixel channel quality*, and the *pixel colour quality*.

    * The probability distributions based on the geometric information of the samples have enabled us to define the *image plane geometry entropy*, the *pixel geometry entropy*, and the *pixel geometry quality*.

    * Complementary to the pixel qualities, concepts about contrast have been defined: the *pixel channel contrast*, the *pixel colour contrast*, and the *pixel geometry contrast*.

    * Several variants of contrast have also been presented. The combination between colour and geometric contrasts has been defined as a *pixel contrast*. Assigning more weight to one option than the other, the aspects of colour or geometry stand out. The measures of quality as much as contrast can be extended to any process that requires an evaluation of these types of characteristics, simply by adapting the probability distributions to the relevant information.

  – An *entropy-based supersampling* method based on the pixel contrast has been presented for ray-tracing. The supersampling of each pixel is carried out directly proportional to its pixel contrast. This measure shows a very good behaviour in the selection of what needs to be supersampled.

  – An *entropy-based adaptive sampling* method has been presented in the same context. The pixel contrast is used as a refinement criterion of a region. Its sampling densities are locally adapted until a sufficiently high quality is achieved. The entropy is shown to be a natural measure for the criterion used in the refinement tree thanks to the grouping property. The results obtained show that the new refinement algorithm improves substantially over uniform sampling and also on classic adaptive refinement techniques.

- The application of a generalised entropy, the Harvda-Charvát-Tsallis entropy, has been studied as a refinement criterion in hierarchical radiosity and compared with three classic approaches.

  - The interpretation of the scene as an information channel (§2.6) allows the application of the HCT entropy and its associated generalised mutual information. Analogous to the Shannon entropy (§2.6), both measures have allowed us to define (discrete and continuous):
    * The *scene HCT entropy*.
    * The *scene generalised mutual information*.

  - HCT entropy introduces the concepts of α-*information* and *entropic index* to the scene. The probabilities considered are those corresponding to the scene information channel considering the elements of the hierarchical adaptive mesh as patches. The concepts of α-*information content* and α-*information transfer* correspond to the HCT entropy and generalised mutual information, respectively.

  - The *transported information* oracle has been defined from a transported power approach. It is based on the scene HCT entropy at patch level. Its kernel considers the α-information content between the source and receiver elements of the hierarchical mesh and the area of the receiver element.

  - The *information smoothness* oracle has been defined from a kernel-smoothness-based approach. It is also based on the discrete scene HCT entropy at patch level. Its kernel is made up from a variation of the α-information content between two elements of the hierarchical mesh and the area of the receiver element.

  - The *mutual information* oracle has been defined from the approach based on smoothness of received radiosity. With the aim of reducing cost, it is based on minimising the generalised discretisation error. This measure has been defined from the difference between the continuous and discrete versions of the generalised mutual information of a scene. It expresses the loss of α-information transfer in a scene due to the discretisation and, between two elements (patch level), constitutes the kernel of this oracle together with the area of both elements.

  - The results obtained for the three information-theoretic oracles improve on the respective classic methods. The mutual information based oracle obtains the most significant results among all of them, for values of subextensivity ($\alpha < 1$), even improving the particular case of Shannon's mutual information oracle. The cost of any of the information-theoretic oracles does not go higher than the respective classic ones.

- The application of Csiszár's *f-divergences* as refinement criteria in rendering has been analysed. Their good behaviour in hierarchical radiosity and adaptive sampling in ray-tracing approaches has been validated for the Kullback-Leibler, chi-square, and Hellinger divergences. The basis for the three refinement criteria consists in evaluating the divergence between a uniform distribution (homogeneity) with respect to a defined distribution from a sample set.

  - In hierarchical radiosity, each one of the three *f*-divergences has produced a refinement criterion. The new kernel is defined from the calculation of the divergence between the uniform distribution and that defined from the normalised point-to-point form factor between two patches of the adaptive mesh. The oracles based on the three divergences have been tested against the kernel-smoothness-based and variance-based oracles showing a better behaviour on the whole.

  - The application of the three *f*-divergences in the adaptive sampling techniques of ray-tracing has produced three new refinement criteria. The criterion is led by the divergence between uniform distribution and that represented by the value of luminance of a sample with respect to the global luminance in a specific region. With regard to the methods of classic contrast and confidence test, the results show a better behaviour for the square roots of the three divergences, especially for the Hellinger case.

7.2   Contributions

According to the previous conclusions, the principal contributions of this thesis are described below. We also indicate the papers related to each contribution.

Scene complexity The concept of complexity for a 3D and 2D scene has been analysed from a geometric visibility point of view. Three aspects have been considered (§3):

> **Point complexity** The concepts of entropy and mutual information fields at an interior point of a scene have been defined (§3.1). They represent the information content and information transfer at a point, respectively. The continuous mutual information field at a point expresses its complexity. From [174].

> **Animation complexity** This represents the complexity of a sequence of frames for a discrete scene (§3.2). Two measures have been defined: animation complexity, based on the discrete scene mutual information, and the Euclidean distance of an animation, based on the form factors. From [177].

> **Region complexity** This expresses the complexity of a region of a scene from two perspectives (§3.3): surface-to-surface complexity (segment-to-segment complexity in 2D), based on the continuous scene mutual information between the surface of the regions; and spatial complexity, based on the complexity of the interior points which defines the region itself. From [176].

Entropy-based refinement criteria in ray-tracing A set of measures of pixel quality and pixel contrast have been introduced from the homogeneity of the received information (§4.1 and §4.2). The Shannon entropy has been used as a measure to capture this homogeneity in a region considering two kinds of information: colour and geometry. A combination of pixel colour and pixel geometry contrasts has been defined as a basic measure. This has been applied as a refinement criterion for supersampling in ray-tracing applications showing, with respect to the classic methods, very good behaviour in isolating the areas that need a density of specific sampling (§4.3 and §4.4). These measures can be adapted to any application which requires quality or contrast criteria on taking decisions on a sample set. From [179, 178, 180].

Entropy-based adaptive sampling algorithm The result of the study of pixel contrast as a refinement criteria, a new adaptive stochastic sampling algorithm for ray-tracing, based on the recursive decomposition of the entropy, has been presented (§4.4). Entropy is shown to be a natural measure for establishing the refinement tree bringing a sound theoretical framework to the procedure and, in practise, a good rate quality versus cost (1.1). Our method is orthogonal to the particular sampling and ray-tracing algorithm used. From [178, 180].

Refinement criteria based on generalised entropy in hierarchical radiosity Based on the HCT generalised entropy, a group of new information-theoretic oracles for hierarchical radiosity (based on transported information, information smoothness, and mutual information) have been presented (§5) in correspondence with three classic approaches (based on transported power, kernel smoothness, and received radiosity smoothness). The transported information and information smoothness oracles use the information content (entropy) between two elements of the hierarchical adaptive mesh while the mutual information oracle is based on minimising the loss of information transfer between them, defined from the generalised mutual information (derived from HCT entropy). The results obtained for these oracles, especially for the mutual information oracle, improve the ones obtained from the analysed classic oracles. This study gives strength to the proposal to use information-theoretic oracles to deal with the radiosity problem. From [181].

f-Divergence-based refinement criteria New refinement criteria based on three f-divergences are introduced: *Kullback-Leibler*, *chi-square*, and *Hellinger*. We have applied these criteria to hierarchical radiosity (§6.3) and to adaptive sampling in ray-tracing (§6.4). In both areas, the results obtained with the f-divergence-based criteria show a better behaviour compared to the analysed classic ones. From [182, 183].

7.3 Publications

The set of publications that support the contents of this work is the following:

- *Visibility Complexity of a Region in Flatland.* Jaume Rigau, Miquel Feixas, and Mateu Sbert. Short Presentations of Eurographics, EG Digital Library, 2000 [176].

- *Information Theory Point Measures in a Scene.* Jaume Rigau. Miquel Feixas, and Mateu Sbert. Research Report of the *Institut d'Informàtica i Aplicacions*, University of Girona, 2000 [174].

- *Visibility Complexity of Animation in Flatland.* Jaume Rigau, Miquel Feixas, and Mateu Sbert. Journal of WSCG (Proceedings of Winter School on Computer Graphics and CAD Systems '01), Union Agency - Science Press, 2001 [177].

- *New Contrast Measures for Pixel Supersampling.* Jaume Rigau, Miquel Feixas, and Mateu Sbert. Advances in Modeling, Animation and Rendering (Proceedings of CGI '02), Springer-Verlag, 2002 [179].

- *Entropy-Based Adaptive Supersampling.* Jaume Rigau, Miquel Feixas, and Mateu Sbert. The 13th Eurographics Workshop on Rendering (poster papers proceedings), National Research Council of Italy, 2002 [178].

- *Information-Theory-Based Oracles for Hierarchical Radiosity.* Jaume Rigau, Miquel Feixas, and Mateu Sbert. Computational Science and Its Applications - ICCSA 2003, Springer-Verlag (Lecture Notes in Computer Science), 2003 [181].

- *Entropy-Based Adaptive Sampling.* Jaume Rigau, Miquel Feixas, and Mateu Sbert. Graphics Interface, A. K. Peters Ltd., 2003 [180].

- *Refinement Criteria Based on f-Divergences.* Jaume Rigau, Miquel Feixas, and Mateu Sbert. Rendering Techniques 2003 (14th Eurographics Symposium on Rendering), ACM New-York, 2003 [182].

- *Refinement Criteria for Global Illumination Using Convex Functions.* Jaume Rigau, Miquel Feixas, and Mateu Sbert. The First Compositional Data Analysis Workshop (CoDaWork '03), Universitat de Girona, 2003 [183].

7.4 Concurrent Developments

The main stem of this work is the application of information-theoretic measures to rendering. Along with this development, the discussions and collateral tasks developed have generated new lines of work with interesting results. Here, we include some hints of these concurrent works, some of which are still open for further investigation.

- The concept of *image complexity* has been introduced [185]. We have presented a *partitioning algorithm* where the image is structured into homogeneous regions, by maximising the mutual information gain of the channel going from the histogram bins to the regions of the partitioned image [184]. Algorithms based on mutual information for *image segmentation* have been also designed [184]. The partitioning and segmentation algorithms have been applied to pre-process the medical images for multi-modal registration [188, 10].

- Definition of geometric information-theoretic measures for the recognition of objects [186, 187].

- New sampling systems for image synthesis are studied [197].

- Information-theoretic measures for scene discretisation in flatland have been analysed [173].

Publications in which I have participated are:

- *View-Dependent Information Theory Measures for Pixel Sampling and Scene Discretization in Flatland.* Jaume Rigau, Miquel Feixas, Philippe Bekaert, and Mateu Sbert. Proceedings of Spring Conference on Computer Graphics, IEEE Computer Society, 2001 [173].

- *Medical Image Segmentation Based on Mutual Information Maximization.* Jaume Rigau, Miquel Feixas, Mateu Sbert, Anton Bardera, and Imma Boada. 7th International Conference on Medical Image Computing and Computer-Assisted Intervention (MICCAI '04), Springer-Verlag (Lecture Notes in Computer Science), 2004 [188].

- *An Information Theoretic Framework for Image Segmentation.* Jaume Rigau, Miquel Feixas, and Mateu Sbert. IEEE International Conference on Image Processing (ICIP '04), IEEE Press, 2004 [184].

- *An Information Theoretic Framework for Image Complexity.* Jaume Rigau, Miquel Feixas, and Mateu Sbert. Computational Aesthetics 2005 - First Eurographics Workshop on Computational Aesthetics in Graphics, Visualization and Imaging (CAGVI' 05), Eurographics Association, 2005 [185].

- *Shape Complexity Based on Mutual Information.* Jaume Rigau, Miquel Feixas, and Mateu Sbert. International Conference on Shape Modeling and Applications (SMI '05), IEEE Computer Society, 2005 [186].

- *An Information-Theoretic Approach to Shape Complexity.* Jaume Rigau, Miquel Feixas, and Mateu Sbert. Computer Graphics & Geometry, Scientific Electronic Library eLibrary.Ru, 2006 [187].

- *Systematic Sampling in Image-Synthesis.* Mateu Sbert, Jaume Rigau, Miquel Feixas, and László Neumann. Computational Science and Its Applications - ICCSA '06, Springer-Verlag (Lecture Notes in Computer Science), 2006 [197].

- *Medical Image Registration Based on BSP and Quad-tree Partitioning.* Anton Bardera, Miquel Feixas, Imma Boada, Jaume Rigau, and Mateu Sbert. Biomedical Image Registration - Third International Workshop (WBIR '06), Springer-Verlag (Lecture Notes in Computer Science), 2006 [10].

7.5   Future Work

Our work is one more step towards the incorporation of information-theoretic measures in the study of the complexity of a scene, as well into refinement criteria used for its rendering. In a new phase, some possibilities of future work are:

- From the scene complexity measures, the point complexity can be applied directly to robot vision, design, crowd rendering and simulation, etc. Many options appear on dealing with the problem of finding the best viewpoint (e.g., security cameras, television retransmissions, and recognition of objects). From a theoretical point of view, the scene complexity at a point could be extended to global illumination. Along other lines, we can look for the correlation between the animation complexity measures (i.e., animation complexity and Euclidean distance) and also the correlation with respect to the computational cost of the animation. With regard to region complexity, it could be applied in the field of architecture to search for a relationship between the complexity of a design and the distribution of spaces. Finally, radiosity could be incorporated into the complexity measures in the way indicated in [61].

- The application of the HCT entropy as a refinement criteria in hierarchical radiosity brings with it many questions to be answered. The most interesting one would be to analyse the characterisation, geometrical and/or physical, of a scene with respect to the entropic index as well as to search for a correlation between this and scene complexity. It would also be necessary to analyse the existence of an association between the theoretical entropic index of a scene and its results as a refinement criteria for the methods presented with special attention given to the behaviour of the mutual information-based oracle.

- The introduction of three f-divergences as an refinement criteria in hierarchical radiosity and ray-tracing presents the following question: How would other families of f-divergences behave?

  In hierarchical radiosity, f-divergences based on generalised entropies (e.g., Rényi entropy [172]) would they behave similarly to HCT entropy-based ones? In adaptive ray-tracing, can the generalisation of the f-divergences, which include taking the α power of the basic divergence [122, 95], shed light on the good behaviour of the exponent value $\frac{1}{2}$ used in the ray-tracing case? Why does the criterion based on true distance behave better than the ones based on pseudo-distances? The answers to these questions make up a whole second phase of analysis with respect to the use of f-divergences.

- In general, refinement criteria require a threshold in order to be able to calibrate the final result with the quality that the user desires with respect to the cost (1.1). Our case is not different and so the possibility of calculating a previous threshold, analytically, is an open investigation. An automatic option could be considered by doing a prior study of the scene (e.g., trying out tendencies for predetermined values with low densities of sampling). Other options would be to go through a previous classification of the scenes in accordance with a parameter that is dependent on refinement criteria (e.g., the entropic index). Nevertheless, additional costs would be inevitable.

- The concepts of complexity of a scene, pixel quality, and pixel contrast defined can be applied to imaging. In recent years, growth in this field has been remarkable (e.g., photography, images by satellite, and medical images). From these concepts, applications to image complexity, medical image registration, image compression, and computational aesthetics are viable. Some of these lines of research have been taken up (§7.4).

Appendix A

Geometry

In this section, we compile the basic geometric notation[1] used in this work on a modelled scene $\mathcal{S}$ (closed environment). Detailed definitions can be found in the bibliography of computer graphics and related fields. Within the context of rendering, we should mention particularly Sillion and Puech [215], Glassner [74], Bekaert [12], Szirmay-Kalos [223], and Dutre et al. [53].

- A_{s} is the surface of $\mathcal{S}$ and A_{T} its area.
- S is an enumeration of the set of patches of a discretisation of $\mathcal{S}$ (finite countable with $|S| = N_{\mathrm{p}} > 1$).
- A_i is a surface of i-element of a partition or discretisation (by default, a patch of S).
- n_x is the normal at surface point $x \in A_{\mathrm{s}}$.
- $\mathrm{d}A_x$ is the differential area at surface point $x \in A_{\mathrm{s}}$.
- $\overrightarrow{xy}$ is the normalised direction vector $y - x$.
- r_{xy} is $\| x - y \|$ (i.e., distance between x and y).
- Θ, Υ represent normalised direction vectors. By default, with respect to a point $x \in A_{\mathrm{s}}$, Θ and Υ represent outgoing and incoming directions, respectively.
- θ_Θ^Υ is the angle between the direction vectors Θ and Υ. A usual case is $\theta_{n_x}^{\overrightarrow{xy}}$ for $x, y \in A_{\mathrm{s}}$.
- r_x^Θ represents a *ray* from point x in direction Θ: set of points $\{x + \alpha\Theta \mid \alpha \in \mathbb{R}^+\}$.
- $\Lambda(x, \Theta)$ is the *closest visible surface point function* (from x in direction Θ). The value is defined[2] by $y. y \in D \wedge r_{xy} = \min_{z \in D}\{r_{xz}\}$, where $D = r_x^\Theta \cap A_{\mathcal{S}}$. If $y = \Lambda(x, \Theta)$ and $x \in A_{\mathcal{S}}$, then $x = \Lambda(y, -\Theta)$.
- $V(x, y)$ is the *visibility function* for all x and y of $A_{\mathcal{S}}$. Defined by 1 if x and y are mutually visible (i.e., $\exists\Theta. y = \Lambda(x, \Theta)$) and 0 otherwise.
- $\mathcal{I}_{\mathcal{S}}$ is the set of interior points of the spatial region defined by $\mathcal{S}$ ($\mathcal{I}_{\mathcal{S}}^{\mathrm{2D}}$ for a 2D-region).
- Ω is a solid angle (steradians $\mathtt{sr}$).
- Ω_x is the hemispherical solid angle at surface point x ($2\pi\ \mathtt{sr}$).
- $\Omega_{x \to A}$ is the solid angle with apex at surface point x and subtended by surface A.
- $\mathcal{S}_x^2$ is the solid angle of the unit sphere at surface point x ($4\pi\ \mathtt{sr}$).

- $\mathrm{d}\omega_\Theta$ is the differential solid angle with direction Θ. It is equivalent to differential area $\frac{\cos\theta_{n_y}^{\overrightarrow{yx}}}{r_{xy}^2}\mathrm{d}A_y$, where x is the apex of $\mathrm{d}\omega_\Theta$ and $y = \Lambda(x, \Theta)$.

Fig. A.1 illustrates part of this notation. The same concepts are valid in flatland with analogous interpretations and the respective changes of areas for lengths, solid angles for angles, spheres for circles, etc.

---

[1] As a starting point we have taken Dutre [52].
[2] In an open environment, this function might be undefined.

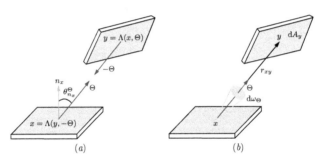

Figure A.1: Geometry in a scene. (a) Between surface points. (b) Differential solid angle and differential surface.

Appendix B

Probability

An enumeration of some probability concepts which are used throughout this work follows.

- A set is *countable* if there is a bijective correspondence with a subset of $\mathbb{N}$. A countable set can be finite or infinite.
- An *alphabet* is a finite nonempty set.
- A *sample space* is a set that includes all possible outcomes of an experiment.
- An *event* is a subset of a sample space.
- If $S \subset \mathbb{R}$ is a finite set, we denote as $S_{\min} = \min\{s \in S\}$, $S_{\max} = \max\{s \in S\}$, and $\overline{S} = \frac{1}{|S|}\sum_{s \in S} s$ its minimum, maximum, and average values, respectively.
- A *random variable* X describes the outcome of an experiment in a sample space $\mathcal{X}$ where each element x has a *probability* of occurring (i.e., $Pr\{X = x\}$). Thus, X is characterised by a pair $(\mathcal{X}, p_X)$ where the probability of occurrence or success is measured by the function $p_X : \mathcal{X} \to [0, 1]$, called *probability distribution*. For all $x \in \mathcal{X}$, we have $p_X(x) = Pr\{X = x\} \geq 0$ and p_X must be the sum of 1 over the domain of $\mathcal{X}$.
- The *cumulative distribution* of a random variable X is the function $P_X : \mathcal{X} \to [0, 1]$ where $P_X(x) = Pr\{X \leq x\}$.
- A *discrete random variable* X is a random variable $(\mathcal{X}, p_X)$ with a countable sample space. Its probability distribution is called *probability mass function* satisfying:

  - $\sum_{x \in \mathcal{X}} p_X(x) = 1$
  - $\forall \mathcal{Y} \subset \mathcal{X}. \sum_{y \in \mathcal{Y}} p_X(y) = Pr\{X \in \mathcal{Y}\}$

  If there is no ambiguity, it is usual to refer to a probability mass function simply as a probability distribution.
- A *continuous random variable* X is a random variable $(\mathcal{X}, p_X)$ with a cumulative continuous distribution P_X. When the derivative $P'_X = p_X$ is defined and integrates to 1, then p_X is called the *probability density function* (pdf) of X:

  - $\int_{-\infty}^{\infty} p_X(x)\mathrm{d}x = 1$
  - $\forall \mathcal{Y} \subset \mathcal{X}. \int_{\mathcal{Y}} p_X(y)\mathrm{d}y = Pr\{X \in \mathcal{Y}\}$

  The set where $p_X(x) > 0$ is the support set of X.
- The *expectance* or *expected value* of a random variable $X = (\mathcal{X}, p_X)$ is $E[X]$ defined as:

  - Discrete: $\sum_{x \in \mathcal{X}} p_X(x_i)x_i$
  - Continuous: $\int_{x \in \mathcal{X}} p_X(x)x\mathrm{d}x$

○ The *variance* of X is the expected square deviation from the expectation:

$$\sigma^2 [X] = E\left[(X - E[X])^2\right] = E\left[X^2\right] - E[X]^2. \tag{B.1}$$

Always[1] $\sigma^2 \geq 0$.

○ An *estimator* is a random variable $\widehat{X}$ which expected value is used to estimate an unknown population parameter x. The *bias* of an estimator is $E[\widehat{X}] - x$.

○ The *sample variance* of a set of random samples S ($|S| > 1$) is the unbiased estimator of the variance:

$$s^2 [S] = \frac{1}{|S| - 1} \sum_{s \in S} (s - \overline{S})^2. \tag{B.2}$$

○ The *standard deviation* σ of a random variable is the square root of the average squared deviation from the expectation (i.e., the variance square root).

○ The *mean square error* (MSE) of an estimator $\widehat{X}$ of a value x is given by

$$MSE(\widehat{X}) = E\left[(\widehat{X} - x)^2\right] \tag{B.3}$$

and it is equal to the variance when the estimator is unbiased (i.e., $E[\widehat{X}] = x$). The *root mean square error* (RMSE), $\sqrt{MSE}$, is normally used to measure the good functioning of the estimator.

○ If (X, Y) is a pair of random variables with respective events E_X and E_Y, we can define:

  - The *joint probability* is the probability of an event of X in conjunction with one of Y: $Pr\{E_X, E_Y\}$. We denote p_{XY} for the probability distribution where $p_{XY}(x_i, y_j) = Pr\{X = x_i, Y = y_j\}$.
  - The *conditional probability* is the probability of event E_X, assuming event E_Y: $Pr\{E_X|E_Y\} = \frac{Pr\{E_X, E_Y\}}{Pr\{E_Y\}}$. We denote $p_{X|Y}$ for the probability distribution where $p_{X|Y}(x_i|y_j) = Pr\{X = x_i|Y = y_j\}$.
  - The *marginal probability* is the probability of one event, ignoring any information about the other event[2]: $Pr\{E_X\}$ ($Pr\{E_Y\}$). We denote p_X (q_Y) for the marginal probability distributions where $p_X(x_i) = Pr\{X = x_i\}$ ($q_Y(y_i) = Pr\{Y = y_i\}$).

○ Two events are *independent* if $Pr\{E_X, E_Y\} = Pr\{E_X\}Pr\{E_Y\}$. With probability distributions: $p_{XY}(x, y) = p_X(x)q_Y(y)$. The discrete random variables X and Y are independent if $p_{XY} = p_X q_Y$.

○ **Theorem 4 (Bayes)** *The inverse probability law is*

$$Pr\{E_X|E_Y\} = \frac{Pr\{E_X\}Pr\{E_Y|E_X\}}{Pr\{E_Y\}}. \tag{B.4}$$

The proof is based on $Pr\{E_X, E_Y\} = Pr\{E_Y\}Pr\{E_X|E_Y\}$. In terms of pdfs, we have

$$p_{XY}(x, y) = q_Y(y)p_{X|Y}(x|y) = p_X(x)p_{Y|X}(y|x). \tag{B.5}$$

○ A *stochastic process* is an indexed collection of random variables, each of which is defined on the same probability space and takes values in the same domain. A particular stochastic process is determined by specifying the joint probability distribution. An important case is the discrete set where the collection runs over a discrete index set. In a continuous stochastic process, the index set is continuous (usually time or space), resulting in an uncountable set of random variables [31, 249].

○ A *random walk* is a stochastic process consisting of a sequence of discrete steps of fixed length. One o more characteristics (e.g., magnitude or direction) are determined at random [31, 190, 98, 57].

---

[1] Non-negativity of variance. From the convex function $f(x) = x^2$ and Jensen's inequality (D.4), with equality for a constant random variable.

[2] Marginal probability is obtained by summing (discrete) or integrating (continuous) the joint probability for the ignored event.

∘ A *discrete Markov chain* $X_1 \to X_2 \to \ldots$ is a sequence of random variables $X_1, X_2, \ldots$ which makes up a discrete-time stochastic process with the *Markov property*: the past is irrelevant for predicting the future given knowledge of the present [128, 31, 37, 137, 249]. Thus, for time $n = 1, 2, \ldots$ we have

$$Pr\{X_{n+1} = x_{n+1} | X_n = x_n, X_{n-1} = x_{n-1}, \ldots, X_1 = x_1\} =$$
$$Pr\{X_{n+1} = x_{n+1} | X_n = x_n\} \quad \forall (x_1, \ldots, x_n, x_{n+1}) \in \mathcal{X}^{n+1}. \quad \text{(B.6)}$$

Then, $p_{X_1 X_2 \ldots X_n} = p_{X_1} p_{X_2 | X_1} \cdots p_{X_n | X_{n-1}}$. A Markov chain is characterised by the conditional distribution called the *transition probability* of the process: $p_{X_{n+1} | X_n}$. If the state space is finite, the transition probability is a finite matrix, called the *transition probability matrix P*.

The *stationary distribution* is a vector which satisfies $\pi^* P = \pi^*$, where the stationary distribution π^* is a left eigenvector of the transition matrix, associated with the eigenvalue 1.

The Markov chain can also be interpreted as a random walk with an infinite countable sequence of random variables $X_{k \geq 0}$, in which each $X_{k > 0}$ depends only on the previous X_{k-1} and not on the ones before. The random variables X_k indicate the probability of finding an imaginary particle in each state after k steps from an initial distribution given by X_0.

Assuming that any probability function has a random variable associated with it, if there is no ambiguity, we can simply note p and q by p_X and q_Y, respectively. However, when the sample space is an alphabet $\mathcal{X}$ with cardinality n, the associated function p_X is the correspondence $p = \{(x_i, p_i) \mid i \in \{1, \ldots, n\}\}$ which allows us to consider, depending on the context, the usual and simplified notations: $p_i = p(x_i) = p_X(x_i)$, $p = \{p_i, \ldots, p_n\}$, and $p = \{p_i\}$. This can be extended to join, conditional, and marginal probabilities.

Appendix C

Statistics

Some statistical concepts mentioned in this work are [82]:

Confidence interval This is an estimated range of values, obtained from a set of samples, which is likely to include an unknown parameter. The *confidence limits* are the lower and upper boundaries and the *confidence level* is the probability value associated $1 - \alpha$ (i.e., for $\alpha = 0.05$ it is the 95% confidence level).

Gamma function It was introduced by Leonhard Euler (1707-1783) when he aimed at generalising the factorial to non-integer values (Fig. C). It is defined over $\mathbb{C}$ except for the nonpositive integers:

$$\Gamma(z) = \int_0^\infty e^{-t} t^{z-1} \mathrm{d}t. \tag{C.1}$$

Euler's following limit form is valid for all complex numbers including the nonpositive integers:

$$\Gamma(z) = \lim_{n \to \infty} \frac{n! n^z}{\Pi_{k=0}^n (z+k)}. \tag{C.2}$$

The Gamma function satisfies $\Gamma(z+1) = z\Gamma(z) = z!$ for all complex numbers except nonpositive integers. In particular, $\Gamma(n+1) = n!$ for any positive integer ($\Gamma(1) = 1$).

Student's distribution It is used to estimate the mean of a normally distributed population when the sample size is small (William Sealey Gosset[1], 1908). Let $X = \{x_1, \ldots, x_n\}$ be a set of independent

---

[1] He was an employer of Guinness Breweries and had to publish under a pseudonym: Student.

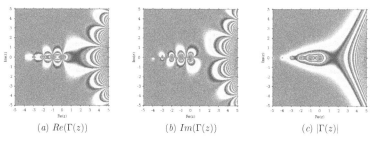

| (a) $Re(\Gamma(z))$ | (b) $Im(\Gamma(z))$ | (c) $|\Gamma(z)|$ |

Figure C.1: The gamma function in complex plane: (a) the real component, (b) the imaginary component, and (c) the absolute value.

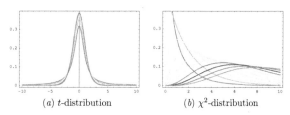

(a) t-distribution (b) χ^2-distribution

Figure C.2:   Ten degrees of freedom from $r = 1$ (red) to $r = 10$ (green-yellow) for (a) the t-distribution and (b) the χ^2-distribution.

measurements that are normally distributed[2]. The estimation of the true mean is $\frac{\overline{X}-\mu}{\sigma/\sqrt{n}}$. Using the sample variance s^2 (§B) we have the following value

$$t = \frac{\overline{X} - \mu}{s(X)/\sqrt{n}}. \tag{C.3}$$

Student's distribution is defined as the distribution of the random variable t and it approaches the normal distribution when n increases. Its pdf, called t-distribution, is:

$$f_r(t) = \frac{\Gamma((r+1)/2)}{\sqrt{r\pi}\Gamma(r/2)}(1 + t^2/r)^{-\frac{r+1}{2}}, \tag{C.4}$$

where $r = n - 1$ are the degrees of freedom (Fig. C.2.a). The support set is $(-\infty, +\infty)$, $\mu = 0$, and $\sigma^2 = \frac{r}{r-2}$. Its importance is rooted in the fact that it does not depend on μ neither σ, but on r and that it is the best approximation without knowing σ.

χ^2-**distribution**   It is the probability distribution of the random variable

$$\chi^2_r = \sum_{i=1}^{r} X_i^2, \tag{C.5}$$

where the X_i are normal independent distributions[2]. The corresponding pdf is

$$f_r(x) = \frac{x^{\frac{r}{2}-1}e^{-\frac{x}{2}}}{\Gamma(r/2)2^{\frac{r}{2}}}, \tag{C.6}$$

where r are the degrees of freedom (Fig. C.2.b). The support set is $[0, +\infty)$, $\mu = r$, and $\sigma^2 = 2r$.

---

[2] $\mu = 0$ and $\sigma^2 = 1$.

Appendix D

Convexity

The property of convexity is widely applied to mathematics, information theory, and different engineering areas to obtain divergence measures.

Definition 81 *A function $f : D \subset \mathbb{R}^n \to \mathbb{R}$ is convex if*

$$x, y \in D \wedge \lambda \in [0, 1] \Rightarrow \lambda x + (1 - \lambda)y \in D$$
$$f(\lambda x + (1 - \lambda)y) \leq \lambda f(x) + (1 - \lambda)f(y) \tag{D.1}$$

A function is strictly convex if equality holds, only if $\lambda = 0$ or $\lambda = 1$ for $x \neq y$.

For $n = 1$, the graph of a convex function lies below any chord. The functions x^2, e^x, and $x \log x$ for $x > 0$ are strictly convex (Fig. D.1).

Definition 82 *A function $f(x)$ is (strictly) concave if and only if $-f(x)$ is (strictly) convex.*

For $n = 1$, the graph of a concave function lies above any chord. For instance, $\log x$ for $x > 0$ is a strictly concave function (Fig. D.1). An important inequality with convexity (concavity) is:

Theorem 5 (Jensen's inequality) *If f is a convex function on the interval $[a, b]$, then*

$$\sum_{i=1}^{n} \lambda_i f(x_i) - f\left(\sum_{i=1}^{n} \lambda_i x_i\right) \geq 0, \tag{D.2}$$

where $0 \leq \lambda \leq 1$, $\sum_{i=1}^{n} \lambda_i = 1$, and $x_i \in [a, b]$. If f is a concave function, the inequality is reversed.

Proof in [105]. A very special case of this inequality is when $\lambda_i = \frac{1}{n}$ because then

$$\frac{1}{n} \sum_{i=1}^{n} f(x_i) - f\left(\frac{1}{n} \sum_{i=1}^{n} x_i\right) \geq 0. \tag{D.3}$$

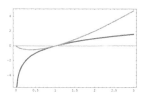

Figure D.1: The behaviour of two logarithmic functions for $x \in (0, 3]$: the $x \log x$ (red), a strictly convex function, and the $\log x$ (blue), a strictly concave function.

The value of the function at the mean of the x_i is less than or equal to the mean of the values of the function at each x_i. In particular,

Theorem 6 *If f is convex on the range of a random variable $X \in \mathbb{R}^n$, then*

$$E[f(X)] \geq f(E[X]). \tag{D.4}$$

For f concave, the reverse inequality holds.

Proof in [37, p.25–26] by induction on the number of mass points. If f is strictly convex (concave), then equality in (D.4) implies that $X = E[X]$ (i.e., X is a constant). Important properties are derived from this inequality (e.g., the non-negativity of variance (B.1) and other information-theoretic measures (2.72, 2.79). Another important inequality can be obtained from Jensen's inequality:

Theorem 7 (The log-sum inequality) *If $a_1, \ldots, a_n$ and $b_1, \ldots, b_n$ are nonnegative numbers with $A = \sum_{i=1}^{n} a_i$ and $B = \sum_{i=1}^{n} a_i$, then*[1]

$$\sum_{i=1}^{n} a_i \log \frac{a_i}{b_i} \geq A \log \frac{A}{B}, \tag{D.5}$$

with equality if and only if $\frac{a_i}{b_i}$ is constant.

Proof [37, p.28] is obtained using the strict convexity of $x \log x$ and Jensen's inequality (Th. 5). Note that the conditions in this inequality are much weaker than for Jensen's inequality. The expression (D.5) can be rewritten as

$$\sum_{i=1}^{n} \frac{a_i}{A} \log \frac{a_i/A}{b_i/B} \geq 0, \tag{D.6}$$

from which properties of non-negativity are derived in information theory (§2.5).

---

[1] With the convention, from continuity, that $0 \log 0$ and $0 \log \frac{0}{0}$ is 0, and $x \log \frac{a}{0} = \infty$ for $a > 0$.

Bibliography

[1] János Aczél and Zoltan Daróczy. Ueber Verallegmeinerte Quasilineare Mittelwerte die mit Gewichtsfunktionnen Gebildet sind[1]. *Publications Mathematicæ*, 10:171–190, 1963.

[2] Takaaki Akimoto, Kenji Mase, and Yaushito Suenaga. Pixel selected ray tracing. *IEEE Computer Graphics and Applications*, 11(4):14–22, 1991.

[3] Mohamed S. Ali and Samuel D. Silvey. A general class of coefficient of divergence of one distribution from another. *Journal of Royal Statistical Society (Serie B)*, 28(1):131–142, 1966.

[4] Celia B. Anteneodo and Angel R. Plastino. Some features of the López Ruiz-Mancini-Calbet (LMC) statistical measure of complexity. *Physics Letters A*, 223:348–354, 1996.

[5] Tal Arbel and Frank P. Ferrie. Viewpoint selection by navigation through entropy maps. In *Proceedings of 7th International Conference on Computer Vision*, pages 248–254, September 1999.

[6] Jacqueline Argence. Antialiasing for ray tracing using CSG modeling. In N. Magnenat-Thalmann and D. Thalmann, editors, *New Trends in Computer Graphics (Proceedings of CGI '88)*, pages 199–208, New York (NY), USA, 1988. Springer-Verlag.

[7] Christoph Arndt. *Information Measures*. Signals and Communication Technology. Springer-Verlag, Berlin, Germany, 2001.

[8] James Arvo and David Kirk. A survey of ray tracing acceleration techniques. In Andrew S. Glassner, editor, *An Introduction to Ray Tracing*, pages 201–262. Academic Press Ltd., San Diego (CA), USA, 1989.

[9] Remo Badii and Antonio Politi. *Complexity. Hierarchical Structures and Scaling in Physics*. Cambridge University Press, 1997.

[10] Anton Bardera, Miquel Feixas, Imma Boada, Jaume Rigau, and Mateu Sbert. Medical image registration based on BSP and quad-tree partitioning. In Per Josien Pluima, Boštjan Likar, and Frans Gerritsen, editors, *Biomedical Image Registration - Third International Workshop (WBIR '06)*, volume 4057 of *Lecture Notes in Computer Science*, pages 1–8. Springer-Verlag, July 2006.

[11] Neil S. Barnett, Pietro Cerone, Sever S. Dragomir, and Anthony Sofo. Approximating Csiszár f-divergence by the use of Taylor's formula with integral remainder. *Mathematical Inequalities and Applications*, 5(3):417–434, 2002.

[12] Philippe Bekaert. *Hierarchical and Stochastic Algorithms for Radiosity*. PhD thesis, Katholieke Universiteit Leuven, Leuven, Belgium, December 1999.

[13] Philippe Bekaert, László Neumann, Attila Neumann, Mateu Sbert, and Yves D. Willems. Hierarchical Monte Carlo radiosity. In George Drettakis and Nelson Max, editors, *Rendering Techniques '98 (Proceedings of the 9th Eurographics Workshop on Rendering)*, pages 259–268, New York (NY), USA, June 1998. Springer-Verlag.

---

[1] About generalised quasi-linear averages that are formed with weight functions.

[14] Philippe Bekaert and Yves D. Willems. Error control for radiosity. In Xavier Pueyo and Peter Schröder, editors, *Rendering Techniques '96 (Proceedings of the 7th Eurographics Workshop on Rendering)*, pages 153–164, New York (NY), USA, June 1996. Springer-Verlag.

[15] Charles H. Bennett. Logical depth and physical complexity. In Rolf Herken, editor, *The Universal Turing Machine, a Half-Century Survey*, pages 227–257. Oxford University Press, Oxford, UK, 1988.

[16] Pedro Bernaola, José L. Oliver, and Ramón Román. Decomposition of DNA sequence complexity. *Physical Review Letters*, 83(16):3336–3339, October 1999.

[17] Gonzalo Besuievsky and Mateu Sbert. The multi-frame lighting method: A Monte Carlo based solution for radiosity in dynamic environments. In Xavier Pueyo and Peter Schröder, editors, *Rendering Techniques '96 (Proceedings of the 7th Eurographics Workshop on Rendering)*, pages 185–194, London, UK, June 1996. Springer-Verlag.

[18] Richard E. Blahut. *Principles and Practice of Information Theory*. Addison-Wesley, Reading (MA), USA, 1987.

[19] James F. Blinn. Models of light reflection for computer synthesized pictures. In *Proceedings of the 4th Annual Conference on Computer Graphics and Interactive Techniques (SIGGRAPH '77)*, pages 192–198, New York (NY), USA, 1977. ACM Press.

[20] Mark A. Bolin and Gary W. Meyer. An error metric for Monte Carlo ray tracing. In Julie Dorsey and Philipp Slusallek, editors, *Rendering Techniques '97 (Proceedings of the 8th Eurographics Workshop on Rendering)*, pages 57–68, New York (NY), USA, June 1997. Springer-Verlag.

[21] Mark R. Bolin and Gary W. Meyer. A perceptually based adaptive sampling algorithm. In Michael Cohen, editor, *SIGGRAPH '98 Conference Proceedings*, Annual Conference Series, pages 299–309, New York (NY), USA, July 1998. ACM SIGGRAPH, ACM Press.

[22] Christian Bouville, Pierre Tellier, and Kadi Bouatouch. Low sampling densities using a psychovisual approach. In Frits H. Post and Wilhelm Barth, editors, *Eurographics '91 (Proceedings of European Computer Graphics Conference and Exhibition)*, pages 167–182, Amsterdam, Holland, September 1991. Elsevier North-Holland.

[23] Matevž Bren and Vladimir Batagelj. The metric index. Technical Report 35-561, Institute of mathematics, physics, and mechanics, Department of mathematics, University of Ljubljana, Ljubljana, Slovenia, 1997.

[24] Jacob Burbea. *J*-divergences and related concepts. In Samuel Kotz, Norman L. Johnson, and Campbell B. Read, editors, *Encyclopedia of Statistical Sciences*, volume 4, pages 290–296. Wiley Interscience, New York (NY), USA, 1983.

[25] Terrence M. Caelli. *Visual Perception: Theory and Practice*. Pergamon Press, Oxford, UK, 1981.

[26] Frederic Cazals and Mateu Sbert. Some integral geometry tools to estimate the complexity of 3D scenes. Research Report 3204, INRIA, July 1997.

[27] CIE Technical Committee 3.1. An analytic model for describing the influence of lighting parameters upon visual performance. Technical Report 19.21–19.22, Commission Internationale de L'Éclairage, Paris, France, 1981.

[28] James J. Clark, Matthew R. Palmer, and Peter D. Lawrence. A transformation method for the reconstruction of functions from nonuniformly spaced samples. *IEEE Transactions on Acoustics, Speech, and Signal Processing*, 33(4):1151–1165, October 1985.

[29] Michael F. Cohen and Donald P. Greenberg. The hemi-cube: A radiosity solution for complex environments. *Computer Graphics (Proceedings of SIGGRAPH '85)*, 19(3):31–40, July 1985.

[30] Michael F. Cohen and John R. Wallace. *Radiosity and Realistic Image Synthesis*. Academic Press Professional, Boston (MA), USA, 1993.

[31] Robert Coleman. *Stochastic Processes*. George Allen & Unwin Ltd., London, UK, 1974.

[32] International Electrotechnical Commission. Default RGB colour space - sRGB. In *Colour Management in Multimedia Systems*, chapter Part 2.1. IEC, Geneva, Switzerland, 1998. IEC/PT61966(PL)34.

[33] Computer Graphics Research Group. Renderpark: A photorealistic rendering tool. Software, Department of Computer Science, Katholieke Universiteit Leuven, Leuven, Belgium, 2000. http://www.renderpark.be.

[34] Robert L. Cook. Stochastic sampling in computer graphics. *ACM Transactions on Graphics*, 5(1):51–72, January 1986.

[35] Robert L. Cook, Thomas Porter, and Loren Carpenter. Distributed ray tracing. *Computer Graphics (Proceedings of SIGGRAPH '84)*, 18(3):137–145, July 1984.

[36] Robert L. Cook and Kenneth E. Torrance. A reflectance model for computer graphics. *ACM Transactions on Graphics*, 1(1):7–24, January 1982.

[37] Thomas M. Cover and Joy A. Thomas. *Elements of Information Theory*. Wiley Series in Telecommunications, 1991.

[38] Franklin C. Crow. The aliasing problem in computer-generated shaded images. *Communications of the ACM*, 20(11):799–805, November 1977.

[39] Franklin C. Crow. A comparison of antialiasing techniques. *IEEE Computer Graphics and Applications*, 1(1):40–48, January 1981.

[40] Imre Csiszár. Eine Informationsheoretische Ungleichung und ihre Anwendungen auf den Beweis der Ergodizität von Markoffschen Ketten[2]. *Magyar Tudományos Akadémia Közleményei*, 8:85–108, 1963.

[41] Imre Csiszár. Information-type measure of difference of probability distributions and indirect observations. *Studia Scientiarum Mathematicarum Hungarica*, 2:299–318, 1967.

[42] Imre Csiszár. Information measures: A critical survey. *Transactions of the Seventh Prague Conference on Information Theory, Statistical Decision Functions, Random Processes and the European Meeting of Statisticians*, A:73–86, 1974.

[43] Cyrille Damez and François X. Sillion. Space-time hierarchical radiosity for high-quality animations. In Dani Lischinski and Greg Ward, editors, *Rendering Techniques '99 (Proceedings of the 10th Eurographics Workshop on Rendering)*, pages 235–246, New York (NY), USA, June 1999. Springer-Verlag.

[44] Zoltan Daróczy. Generalized information measures. *Information and Control*, 16:36–51, 1970.

[45] Lucia Darsa and Bruno Costa. Multi-resolution representation and reconstruction of adaptively sampled images. In *Proceedings of IX Brazilian Symposium on Computer Graphics and Image Processing (SIBGRAPI '96)*, pages 321–328, October 1996.

[46] Lucia Darsa, Bruno Costa, and Amitabh Varshney. Navigating static environments using image-space simplification and morphing. In Michael Cohen and David Zeltzer, editors, *1997 Symposium on Interactive 3D Graphics*, pages 25–34. ACM SIGGRAPH, April 1997.

[47] Gunther Wyszecki Deane B. Judd. *Color in Business, Science, and Industry*. John Wiley & Sons Inc., New York (NY), USA, 3 edition, 1975.

---

[2]An information-theoretic inequality and its application to the proof of the ergodicity of Markov chains.

[48] Esteve del Acebo, Miquel Feixas, and Mateu Sbert. Form factors and information theory. In *The 3rd International Conference on Computer Graphics and Artificial Intelligence (3IA '98)*, Limoges, France, 1998.

[49] Mark A. Z. Dippé and Erling H. Wold. Antialiasing through stochastic sampling. *Computer Graphics (Proceedings of SIGGRAPH '85)*, 19(3):69–78, July 1985.

[50] Sever S. Dragomir. Some inequalities for the Csiszár f-divergence. In *Inequalities for Csiszár f-Divergence in Information Theory*. Research Group in Mathematical Inequalities and Applications, Melbourne, Australia, 2000. http://rgmia.vu.edu.au/monographs/csiszar_list.html.

[51] Dan E. Dudgeon and Russell M. Mersereau. *Multidimensional Digital Signal Processing*. Prentice Hall Inc., Englewood Cliffs (NJ), USA, 1990.

[52] Philip Dutré. Global illumination compendium. World wide web document, Computer Graphics, Department of Computer Science, Katholieke Universiteit Leuven, Leuven, Belgium, 2003. http://www.cs.kuleuven.ac.be/~phil/.

[53] Philip Dutré, Kavita Bala, and Philippe Bekaert. *Advanced Global Illumination*. A. K. Peters, Ltd., Natick (MA), USA, 2002.

[54] Philip Dutré, Eric P. Lafortune, and Yves D. Willems. Monte Carlo light tracing with direct computation of pixel intensities. In *Proceedings of 3th International Conference on Computational Graphics and Visualization Techniques (Compugraphics '93)*, pages 128–137, December 1993.

[55] Albert Einstein. Zur Elektrodynamik Bewegter Körper[3]. *Annalen der Physik*, 17(10):891–921, September 1905.

[56] Tapio Elomaa and Juho Rousu. General and efficient multisplitting of numerical attributes. *Machine Learning*, 36(3):201–244, 1999.

[57] Farlex, Inc. *The Free Dictionary*[TM]. Huntingdon Valley, PA, USA, 2005. http://encyclopedia.thefreedictionary.com © 2003 by Farlex, Inc.

[58] Hans G. Feichtinger and Karlheinz Gröchenig. Iterative reconstruction of multivariate band-limited functions from irregular sampling values. *SIAM Journal on Mathematical Analysis*, 23(1):244–261, January 1992.

[59] Hans G. Feichtinger and Karlheinz Gröchenig. Theory and practice of irregular sampling. In John J. Benedetto and Michael W. Frazier, editors, *Wavelets: Mathematics and Applications*, pages 305–363. CRC Press, Boca Raton (FL), USA, 1994.

[60] Miquel Feixas. *An Information-Theory Framework for the Study of the Complexity of Visibility and Radiosity in a Scene*. PhD thesis, Universitat Politècnica de Catalunya, Barcelona, Spain, Desember 2002.

[61] Miquel Feixas, Esteve del Acebo, Philippe Bekaert, and Mateu Sbert. An information theory framework for the analysis of scene complexity. *Computer Graphics Forum (Proceedings of Eurographics '99)*, 18(3):95–106, September 1999.

[62] Miquel Feixas, Esteve del Acebo, and Mateu Sbert. Entropy of scene visibility. In *Proceedings of Winter School on Computer Graphics and CAD Systems (WSCG '99)*, pages 25–34, Plzen-Bory, Czech Republic, February 1999.

[63] Miquel Feixas, Jaume Rigau, Philippe Bekaert, and Mateu Sbert. Information-theoretic oracle based on kernel smoothness for hierarchical radiosity. In *Short Presentations (Eurographics '02)*, pages 325–333, September 2002.

---

[3]On the electrodynamics of moving bodies.

[64] David P. Feldman. A brief introduction to: Information theory, excess entropy and computational mechanics. Lecture notes, Department of Physics, University of California, Berkeley (CA), USA, 1997.

[65] David P. Feldman and James P. Crutchfield. Discovering noncritical organization: Statistical mechanical, information theoretic and computational views of patterns in one-dimensional spin systems. Working Paper 98–04–026, Santa Fe Institute, Santa Fe (NM), USA, April 1998.

[66] David P. Feldman and James P. Crutchfield. Statistical measures of complexity: Why? *Physics Letters A*, 238(4/5):244–252, 1998.

[67] Richard P. Feynman, Robert B. Leighton, and Matthew Sands. *The Feyman Lectures on Physics*. Addison-Wesley, Reading (MA), USA, 1964.

[68] Sarah F. Frisken and Roger J. Hubbold. Efficient hierarchical refinement and clustering for radiosity in complex environments. *Computer Graphics Forum*, 15(5):297–310, 1996.

[69] Shigeru Furuichi, Kenjiro Yanagi, and Ken Kuriyama. Fundamental properties of Tsallis relative entropy. *Journal of Mathematical Physics*, 45(12):4868–4877, 2004.

[70] Robert A. Gabel and Richard A. Roberts. *Signals and Linear Systems*. John Wiley & Sons Inc., New York (NY), USA, 1980.

[71] Murray Gell-Mann and James P. Crutchfield. Computation in physical and biological systems: Measures of complexity. World wide web document, Santa Fe Insitute, Santa Fe (NM), USA, 2001. http://www.santafe.edu/sfi/research/focus/compPhysics.

[72] Alison L. Gibbs and Francis E. Su. On choosing and bounding probability metrics. *International Statistical Review*, 70:419–435, 2001.

[73] Andrew S. Glassner. An overview of ray tracing. In Andrew S. Glassner, editor, *An Introduction to Ray Tracing*, pages 1–32. Academic Press Ltd., San Diego (CA), USA, 1989.

[74] Andrew S. Glassner. *Principles of Digital Image Synthesis*. Morgan Kaufmann Publishers, San Francisco (CA), USA, 1995.

[75] Cindy M. Goral, Kenneth E. Torrance, Donald P. Greenberg, and Bennett Battaile. Modelling the interaction of light between diffuse surfaces. *Computer Graphics (Proceedings of SIGGRAPH '84)*, 18(3):213–222, July 1984.

[76] Steven J. Gortler, Peter Schröder, Michael F. Cohen, and Pat Hanrahan. Wavelet radiosity. In James T. Kajiya, editor, *Computer Graphics (Proceedings of SIGGRAPH '93)*, volume 27 of *Annual Conference Series*, pages 221–230, August 1993.

[77] John C. Gower. Measures of similarity, dissimilarity, and distance. In Samuel Kotz, Norman L. Johnson, and Campbell B. Read, editors, *Encyclopedia of Statistical Sciences*, volume 5, pages 397–405. Wiley Interscience, New York (NY), USA, 1985.

[78] Rex Graham. Constantino Tsallis. Describing a new entropy. World wide web document, Santa Fe Institute, Santa Fe (NM), USA, 2002. http://www.santafe.edu/research/publications/bulletin/fall00/tsallis.php.

[79] Peter Grassberger. Toward a quantitative theory of self-generated complexity. *International Journal of Theoretical Physics*, 25(9):907–938, 1986.

[80] Robert M. Gray. *Entropy and Information Theory*. Springer-Verlag, New York (NY), USA, 1990.

[81] Ned Greene and Paul S. Heckbert. Creating raster omnimax images from multiple perspective views using the elliptical weighted average filter. *IEEE Computuer Graphics and Applications*, 6(6):21–27, June 1986.

[82] GuruNet Corp. *Answers.com*^{TM}. New York (NY), USA, 2005. http://www.answers.com © 1999-2005 by GuruNet Corp.

[83] Roy Hall. *Illumination and Color in Computer Generated Imagery*. Springer-Verlag, New York (NY), USA, 1989.

[84] John M. Hammersley and David C. Handscomb. *Monte Carlo Methods*. Methuen & Co., London, UK, 1964.

[85] Pat Hanrahan. Rendering concepts. In Michael F. Cohen, John Wallace, and Pat Hanrahan, editors, *Radiosity and Realistic Image Synthesis*. Academic Press Professional, Inc., San Diego (CA), USA, 1993.

[86] Pat Hanrahan, David Salzman, and Larry Aupperle. A rapid hierarchical radiosity algorithm. *Computer Graphics (Proceedings of SIGGRAPH '91)*, 25(4):197–206, July 1991.

[87] Akihiko Hashimoto, Taka-aki Akimoto, Kenji Mase, and Yasuhito Suenaga. Vista ray-tracing: High speed ray tracing using perspective projection image. In Rae A. Earnshaw and Brian Wyvill, editors, *New Advances in Computer Graphics (Proceedings of CGI '89)*, pages 549–561. Springer-Verlag, New York (NY), USA, 1989.

[88] Jan Havrda and František Charvát. Quantication method of classication processes. Concept of structural α-entropy. *Kybernetika*, pages 30–35, 1967.

[89] Yun He, A. Ben Hamza, and Hamid Krim. A generalized divergence measure for robust image registration. *IEEE Transactions on Signal Processing*, 51(5):1211–1220, May 2003.

[90] Paul S. Heckbert. Fundamentals of texture mapping and image warping. Master's thesis, University of California, Berkeley (CA), USA, June 1989.

[91] Paul S. Heckbert. Adaptive radiosity textures for bidirectional ray tracing. *Computer Graphics (Proceedings of SIGGRAPH '90)*, 24(4):145–154, August 1990.

[92] Paul S. Heckbert. Simulating global illumination using adaptive meshing. Technical Report UCB/CSD 91/636, Computer Science Division (EECS), University of California, Berkeley (CA), USA, 1991.

[93] Werner Heisenberg. *The Physical Principles of the Quantum Theory*. University of Chicago Press, 1930. 23 March 1927, receipt of Heisenberg's paper on the uncertainty principle (Zs. f. Phys., 43, 172–198).

[94] Ernst D. Hellinger. Neue Begründung der Theorie der Quadratischen Formen von Unendlichen Vielen Veränderlichen[4]. *Journal für Reine und Angewandte Mathematik*, 136:210–271, 1909.

[95] Alfred O. Hero, Bing Ma, Olivier Michel, and John Gorman. Alpha-divergence for classification, indexing and retrieval. Technical Report CSPL-328, Communications and Signal Processing Laboratory, Ann Arbor (MI), USA, May 2001.

[96] Nicolas Holzschuch and François X. Sillion. An exhaustive error-bounding algorithm for hierarchical radiosity. *Computer Graphics Forum*, 17(4):197–218, 1998.

[97] John E. Hopcroft and Jeffrey D. Ullmann. *Introduction to Automata Theory, Languages, and Computation*. Addison-Wesley, Reading (MA), USA, 1979.

[98] Barry D. Hughes. *Random Walks and Random Environments. Volum I: Random Walks*. Oxford University Press, Oxford, UK, 1995.

---

[4]A new foundation of the theory of quadratic forms of infinite many variables.

[99] Frederik W. Jansen and Jarke J. van Wijk. Fast previewing techniques in raster graphics. In Paul J. W. ten Hagen, editor, *Proceedings of Eurographics '83*, pages 195–202, Amsterdam, Holland, September 1983. North-Holland.

[100] Edwin T. Jaynes. Information theory and statistical mechanics. *Physical Review*, 106:620–630, 1957.

[101] Edwin T. Jaynes. Information theory and statistical mechanics - II. *Physical Review*, 108:171–190, 1957.

[102] Henrik W. Jensen. Global illumination using photon maps. In Xavier Pueyo and Peter Schröder, editors, *Rendering Techniques '96 (Proceedings of the 7th Eurographics Workshop on Rendering)*, pages 21–30, London, UK, June 1996. Springer-Verlag.

[103] Henrik W. Jensen and Niels J. Christensen. Photon maps in bidirectional Monte Carlo ray tracing of complex objects. *Computers and Graphics*, 19(2):215–224, 1995.

[104] Henrik W. Jensen and Per H. Christensen. Efficient simulation of light transport in scenes with participating media using photon maps. In Michael Cohen, editor, *SIGGRAPH '98 Conference Proceedings*, Annual Conference Series, pages 311–320, New York (NY), USA, July 1998. ACM SIGGRAPH, ACM Press.

[105] Johan L. W. V. Jensen. Sur les fonctions convexes et les inégalités entre les valeurs moyennes[5]. *Acta Mathematica*, 30:175–193, 1906.

[106] James T. Kajiya. The rendering equation. *Computer Graphics (Proceedings of SIGGRAPH '86)*, 20(4):143–150, August 1986.

[107] James T. Kajiya. Radiometry and photometry for computer graphics. In Andrew S. Glassner, editor, *SIGGRAPH '90 Advances Topics in Ray Tracing (course notes)*, chapter 2. ACM Siggraph, New York (NY), USA, August 1990.

[108] Shizuo Kakutani. On equivalence of infinite product measures. *Annals of Mathematics*, 49:214–224, 1948.

[109] Malvin H. Kalos and Paula A. Whitlock. *The Monte Carlo Method*. John Wiley & Sons Inc., 1986.

[110] Alexander Keller and Stefan Heinrich. Quasi-Monte Carlo methods in computer graphics, Part I: The QMC-buffer. Technical Report 242/94, University of Kaiserslautern, Kaiserslautern, Germany, 1994.

[111] David Kirk and James Arvo. Unbiased variance reduction for global illumination. In *Proceedings of the 2nd Eurographics Workshop on Rendering*, pages 153–156, May 1991.

[112] Andrei N. Kolmogorov. On the Shannon theory of information transmission in the case of continuous signals. *IRE Transactions on Information Theory*, 2:102–108, 1956.

[113] Solomon Kullback and Richard A. Leibler. On information and sufficiency. *Annals of Mathematical Statistics*, 22:76–86, 1951.

[114] Eric P. Lafortune and Yves D. Willems. Bi-directional path tracing. In *Proceedings of 3th International Conference on Computational Graphics and Visualization Techniques (Compugraphics '93)*, pages 145–153, December 1993.

[115] Lucien M. Le Camp and Grace L. Yang. *Asymptotics in Statistics: Some Basic Concepts*. Springer-Verlag, New York (NY), USA, 1990.

[116] Mark E. Lee and Richard A. Redner. Filtering: A note on the use of nonlinear filtering in computer graphics. *IEEE Computer Graphics and Applications*, 10(3):23–29, May 1990.

---

[5]On the convex functions and the inequalities between the averages.

[117] Mark E. Lee, Richard A. Redner, and Samuel P. Uselton. Statiscally optimized sampling for distributed ray tracing. *Computer Graphics (Proceedings of SIGGRAPH '85)*, 19(3):61–67, July 1985.

[118] François LeGland. Stability and approximation of nonlinear filters: an information theoretic approach. In *Proceedings of the 38th IEEE Conference on Decision and Control*, pages 1889–1894, December 1999.

[119] Oscar A. Z. Leneman. Random sampling of random processes: Impulse processes. *Information and Control*, 9(4):347–363, August 1966.

[120] Ming Li and Paul Vitányi. *An Introduction to Kolmogorov Complexity and Its Applications*. Graduate Texts in Computer Science. Springer-Verlag, New York (NY), USA, 1997.

[121] Wentian Li. On the relationship between complexity and entropy for Markov chains and regular languages. *Complex Systems*, 5(4):381–399, 1991.

[122] Friedrich Liese and Igor Vajda. *Convex Statistical Distances*. Teubner Verlagsgesellschaft, Leipzig, Germany, 1987.

[123] Daniel Lischinski, Brian Smits, and Donald P. Greenberg. Bounds and error estimates for radiosity. In *Computer Graphics (Proceedings of SIGGRAPH '94)*, volume 28 of *Annual Conference Series*, pages 67–74, July 1994.

[124] Daniel Lischinski, Filippo Tampieri, and Donald P. Greenberg. Combining hierarchical radiosity and discontinuity meshing. In James T. Kajiya, editor, *Computer Graphics (Proceedings of SIGGRAPH '93)*, volume 27 of *Annual Conference Series*, pages 199–208, August 1993.

[125] Seth Lloyd and Heinz Pagels. Complexity as thermodymanic depth. *Annals of Physics*, 188:186–213, 1988.

[126] Jean-Luc Maillot, Laurent Carraro, and Bernard Peroche. Progressive ray tracing. In Alan Chalmers, Derek Paddon, and François X. Sillion, editors, *Proceedings of the 3th Eurographics Workshop on Rendering*, pages 9–20, Amsterdam, Holland, May 1992. Elsevier.

[127] Thomas J. V. Malley. *A Shading Method for Computer Generated Images*. PhD thesis, University of Utah, Logan (UT), USA, 1988.

[128] Andrei A. Markov. Rasprostranenie zakona bol'shih chisel na velichiny, zavisyaschie drug ot druga[6]. *Izvestiya Fiziko-Matematicheskogo Obschestva pri Kazanskom Universitete*, 15(2):135–156, 1906.

[129] Josep A. Martín. *Medidas de Diferencia y Clasificación no Paramétrica de Datos Composicionales[7]*. PhD thesis, Universitat Politècnica de Catalunya, Barcelona, Spain, 2001.

[130] Stefan Martin, Gordon Morison, William H. Nailon, and Tariq S. Durrani. Fast and accurate image registration using Tsallis entropy and simultaneous perturbation stochastic approximation. *IEE Electronics Letters (Simultaneous Perturbation Stochastic Approximation)*, 40(10):595–597, May 2004.

[131] Farokh Marvasti, Mostafa Analoui, and Mohsen Gamshadzahi. Recovery of signals from nonuniform samples using iterative methods. *IEEE Transactions on Signal Processing*, 39(4):872–878, April 1991.

[132] Nelson Max. An optimal filter for image reconstruction. In James Arvo, editor, *Graphics Gems II*, pages 101–104. Academic Press, San Diego (CA), USA, 1991.

---

[6]Extension of the law of large numbers to dependent events.
[7]Measures of difference and non-parametric clasification of compositional data.

[133] Michael McCool and Eugene Fiume. Hierarchical Poisson disk sampling distributions. In *Proceedings of Graphics Interface '92*, pages 94–105, May 1992.

[134] Merriam-Webster, Inc. *Merriam-Webster Online Dictionary*. Springfield (MA), USA, 2005. http: //www.m-w.com © 2005 by Merriam-Webster, Inc.

[135] Don P. Mitchell. Generating antialiased images at low sampling densities. *Computer Graphics (Proceedings of SIGGRAPH '87)*, 21(4):65–72, July 1987.

[136] Don P. Mitchell and Arun N. Netravali. Reconstruction filters in computer graphics. *Computer Graphics (Proceedings of SIGGRAPH '88)*, 22(4):221–228, July 1988.

[137] Rajeev Motwani and Prabhakar Raghavan. *Randomized Algorithms*. Cambridge University Press, New York (NY), USA, 1995.

[138] László Neumann. Monte Carlo radiosity. *Computing*, 55(1):23–42, 1995.

[139] László Neumann, Martin Feda, and Werner Purgathofer. A new stochastic radiosity method for highly complex scenes. In Stefan Haas, Stefan Mueller, Georg Sakas, and Peter Shirley, editors, *Photorealistic Rendering Techniques (Proceedings of the 5th Eurographics Workshop on Rendering)*, pages 201–213, New York (NY), USA, 1995. Springer-Verlag.

[140] László Neumann, Attila Neumann, and Philippe Bekaert. Radiosity with well distributed ray sets. *Computer Graphics Forum (Proceedings of Eurographics '97)*, 16(3):261–270, 1997.

[141] Ludo Niepel, Jozef Martinka, Andrej Ferko, and Pavol Elias. On scene complexity definition for rendering. In *Proceedings of Winter School on Computer Graphics and CAD Systems (WSCG '95)*, pages 209–217, Plzen-Bory, Czech Republic, June 1995.

[142] Tomoyuki Nishita and Eihachiro Nakame. Continuous tone representation of 3-D objects taking account of shadows and interreflection. *Computer Graphics (Proceedings of SIGGRAPH '85)*, 19(3):23–30, July 1985.

[143] Harry Nyquist. Certain topics in telegraph transmission theory. *Transactions of American Institute of Electrical Engineers*, 47:617–644, April 1928.

[144] Ryutarou Ohbuchi and Masaki Aono. Quasi–Monte Carlo rendering with adaptive sampling. Technical report, Tokyo Research Laboratory, IBM Japan Ltd., Tokyo, Japan, 1996.

[145] Alan V. Oppenheim and Ronald W. Schafer. *Digital Signal Processing*. Prentice-Hall Inc., Englewood Cliffs (NJ), USA, 1975.

[146] Rachel Orti. *Radiosité Dynamique 2D et Complexe de Visibilité*[8]. PhD thesis, Université Joseph Fourier, Grenoble, France, 1997.

[147] Ferdinand Österreicher. Csiszár's f-divergences - Basic properties. In *Workshop of the Research Group in Mathematical Inequalities and Applications*, Melbourne, Australia, November 2002.

[148] Ferdinand Österreicher. f-Divergences - Representation theorem and metrizability. In *Workshop of the Research Group in Mathematical Inequalities and Applications*, Melbourne, Australia, November 2002.

[149] Ferdinand Österreicher and Igor Vajda. Statistical information and discrimination. *IEEE Transactions on Information Theory*, 39(3):1036–1039, May 1993.

[150] Joseph A. O'Sullivan, Richard E. Blahut, and Donald L. Snyder. Information-theoretic image formation. *IEEE Transactions on Information Theory*, 44(6):2094–2123, October 1998.

---

[8]2D dynamic radiosity and visibility complex.

[151] James Painter and Kenneth Sloan. Antialiased ray tracing by adaptive progressive refinement. *Computer Graphics (Proceedings of SIGGRAPH '89)*, 23(3):281–288, July 1989.

[152] Athanasios Papoulis. A new algorithm in spectral analysis and band-limited extrapolation. *IEEE Transactions on Circuits and Systems*, 22(9):735–7342, September 1975.

[153] Athanasios Papoulis. *Probability, Random Variables, and Stochastic Processes*. McGraw-Hill, New York (NY), USA, 2 edition, 1984.

[154] María del Carmen Pardo and Igor Vajda. About distances of discrete distributions satisfying the data processing theorem of information theory. *IEEE Transactions on Information Theory*, 43(7):1288–1293, 1997.

[155] María del Carmen Pardo and Igor Vajda. On asymptotic properties of information-theoretic divergences. *IEEE Transactions on Information Theory*, 49(7):1860–1868, 2003.

[156] Sumanta N. Pattanaik. *Computational Methods for Global Illumination and Visualisation of Complex 3D Environments*. PhD thesis, Birla Institute of Technology and Science, Pilani, India, 1993.

[157] Sumanta N. Pattanaik and Kadi Bouatouch. Linear radiosity with error estimation. In Pat Hanrahan and Werner Purgathofer, editors, *Rendering Techniques '95 (Proceedings of the 6th Eurographics Workshop on Rendering)*, New York (NY), USA, June 1995. Springer-Verlag.

[158] Sumanta N. Pattanaik and Sudhir P. Mudur. Adjoint equations and random walks for illumination computation. *ACM Transactions on Computer Graphics*, 14(1):77–102, January 1995.

[159] Mark J. Pavicic. Convenient anti-aliasing filters that minimize "bumpy" sampling. In Andrew S. Glassner, editor, *Graphics Gems*, pages 144–146. Academic Press, San Diego (CA), USA, 1990.

[160] Karl Pearson. On the criterion that a given system of deviations from the probable in the case of a correlated system of variables is such that it can be reasonably supposed to have arisen from random sampling. *Philosophical Magazine*, V(1):157–175, 1900.

[161] Bui T. Phong. Illumination for computer generated pictures. *Communications of ACM*, 18(6):311–317, 1975.

[162] Mark S. Pinsker. *Information and Stability of Random Variables and Processes*. Izdatel'stvo Akademii Nauk SSSR, Moscow, Russia, 1960. Translated by A. Feinstein, 1964.

[163] Ángel Plastino and Ángel R. Plastino. Tsallis entropy and Jayne's information theory formalism. *Brazilian Journal of Physics*, 29(1):50–60, 1998.

[164] Ángel R. Plastino, Ángel Plastino, and Constanino Tsallis. The classical N-body problem within a generalized statistical mechanics. *Journal of Physics A: Mathematical and General*, 27:5707–5714, 1994.

[165] Josien P. W. Pluim. *Mutual Information Based Registration of Medical Images*. PhD thesis, Utrecht University, Utrecht, Holland, 2001.

[166] Charles Poynton. *Digital Video and HDTV: Algorithms and Interfaces*. Morgan Kaufmann Publishers, San Francisco (CA), USA, 2003.

[167] Jan Prikryl and Werner Purgathofer. Perceptually based radiosity. State of the art report, Eurographics '98, 1998.

[168] Kari Pulli, Michael F. Cohen, Tom Duchamp, Hugues Hoppe, Linda Shapiro, and Werner Stuetzle. View-based rendering: Visualizing real objects from scanned range and color data. In Julie Dorsey and Philipp Slusallek, editors, *Rendering Techniques '97 (Proceedings of the 8th Eurographics Workshop on Rendering)*, pages 23–34, New York (NY), USA, June 1997. Springer-Verlag.

[169] Werner Purgathofer. A statistical method for adaptive stochastic sampling. *Eurographics '86: Proceedings of the European Conference and Exhibition*, 11(2):157–162, August 1986.

[170] Pushpa N. Rathie and Palaniappan L. Kannappan. A directed-divergence function of type β. *Information and Control*, 20(1):38–45, February 1972.

[171] Rolf-Dieter Reiss. *Approximate Distributions of Order Statistics: With Applications to Nonparametric Statistics*. Springer-Verlag, New York (NY), USA, 1989.

[172] Alfréd Rényi. On measures of entropy and information. In *Proc. Fourth Berkeley Symp. Math. Stat. and Probability' 60*, volume 1, pages 547–561, Berkeley (CA), USA, 1961. University of California Press.

[173] Jaume Rigau, Miquel Feixas, Philippe Bekaert, and Mateu Sbert. View-dependent information theory measures for pixel sampling and scene discretization in flatland. In *Proceedings of Spring Conference on Computer Graphics '01*, pages 173–180, Los Alamitos (CA), USA, April 2001. IEEE Computer Society.

[174] Jaume Rigau, Miquel Feixas, and Mateu Sbert. Information theory point measures in a scene. Research Report IIiA–00–08–RR, Institut d'Informàtica i Aplicacions, Universitat de Girona, Girona, Spain, 2000.

[175] Jaume Rigau, Miquel Feixas, and Mateu Sbert. Scene visibility complexity in flatland. Research Report IIiA–00–03–RR, Institut d'Informàtica i Aplicacions, Universitat de Girona, Girona, Spain, 2000.

[176] Jaume Rigau, Miquel Feixas, and Mateu Sbert. Visibility complexity of a region in flatland. In *Short Presentations of Eurographics '00*, pages 159–163. EG Digital Library, August 2000.

[177] Jaume Rigau, Miquel Feixas, and Mateu Sbert. Visibility complexity of animation in flatland. In *Journal of WSCG (Proceedings of Winter School on Computer Graphics and CAD Systems '01)*, volume 2, pages 352–359, Plzen-Bory, Czech Republic, February 2001. Union Agency - Science Press.

[178] Jaume Rigau, Miquel Feixas, and Mateu Sbert. Entropy-based adaptive supersampling. In Paul Debevec and Simon Gibson, editors, *The 13th Eurographics Workshop on Rendering, Poster Papers Proceedings*, pages 63–70, Pisa, Italy, June 2002. National Research Council of Italy.

[179] Jaume Rigau, Miquel Feixas, and Mateu Sbert. New contrast measures for pixel supersampling. In John Vince and Rae Earnshaw, editors, *Advances in Modeling, Animation and Rendering (Proceedings of CGI '02)*, pages 439–451, London, UK, July 2002. Springer-Verlag London Limited.

[180] Jaume Rigau, Miquel Feixas, and Mateu Sbert. Entropy-based adaptive sampling. In *Graphics Interface*, pages 149–157. Canadian Information Processing Society, A. K. Peters Ltd., June 2003.

[181] Jaume Rigau, Miquel Feixas, and Mateu Sbert. Information-theory-based oracles for hierarchical radiosity. In Vipin Kumar, Marina L. Gavrilova, Chih jeng Kenneth Tan, and Pierre L'Ecuyer, editors, *Computational Science and Its Applications - ICCSA 2003*, number 2669-3 in Lecture Notes in Computer Science, pages 275–284. Springer-Verlag, May 2003.

[182] Jaume Rigau, Miquel Feixas, and Mateu Sbert. Refinement criteria based on f-divergences. In Per H. Christensen and Daniel Cohen-Or, editors, *Rendering Techniques 2003 (14th Eurographics Symposium on Rendering)*, pages 260–269, New York (NY), USA, June 2003. Association for Computing Machinery.

[183] Jaume Rigau, Miquel Feixas, and Mateu Sbert. Refinement criteria for global illumination using convex functions. In Santi Thió and Josep A. Martín, editors, *The First Compositional Data Analysis Workshop (CoDaWork '03)*, Girona, Spain, October 2003. Universitat de Girona.

[184] Jaume Rigau, Miquel Feixas, and Mateu Sbert. An information theoretic framework for image segmentation. In *IEEE International Conference on Image Processing (ICIP '04)*, volume 2, pages 1193–1196, Victoria (British Columbia), Canada, October 2004. IEEE Press.

[185] Jaume Rigau, Miquel Feixas, and Mateu Sbert. An information theoretic framework for image complexity. In *Computational Aesthetics 2005 - First Eurographics Workshop on Computational Aesthetics in Graphics, Visualization and Imaging (CAGVI '05)*, pages 177–184, Aire-la-Ville, Switzerland, May 2005. Eurographics Association.

[186] Jaume Rigau, Miquel Feixas, and Mateu Sbert. Shape complexity based on mutual information. In *International Conference on Shape Modeling and Applications (SMI '05)*, pages 355–360, Los Alamitos (CA), USA, June 2005. IEEE Computer Society.

[187] Jaume Rigau, Miquel Feixas, and Mateu Sbert. An information-theoretic approach to shape complexity. *Computer Graphics & Geometry*, 8(1):10–21, May 2006. World Wide Web journal.

[188] Jaume Rigau, Miquel Feixas, Mateu Sbert, Anton Bardera, and Imma Boada. Medical image segmentation based on mutual information maximization. In Christian Barillot, David R. Haynor, and Pierre Hellier, editors, *7th International Conference on Medical Image Computing and Computer-Assisted Intervention (MICCAI '04)*, number 3216 in Lecture Notes in Computer Science, pages 135–142. Springer-Verlag, September 2004.

[189] Scott D. Roth. Ray casting for modeling solids. *Computer Graphics and Image Processing*, 18(2):109–144, February 1982.

[190] Reuven Y. Rubinstein. *Simulation and the Monte Carlo Method*. John Wiley & Sons Inc., New York (NY), USA, 1981.

[191] Holly E. Rushmeier and Kenneth E. Torrance. The zonal methods for calculating light intensities in the presence of a participating medium. *Computer Graphics (Proceedings of SIGGRAPH '87)*, 21(4):293–302, July 1987.

[192] Lluís Santaló. *Integral Geometry and Geometric Probability*. Addison-Wesley, Reading (MA), USA, 1976.

[193] Ken D. Sauer and Jan P. Allebach. Iterative reconstruction of bandlimited images from nonuniformly spaced samples. *IEEE Transactions on Circuits and Systems*, 34(12):1497–1506, December 1987.

[194] Mateu Sbert. An integral geometry based method for fast form-factor computation. *Computer Graphics Forum (Proceedings of Eurographics '93)*, 12(3):409–420, 1993.

[195] Mateu Sbert. *The Use of Global Random Directions to Compute Radiosity. Global Monte Carlo Methods*. PhD thesis, Universitat Politècnica de Catalunya, Barcelona, Spain, November 1996.

[196] Mateu Sbert, Philippe Bekaert, and John Halton. Reusing paths in radiosity and global illumination. In *4th IMACS Seminar on Monte Carlo Methods*, September 2003.

[197] Mateu Sbert, Jaume Rigau, Miquel Feixas, and László Neumann. Systematic sampling in image-synthesis. In Marina Gavrilova, Osvaldo Gervasi, Vipin Kumar, C. J. Kenneth Tan, David Taniar, Antonio Laganà, Youngsong Mun, and Hyunseung Choo, editors, *Computational Science and Its Applications - ICCSA 2006*, number 3980-1 in Lecture Notes in Computer Science, pages 449–458. Springer-Verlag, May 2006.

[198] Christophe Schlick. An adaptive sampling technique for multidimensional ray tracing. In *Proceedings of the 2nd Eurographics Workshop on Rendering*, pages 48–56, May 1991.

[199] Peter Schröder and Pat Hanrahan. On the form factor between two polygons. In James T. Kajiya, editor, *Computer Graphics Proceedings (Proceedings of SIGGRAPH '93)*, volume 27 of *Annual Conference Series*, pages 163–164, August 1993.

[200] Claude E. Shannon. A mathematical theory of communication. *The Bell System Technical Journal*, 27:379–423 (part I) and 623–656 (part II), July (part I) and October (part II) 1948.

[201] Claude E. Shannon. Communication in the presence of noise. *Proceedings Institute of Radio Engineers*, 37(1):10–21, January 1949.

[202] Bhu D. Sharma and Dharam P. Mittal. New non-additive measures of entropy for a discrete probability distribution. *Journal of Mathematical Sciences (India)*, 10:28–40, 1975.

[203] Bhu D. Sharma and Inder J. Taneja. Entropy of type (α, β) and other generalized measures in information theory. *Metrika*, 22(1):205–215, 1975.

[204] Peter Shirley. Physically based lighting calculations for computer graphics: A modern perspective. In Kadi Bouatouch and Christian Bouville, editors, *Eurographics Workshop on Photosimulation, Realism and Physics in Computer Graphics*, pages 67–81, Amsterdam, Holland, 1990. Elsevier.

[205] Peter Shirley. A ray tracing method for illumination calculation in diffuse-specular scenes. In *Proceedings of Graphics Interface '90*, pages 205–212, Toronto (Ontario), Canada, May 1990. Canadian Information Processing Society.

[206] Peter Shirley. Discrepancy as a quality measure for sample distributions. In Frits H. Post and Wilhelm Barth, editors, *Eurographics '91 (Proceedings of European Computer Graphics Conference and Exhibition)*, pages 183–194, Amsterdam, Holland, September 1991. Elsevier North-Holland.

[207] Peter Shirley. *Physically Based Lighting Calculations for Computer Graphics*. PhD thesis, University of Illinois, Urbana-Champaign (IL), USA, 1991.

[208] Peter Shirley. A ray tracing framework for global illumination systems. In Brian Wyvill, editor, *Proceedings of Graphics Interface '91*, pages 117–128, Toronto (Ontario), Canada, May 1991. Canadian Information Processing Society.

[209] Peter Shirley. *Realistic Ray Tracing*. A. K. Peters, Ltd., Natick (MA), USA, 2000.

[210] Peter Shirley and Changyaw Wang. Distribution ray tracing: Theory and practice. In Alan Chalmers, Derek Paddon, and François X. Sillion, editors, *Proceedings of the 3th Eurographics Workshop on Rendering*, pages 33–43, Amsterdam, Holland, May 1992. Elsevier.

[211] Renben Shu and Alan Liu. A fast ray casting algorithm using adaptive isotriangular subdivision. In *Proceedings of the 2nd conference on Visualization '91*, pages 232–238, Los Alamitos (CA), USA, 1991. IEEE Computer Society Press.

[212] Robert Siegel and John R. Howell. *Thermal Radiation Heat Transfer*. Hemisphere Publishing Corporation, New York (NY), USA, 3 edition, 1992.

[213] François X. Sillion, James R. Arvo, Stephen H. Westin, and Donald P. Greenberg. A global illumination solution for general reflectance distributions. *Computer Graphics (Proceedings of SIGGRAPH '91)*, 25(4):187–196, July 1991.

[214] François X. Sillion and Claude Puech. A general two-pass method integrating specular and diffuse reflection. *Computer Graphics (Proceedings of SIGGRAPH '89)*, 23(3):335–344, July 1989.

[215] François X. Sillion and Claude Puech. *Radiosity and Global Illumination*. Morgan Kaufmann Publishers, San Francisco (CA), USA, 1994.

[216] Maryann Simmons and Carlo H. Séquin. Tapestry: A dynamic mesh-based display representation for interactive rendering. In Bernard Péroche and Holly Rushmeier, editors, *Rendering Techniques 2000 (Proceedings of the 11th Eurographics Workshop on Rendering)*, pages 329–340, New York (NY), USA, June 2000. Springer-Verlag.

[217] Brian E. Smits, James Arvo, and David Salesin. An importance-driven radiosity algorithm. *Computer Graphics (Proceedings of SIGGRAPH '92)*, 26(2):273–282, July 1992.

[218] Herbert Solomon. *Geometric Probability*, volume 28 of *CBMS-NFS Regional Conference Series in Applied Mathematics*. Society for Industrial and Applied Mathematics (SIAM), Philadelphia (PA), USA, 1978.

[219] Marc Stamminger, Philipp Slusallek, and Hans-Peter Seidel. Bounded radiosity-illumination on general surfaces and clusters. *Computer Graphics Forum (Proceedings of Eurographics '97)*, 16(3):300–317, 1997.

[220] Michael Stokes, Matthew Anderson, Srinivasan Chandrasekar, and Ricardo Motta. A standard default color space for the internet - sRGB. World wide web document, Hewlett-Packard and Microsoft, November 1996. http://www.w3.org/Graphics/Color/sRGB.

[221] Colin Studholme. *Measures of 3D Medical Image Alignment*. PhD thesis, University of London, London, UK, August 1997.

[222] Frank Suykens and Yves D. Willems. Weighted multipass methods for global illumination. *Computer Graphics Forum (Proceedings of Eurographics '99)*, 18(3):209–220, September 1999.

[223] László Szirmay-Kalos. *Monte Carlo Methods in Global Illumination*. Institute of Computer Graphics, Vienna University of Technology, Vienna, Austria, 2000.

[224] Rasmus Tamstorf and Henrik W. Jensen. Adaptive sampling and bias estimation in path tracing. In Julie Dorsey and Philipp Slusallek, editors, *Rendering Techniques '97 (Proceedings of the 8th Eurographics Workshop on Rendering)*, pages 285–295, New York (NY), USA, June 1997. Springer-Verlag.

[225] Inder J. Taneja. Bivariate measures of type α and their applications. *Tamkang Journal of Mathematics*, 19(3):63–74, 1988.

[226] Inder J. Taneja. On generalized information measures and their applications. In *Advances in Electronics and Electron Physics*, volume 76, pages 327–413. Academic Press Ltd., 1989.

[227] Inder J. Taneja. Generalized information measures and their applications. Book on-line, Departamento de Matemática, Universidade Federal de Santa Catarina, Florianópolis (SC), Brazil, 2001. http://www.mtm.ufsc.br/~taneja/book/book.html.

[228] Inder J. Taneja. Tsallis measures are not due to Tsallis: Historical comments. World wide web document, Departamento de Matemática, Universidade Federal de Santa Catarina, Florianópolis (SC), Brazil, 2006. To appear.

[229] Seth J. Teller and Pat Hanrahan. Global visibility algorithms for illumination computation. In James T. Kajiya, editor, *Computer Graphics (Proceedings of SIGGRAPH '93)*, volume 27 of *Annual Conference Series*, pages 239–246, August 1993.

[230] Giulio Tononi, Anthony R. McIntosh, D. Patrick Russell, and Gerald M. Edelman. Functional clustering: Identifying strongly interactive brain regions in neuroimaging data. *Neuroimage*, 7(2):133–149, February 1998.

[231] Flemming Topsøe. Some inequalities for information divergence and related measures of discrimination. *IEEE Transactions on Information Theory*, 46(4):1602–1609, 2000.

[232] Flemming Topsøe. Jensen-Shannon divergence and norm-based measures of discrimination and variation. World wide web document, Institute for Mathematical Sciences, University of Copenhagen, 2003. http://www.math.ku.dk/~topsoe/manuscripts.html.

[233] Constanino Tsallis. Possible generalization of Boltzmann-Gibbs statistics. *Journal of Statistical Physics*, 52(1/2):479–487, 1988.

[234] Constanino Tsallis. Generalized entropy-based criterion for consistent testing. *Physical Review E*, 58:1442–1445, 1998.

[235] Constanino Tsallis. Entropic nonextensivity: A possible measure of complexity. *Chaos, Solitons, & Fractals*, 13(3):371–391, 2002. Update review corresponding to the inaugural talk delivered at the International Workshop on Classical and Quantum Complexity and Nonextensive Thermodynamics, Denton (TX), USA, 2000.

[236] Jack Tumblin and Holly Rushmeier. Tone reproduction for realistic images. *IEEE Computer Graphics and Applications*, 13(6):42–48, 1993.

[237] International Telecommunication Union. Basic parameter values for the HDTV standard for the studio and for international programme exchange. In *ITU-R Recommendation BT.709*. ITU, Geneva, Switzerland, 1990. Formerly Comité Consultatif International Radio.

[238] Igor Vajda. *Theory of Statistical Inference and Information*. Kluwer Academic Publishers, Boston (MA), USA, 1989.

[239] Jan C. A. van der Lubbe. *Information Theory*. Cambridge University Press, Cambridge, UK, 1997.

[240] Theo van Walsum, Peter E. van Nieuwenhuizen, and Frederick W. Jansen. Refinement criteria for adaptive stochastic ray tracing of textures. In Frits H. Post and Wilhelm Barth, editors, *Eurographics '91 (Proceedings of European Computer Graphics Conference and Exhibition)*, pages 155–166, Amsterdam, Holland, September 1991. Elsevier North-Holland.

[241] Eric Veach and Leonidas J. Guibas. Bidirectional estimators for light transport. In Stefan Haas, Stefan Mueller, Georg Sakas, and Peter Shirley, editors, *Photorealistic Rendering Techniques (Proceedings of the 5th Eurographics Workshop on Rendering)*, pages 147–162, New York (NY), USA, 1994. Springer-Verlag.

[242] Eric Veach and Leonidas J. Guibas. Metropolis light transport. In Turner Whitted, editor, *SIGGRAPH '97 Conference Proceedings*, Annual Conference Series, pages 65–76. ACM SIGGRAPH, Addison-Wesley, August 1997.

[243] Sergio Verdú. Fifty years of Shannon theory. *IEEE Transactions on Information Theory*, 44(6):2057–2078, October 1998.

[244] Paul A. Viola. *Alignment by Maximization of Mutual Information*. PhD thesis, Massachusetts Institute of Technology, Massachusetts (MA), USA, 1995.

[245] John R. Wallace, Michael F. Cohen, and Donald P. Greenberg. A two-pass solution to the rendering equation: A synthesis of ray tracing and radiosity methods. *Computer Graphics (Proceedings of SIGGRAPH '87)*, 21(4):311–320, July 1987.

[246] Greg Ward, Rob Shakespeare, Ian Ashdown, and Holly Rushmeier. Materials and geometry format (MGF). World wide web document, Lawrence Berkeley National Laboratory (CA), USA, Indiana University (IN), USA, Ledalite Corp., Langley (British Columbia), Canada, and the National Institute for Standards and Technology, USA, 2005. http://radsite.lbl.gov/mgf/.

[247] William M. Wells III, Paul A. Viola, Hideki Atsumi, Shin Nakajima, and Ron Kikinis. Multi-modal volume registration by maximization of mutual information. *Medical Image Analysis*, 1(1), 1996.

[248] Turner Whitted. An improved illumination model for shaded display. *Communications of the ACM (Graphics and Image Processing)*, 23(6):343–349, June 1980.

[249] Wikimedia Foundation, Inc. *Wikipedia*. St. Petersburg (FL), USA, 2005. http://en.wikipedia.org © 2000-2002 GNU Free Documentation License.

[250] George Wolberg. *Digital Image Warping*. IEEE Computer Society Press, Los Alamitos (CA), USA, 1994.

[251] Günther Wyszecki and Walter S. Stiles. *Color Science: Concepts and Methods, Quantitative Data and Formulæ*. John Wiley & Sons, Inc., New York (NY), USA, 1982.

[252] Geoff Wyvill and Paul Sharp. Fast antialiasing of ray traced images. In Nadia Magnenat-Thalmann and Daniel Thalmann, editors, *New Trends in Computer Graphics (Proceedings of CGI '88)*, pages 579–588, New York (NY), USA, 1988. Springer-Verlag.

[253] Yuhong Yang and Andrew Barron. Information theoretic determination of minimax rates of convergence. *Annals of Statistics*, 27:1546–1599, 1999.

[254] Jui L. Yen. On nonuniform sampling of bandwidth-limited signals. *IRE Transactions on Circuit Theory*, 3(4):251–257, December 1956.

[255] Wojciech H. Zurek. Algorithmic randomness and physical entropy. *Physical Review D*, 40(8):4731–4751, 1989.

Index

Set of words that we consider more relevant. Bold face page numbers indicate pages with a definition or description of the entry, while page numbers in normal (italic) type indicate a textual (footnote) reference.

www.ingramcontent.com/pod-product-compliance
Lightning Source LLC
LaVergne TN
LVHW022312060326
832902LV00020B/3416